The World Language Teacher's Guide to Active Learning

Enhance your students' success and improve the likelihood of retention with the easy-to-implement activities and strategies in this book! Bestselling author Deborah Blaz shows how to create a classroom in which students can actively experience, experiment with, and discover a world language. The new edition features updated strategies based on brain-based research and new ideas for using technology and personalized learning. In addition, the book has been reorganized to help you easily find and pull activities you want to use in your classroom the very next day. You'll learn how to . . .

- mix up your repertoire of activities, games, and exercises to keep students engaged;
- introduce students to the culture of the language you teach by hosting parties and celebrations;
- overcome some of the biggest obstacles in the path to fluency, including verb conjugation, using object pronouns, and the subjunctive mood;
- customize your teaching strategies to accommodate a broader range of talents, skills, and intelligences;
- implement new assessment strategies to improve verbal skills and reading comprehension;
- and more!

Bonus: Downloadable versions of some of the resources in this book are available on the Routledge website at www.routledge.com/9781138049574, so you can print and distribute them for immediate classroom use.

Deborah Blaz has taught French to grades 7 through 12 for the past 38 years in Indiana, and has taught dual credit, AP, and college classes. She also serves as world language department chair at her school. She frequently presents workshops and keynotes, regionally, nationally, and internationally.

Other Eye On Education Books available from Routledge

(www.routledge.com/eyeoneducation)

The World Language Teacher's Guide to Active Learning

Strategies and Activities for
Increasing Student Engagement

Second Edition

Deborah Blaz

Routledge
Taylor & Francis Group

NEW YORK AND LONDON

Second edition published 2018
by Routledge
711 Third Avenue, New York, NY 10017

and by Routledge
2 Park Square, Milton Park, Abingdon, Oxon, OX14 4RN

Routledge is an imprint of the Taylor & Francis Group, an informa business

© 2018 Taylor & Francis

First edition published by Routledge 1999

Library of Congress Cataloging-in-Publication Data
A catalog record has been requested for this book

ISBN: 978-1-138-04956-7 (hbk)
ISBN: 978-1-138-04957-4 (pbk)
ISBN: 978-1-315-16951-4 (ebk)

Typeset in Palatino
by Florence Production Ltd, Stoodleigh, Devon, UK

Visit the eResources: www.routledge.com/9781138049574

Contents

eResources

Several of the tools in this book are also available as free eResources 📥, so you can easily download and print them for classroom use.

You can access them by visiting the book product page: www.routledge.com/9781138049574. Click on the tab that says "eResources" and select the files. They will begin downloading to your computer.

Tools

Meet the Author

Deborah Blaz, a French teacher at Angola High School in Angola, Indiana, received her B.A. in French and German from Illinois State University, a *diplôme* from the Université de Grenoble in Grenoble, France, and, in 1974, an M.A. in French from the University of Kentucky. Ms. Blaz has taught French and English to grades 7 through 12 for the past 38 years in Indiana.

Ms. Blaz, a frequent workshop and keynote presenter, nationally and internationally, was named to the All-USA Teacher team, Honorable Mention, by *USA Today* in 1998. She was also honored as the Indiana French Teacher of the Year in 1996, and received the Project E Excellence in Education award in 2000. She has authored several books for world language teachers, including the bestselling *Differentiated Instruction*: *A Guide for World Language Teachers*.

dblaz@msdsc.us
@AHSBlaz

Action Learning
in Theory and in Practice

I hear . . . I forget.
I see . . . I remember.
I do . . . I understand.
Ancient Chinese proverb

Since the first edition of this book, there have been, of course, new discoveries and inventions that influence world language (also known as WL) teaching and learning, especially involving the Internet, but years of research and results show that keeping students active is still what *really* works in any classroom. I am the first to admit that I love the accessibility of authentic materials online, and use them frequently, but using a computer is more mental than physical (in fact, research shows clearly that taking notes by hand is far superior to doing so on a keyboard, in terms of retention). This second edition of my book will continue to focus on what works best in learning a language: using the language actively.

Definition

So, what *is* "active learning"? Over time, people have muddied what this means, providing their own definition, whether to suit their own teaching styles or attitudes toward learning, or to promote one specific method of language learning. "Active learning" is a phrase so popular and widely used that it gets used interchangeably with "collaborative learning," "cooperative learning," and "hands-on learning" (the phrase my students seem to use most to describe what they like best). Those last three are subsets of active learning, but not the only types.

The standard definition goes like this: a range of teaching methods that engage students, individually or in groups, in the process of learning through activities and/or discussion in class, involving higher-order thinking and all followed by a period of reflecting. Active learning, done well, should be both challenging and enjoyable, too.

In (my favorite definition) the words of Richard Hake (1998) an emeritus professor at Indiana University, it is "heads-on (always) and hands-on (usually) activities that yield immediate feedback through discussion with peers and/or instructors."

In everyday language, that means learners are *doing something* besides sitting and listening passively to the teacher or watching him/her write things on the board, reading a text or a computer screen, *and* they are *thinking* about the things they are doing.

Here is what you will see in an "active learning" situation:

- In the classroom, students are not passive recipients of knowledge, but are engaged learners.
- Teachers are not the sole givers of information, but function more like mentors and coaches.

This does not mean that learners and teachers have equal roles. To keep going with the coach idea above: athletes can't get good at a sport just by listening to the coach talk about it, but they won't get very good if they try to do things all by themselves, either. They have to actively practice with teammates and get feedback from the coach so they can improve. These activities can take place individually, in pairs, or in small or collaborative groups.

There is an assumption that it can only happen in face-to-face instruction, but it is also possible to incorporate it into blended or online instruction if the assignment is engaging and takes into account students' previous knowledge.

Active learning can take many forms but generally involves four basic elements:

- talking and listening
- writing
- reading, and
- reflecting.

For world languages, all of those elements are easily incorporated in a lesson. Active participation primarily means using the language to communicate, principally through speaking and writing. Communication is one of the key components of twenty-first century learning, yet it has not attracted the same level of research or attention as creativity, collaboration, or critical thinking.

Communication means learners:

- express thoughts and ideas successfully using oral, written, and nonverbal communication skills in a variety of forms and contexts;
- listen to decipher meaning, including knowledge, values, attitudes, and intentions;
- use communication for a range of purposes (e.g., to inform, motivate, and persuade);
- employ multiple media and technologies, and know how to judge their effectiveness and assess their impact;
- communicate effectively in varied environments (including multilingual).

Isn't that what any world language teacher (and our administrators) wants to see happening? To do any of those, learners must actively participate.

Does Active Learning Really Work?

There is now a huge body of research on active learning that did not exist when this book was first published. The largest and most comprehensive recent study (Freeman et al., 2014) looked at 225 other studies dealing with STEM (Science, Technology, Engineering and Mathematics) students and here is what they found:

1 Students in a classroom using traditional (primarily lecture) methods are 1.5 times more likely to fail, compared to students in classrooms that use active learning strategies.
2 Students in active learning classes outperform those in traditional lectures on identical exams. On average, students taught with active learning got scores 6 percent higher than students in a traditional class (the difference between a B and a B+, for example).
3 Students from minority ethnic groups, disadvantaged backgrounds, and/or women in male-dominated fields (in the study, also called "underrepresented students") benefit more from and achieve more than other categories of students when active learning is used.

In Freeman's words, (in an interview with D. Lederman, 2014):

> The impact of these data should be like the Surgeon General's report on "Smoking and Health" in 1964—they should put to rest any debate about whether active learning is more effective than lecturing.

In a study by Marzano (2007), careful statistical methods averaged the findings of thousands of the most rigorous studies on active learning. Results showed that, for the best active methods, students in the active learning group scored more than a grade and a half better than those in the group not using active learning.

In another study, however, there was another finding that I feel I must include in this book. Tessa Andrews et al. (2011) noticed that most studies on active learning were done by educators who were very committed to education, experienced, and well informed. How, they wondered, would an "ordinary" instructor do? They studied 29 courses taught at 28 institutions by 33 instructors, and found . . . no difference. They went on to state that their results imply that it only works with instructors who know *why* active learning works. My version of this is: successful active learning depends on an instructor well informed about learning theory, in order to know what best they should ask their students to do. (Again, going back to the sports metaphor, a well-trained coach).

In *Understanding by Design* (Wiggins and McTighe, 2006), the authors make it clear that simply introducing activity into the classroom does not work. An effective activity must be designed with the end (desired outcome) in mind, and encourage thoughtful engagement on the part of the learner.

That is the basic reason for this chapter on theory. In order to construct and use an active learning lesson effectively, you must have some knowledge of how learning happens, and what works best.

In order to achieve this goal, we will need to modify what we do every day in the classroom. We need to implement two very important goals:

1   Be current.
2   Use variety.

Chapters 1, 2, and 6 of this book will deal with information you need to be on the cutting edge of foreign language teaching. Brain research, multiple intelligences, and alternative assessment are all important to know about, and, if implemented, will add a lot to your success as a teacher.

The other chapters in this book will address the issue of using variety. Creating a great class requires imagination, creativity, and innovation—and taking advantage of every teaching opportunity. We must have a classroom that allows students to experience, experiment, fail, or discover without punishment. The teacher who can do this is prepared to meet the challenges of this era in foreign language education. Chapter 2, in presenting multiple intelligences, will also have many ideas you can use daily, and Chapters 3 through 5 present some creative ideas for presenting and practicing in a different way, and which will appeal to your students.

But first, we need to spend some time thinking about learning and cognition and how that applies to the classroom.

Brain Research

Improvements in magnetic resonance imaging (MRI), as well as research in neuroscience and cognitive psychology have confirmed earlier theories of developmental psychology. Watching someone's brain while they are hearing a foreign language, or studying it, or trying to memorize anything, has shown us that the basic strategies we use to teach languages work, but can stand to be improved or modified (such as increasing the frequency of certain types of activities and decreasing others) for better learning. It is logical that the more the brain is stimulated because the learner's environment is rich and varied, the more brain activity there will be.

Knowing how the brain processes information and learns is invaluable in deciding how to structure a lesson, and which materials you'll need.

The brain has priorities for storing material:

1   The highest priority is for anything that is a threat to survival. Unfortunately, menacing students' survival would result in the loss of our jobs. Failing Friday's test is not life threatening, much as we may like to think so.
2   The second highest priority is for information attached to a strong emotion. When emotions such as anger, fear, or joy are evoked, the conscious processing of the brain stops, and the older limbic system takes over. This sort of effect is one that we can achieve in the classroom occasionally; for example, the thrill of discovery of a concept through inductive or deductive teaching would help maximize what material is stored. We all know the value of humor, too. Enjoyable activities bring positive emotions into memory retrieval.

A lot of material is remembered because it has emotional associations attached to it. Think of a word such as "Mom," "holocaust," "abortion," or even "Monday" and a lot of other words, ideas, or pictures will pour into your mind. Helping students make these associations will increase learning. Memory Model, a method explained in Chapter 2, is good for encouraging this type of association.

After this, priority is given to material that the working memory thinks is important. The working memory is what 10 years ago was called the short-term memory. Its capacity changes with age (a high-school student has a larger capacity than a child, for example) and it has a definite time limit. Ebbinghaus (1885), in his research on forgetting, memorized long lists of nonsense syllables (what could be more like a foreign language, at first) and stated that the time limit for memorizing is 45 minutes. Sousa (2016) states that recent research has found that the time limit is actually between 10 and 20 minutes for adolescents and adults (see Figure 1.1).

Figure 1.1 Shows the Value of Changing Teaching Strategies or Topics Within a Longer Class Period

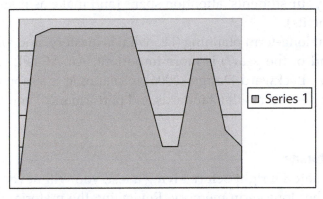

Retention During a 20-Minute Learning Episode

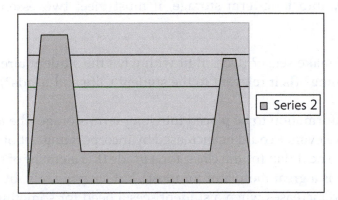

Retention During a 40-Minute Learning Episode with One Lesson

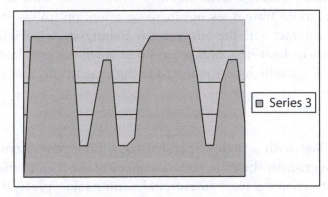

Retention During Two 20-Minute Learning Episodes (40 min.)

From Sousa (2016)

A brain, it seems, is like a cup; you can pour information into it for only so long, and either fatigue or boredom sets in. In order for a person to be able to focus their attention past that time, *change* must take place. By change, I mean that there must be a radical difference in how the material is taught, for example, from a thinking activity to physically dealing with the ideas, or making different connections between the material and other learning.

Sousa states that the average attention span of anyone 14 years or older is roughly 15 minutes! This has profound meaning for all of us, especially those on a block schedule, with 70- to 90-minute classes: variety is not only suggested, it is a necessity. Try appealing to different intelligences (see Chapter 2) or alternate grammar, culture, conversation, reading, and listening activities to maximize your students' attention spans (and make as many of those as active as possible for added benefits).

This also means that long-term planning (i.e., what is mastery, and what do you want them to remember at the end of the year?) is more important. An ACTFL Core Practice is to use Wiggins and McTighe's Backward Design (2006) in planning a lesson or unit, which means that you determine the desired result (standards and performance) and then plan a lesson that will have that result.

Criteria for Long-Term Storage

If you usually review material right before giving a test, you will never know if a student has that material in his or her long-term memory. Reviewing the material re-enters that material in a student's working memory (data retained for immediate use). In order for data to go from the working memory into long-term storage, it must meet two essential conditions. Ask yourself:

1   Does the material make sense? (Does it fit with what the student already knows?)
2   Does it have meaning? (Is it relevant to the student's life and needs?)

In order for the information to be placed into long-term storage, the answer to both questions must be "yes." Relevance could be increased by incorporating action: requiring a student to recite something the next day for the class, for a grade (the element of being on display and possibly embarrassed is a great motivator for most), but *not* passively, by giving a quiz or test over it. Relevance also increases when a student sees a need for something every day, rather than just once.

Data will also not enter the long-term memory without *time*: time to process and rehearse the material. However, more time does not increase retention unless it is time in which the student can personally interact with the information. Ebbinghaus (1885) found that we remember best whatever we see or hear first, and second best is whatever is last (see Figure 1.1 again for the most recent findings which corroborate Ebbinghaus.) With that in mind, Sousa (2016) suggests the following:

Teach New Material First

Instead of beginning class with a review, present something new. Remembering to teach in short (10–20 minute) segments, the new material should take 8 to 10 minutes at most. In the middle of that segment, when the least amount of learning takes place, do your review of previously learned material, or check homework, make announcements, or practice the new material. During the middle time, the brain is still capable of organizing the information for further processing, so it's not wasted time, but no information will be put in long-term storage during that time.

Teach Right to the End of Class and Provide Closure

Giving the students 5 minutes' free time at the end of the class is an absolute waste of those 5 or so minutes at the end, which scientists say are second best for learning. Save something new or important for the end.

Use Chunking

Instead of focusing on teaching a certain number of new items (most will be forgotten overnight, according to Ebbinghaus), a better strategy would be to integrate those items with previously learned structures, in hopes of "chunking" them. An example might be, when teaching descriptive adjectives, to add them to family members: instead of just learning "tall" or "smart," teach them "My father is tall and smart." Highlighting cognates is also a good strategy.

Successful Teaching Practices

Questions like, "Why do we need to know this?" or "Do we need to know this?" reveal students who are having trouble seeing relevancy in the material studied. Dr. Madeline Hunter (2004) of the University of California has also done a lot of research on the interrelationship between teaching strategies and student performance. She suggests, like Sousa did, that teachers:

- Select material to present during the first part of a lesson, condensing it to the smallest possible amount that will have maximum meaning for the students.
- Model the steps to apply to deal with the particular situation being studied, such as putting the correct endings on verbs, making adjectives agree, selecting the correct verb tense, or using a dictionary correctly. A good model is very specific and accurate, and avoids any controversial or emotional issues or words that will distract or redirect the students' attention.
- Bring in examples from students' own experiences to bring previous knowledge into the working memory (i.e., reminding them of another verb tense that is formed in a similar manner).
- Create artificial ways of giving meaning to the material. A good example of this is the use of mnemonic devices, or strategies like Memory Model, found in Chapter 2.
- Insist that students practice in class, in a focused manner. Focus them by standing near them, especially if they are off task. We have all seen how well this works.
- Provide prompt and detailed feedback for students during practice of a concept. If students receive quick corrective and specific feedback, they are more likely to continue working. This also permits students to evaluate their progress.
- Use every available minute of class time. This involves using "sponges," a concept that I have found very helpful.

Sponges

What do your students do while you are taking attendance, writing on the board, accessing a video or web site, talking to a student, parent, or colleague one-on-one, or when moving from whole class to small groups? The answer is probably that they start talking in English, or get off task (their attention wanders). If you have sponges ready to assign, you will be able to get students to use these bits of time to do something constructive in the target language (TL).

SPONGE is an acronym for:

- SHORT, intense, vivid activities, which provide
- PRACTICE of learned material, which students can do
- ON THEIR OWN, and which will also include
- NEW arrivals or those finishing an assignment early, by keeping the
- GROUP involved, and designed to
- ELICIT an immediate response.

Sponge is a good name for them, because they do "soak up" the unused little bits of time during any class. They also are very useful for a short break in a lesson or a change of pace when students' eyes are glazing over, when frustration (for me, usually with technology access) is building. Well-designed sponges also will appeal to a large variety of student learning styles and reinforce your curriculum quite nicely, and you will notice that they all involve active learning.

To write sponges, just think of the chapter in all four aspects: grammar, vocabulary, culture, and literature. Then, consider the five different types of sponge:

1 Say to yourself
2 Say to another
3 Say in chorus
4 Write a response
5 Signal.

NOTE: In the book from this page on, all activities will be notated showing which Common Core (CCSS) or ACTFL standards are being addressed, and sometimes Bloom's level (B) or Depth of Knowledge (DOK)

In the "Say to yourself"-type of sponge, you ask the student to tell themselves something. This type of quiet activity is good for settling down things at the beginning of class, after a fire drill or an announcement, while you are erasing the board, when students are moving into or out of small groups, or after a test while a few slower ones are still finishing.

Here are some examples of this type of sponge:

- Describe to yourself what you see in this picture/poster/video with the sound OFF.
- Look at this handout, and underline all the words you already know (or, the ones you don't know).
- Think of how the character in yesterday's story/movie was feeling when . . .
- Read the story/dialogue/paragraph and make up an appropriate title for it.

> CCSS: RL 1, RL 2, RL 4, RL 6, SL 2, SL 2, SL 3, L1, L4
> ACTFL: 1.1, 1.2, 1.3, 2.1, 2.2, 3.1, 3.2, 4.2
> B: Evaluate; Remember
> DOK 1 if just items, 4 if a scene

Notice that all sponges use action verbs in the command form.

A "Say to another" sponge asks a student to do a short activity with a partner, such as:

- Alternate naming objects, verb endings, colors, favorite foods, etc.
- Take turns describing a family photograph they have brought to class.
- Practice the dialogue. Then switch roles.
- Tell each other the most important thing you learned in this class yesterday/today (very useful, especially if there were several on a field trip or testing the day before).
- One of you, name a category such as "clothing." The other will name as many items as they can that fit in that category.
- Ask your partner a question.
- Taking turns, one of you name a verb, and the other will conjugate it in the _____ tense. Then switch.
- Tell your partner something funny/sad/complimentary/insulting.

> CCSS: SL 1, 2, 3, 4, 5, 6, L4
> ACTFL: 1.1, 1.2, 1.3, 2.1, 2.2, 3.1, 3.2, 4.1, 5.1
> B: Remember
> DOK 1

This sort of activity will involve the students in teaching/correcting each other, which according to the Glasser scale (see Figure 1.2), is quite beneficial.

Figure 1.2 Glasser's Learning Scale

We Learn . . .

10 Percent of What We Read

20 Percent of What We Hear

30 Percent of What We See

50 Percent of What We Both See and Hear

70 Percent of What Is Discussed with Others

80 Percent of What We Experience Personally

90 Percent of What We *Teach* to Someone Else

William Glasser

The third, "Say in chorus," asks students to say, together, things like the alphabet, months or days of the week. They could also sing a song learned in class, chant the verb endings for the preterite, count by fives to a thousand.

Something I like to do is make them do these things forward and backward, to make sure they understand what they are saying, rather than simply memorizing a string of sounds.

> CCSS: SL 1, 4
> ACTFL: 1.1, 1.3, 1.2, 4.1, 5.1
> DOK 1

The "written response" sponge would ask the student to write something like the following:

> CCSS: W 2, 4, L 1, 2, 4, 6
> ACTFL: 1.3, 3.1, 4.1, 5.1
> B: Remember
> DOK 1

- List the four seasons, and typical weather for each one.
- Record what you want your friends/teacher/parents to do for you.
- Make a list of foods that are served (or never served) at the school cafeteria.
- Produce a five-word description of the story/poem we read yesterday.
- Write a five-word description of your favorite place to visit/favorite sandwich/favorite class.
- Finish this sentence: The teacher is . . .
- Use the same noun in the nominative, accusative, and genitive cases.
- Name four famous people and tell what country they are from/what clothing they would wear/what they look like.
- Write eight commands or questions that you often hear from your parents.
- Indicate in writing three things you ought to do some time soon.

"Signal" appeals to almost any student learning style (oral, visual, kinetic, etc.) but most are essentially listening activities. Examples of signals would be hitting the desk, stomping feet, standing up, lifting a piece of paper, or some other sort of physical demonstration to indicate if:

> CCSS: RL1 if word is written, RL3 written, SL2 if oral, SL2 spoken, SL3 spoken, L1, 3
> ACTFL: 1.2, 1.3
> DOK 2

- a word is masculine or feminine, singular or plural, nominative or genitive, etc.;
- a sentence (written or spoken) is true or false;
- a verb is in the past or present, future or conditional, indicative or subjunctive (to differentiate tenses);
- a given situation requires the passé composé/preterite or the imperfect.

In summary, sponge activities keep you from wasting valuable class time as well as requiring students to continue thinking and performing in the language. Make every minute count, and test scores should go up too. This is not a skill you will gain overnight, but don't give up, as you will see a big difference in classroom discipline and in learning.

Figure 1.3 shows some sponge activities I use when doing a unit on families and family members.

Figure 1.3 Family Unit Sponges

Note: These would normally be written in the TL.

Say to Self

- The number of cousins you like, with a separate count of boy cousins and girl cousins.
- How many brothers and sisters you have.
- The name, age, and relationship to you of your favorite relative.
- The name, age, and relationship to you of your least favorite relative.
- Look at the family tree on the screen. You are the person marked with an X. Tell yourself what each person's relationship is to you.
- Look at the picture on the front board. Invent a name for each person in the family, and be ready to tell me their relationships to each other (i.e., Marie is the daughter of Luc and Claire, and the sister of Marc).
- Pick the hardest word in this chapter's vocabulary, and think of a creative way to remember it.

Say to Another

- Describe your family to your partner, and help him or her draw a family tree based on your description. Correct him or her gently if they get something wrong.
- Tell your partner who your favorite relative is, and why.
- Tell your partner who your least favorite relative is, and why.
- Alternate naming people on the family tree. After one of you names a name, the other must tell what family member that person is. For example, Véronique is a daughter, and a sister.
- Alternate saying one of the family vocabulary words. After one of you says a word, the partner must supply the equivalent for the opposite sex. For

example, if Person A says *uncle*, Person B must say *aunt*. Then Person B might say *husband*, and Person A must reply *wife*.

Write

- Draw your family tree. Don't forget the word "my" with each one.
- Pick up one of the cut-out magazine photos on the desk. Each is of a family. In writing, introduce me to the people in the photograph, including their name, age, relationship and profession, if they are an adult.
- Write a postcard to a penpal in France. Tell them about your family.
- Read the story, and draw a family tree based on the information in the story.

Say in Chorus

- List the male family members, from oldest to youngest (Grandpa—Dad—Uncle—Brother—Cousin), forward and backward.
- List the female family members from oldest to youngest, forward and backward.

Signal

- Show me by holding up fingers how many aunts you have.
- Show me by clapping your hands how many uncles you have.
- Show me by stomping your feet how many cousins you have.
- Show me by hitting the desk how many husbands you have.
- Show me by snapping your fingers how many brothers you have.
- Show me by nodding your head how many sisters you have.
- Show me by kicking your left foot how many pets you have.

Spiraling

Dr. Hunter (2004) also discovered that "massed" practice is inferior to "distributed." Massed practice means trying a concept in a variety of different ways, over a short period of time. Distributed practice is when material is practiced over time. According to Dr. Hunter, tests should not only test material in the current chapter, but should also allow/expect students to use material previously learned. This is called a "spiral curriculum" because the ideas and skills are used again and again. Too often learners study a verb or verb tense during one unit, and then the next unit is primarily vocabulary, with no more use of the previous material until several units later. Change an activity in every unit following learning that verb or tense, enabling students to continue to practice it, or supplementing the text or unit with a reading in that tense or a composition requiring it would be an easy way to "spiral" ideas. Integrated Performance Assessments (IPAs) are also good (later in this chapter)

Motivational Factors

Another thing Hunter (2004) discovered was that motivational factors can increase the time that working memory can deal with language.

- Interest: If the learner is interested in the item, he or she is dealing with it in several ways, often making new connections to past learning. Interest will significantly extend a student's attention span. We have all seen it happen: a student who can't listen/write/read for 2 minutes will raptly play a game involving that skill for an hour, especially if it involves working with others. My students love to work collaboratively and cooperatively.
- Accountability: If students believe they will be held accountable for the material, processing time is increased. (Example: drivers ed. classes have both the interest factor and accountability.) To stimulate a feeling of accountability, show students how a skill might be necessary later in life (connecting the present to the future).
- Level of concern: If students are to care about learning, they need to have a little "helpful anxiety." Students who are concerned about doing a better job will try harder to learn more. Too much concern, however, is not good. Here's how you can help students to feel some helpful anxiety:
  - Give consequences. Low-level ones like "Knowing this will help you in the next chapter" raise anxiety less than "This will be on your semester exam."
  - Stand near them. We all know this works well if students are off task.
  - Give the right amount of time to do the task. Too little time raises anxiety, and extending the time will lower it.
  - Help them quickly. This is the most difficult one, as you don't want students to become too dependent on you.

Using Gestures

Research by several American psychologists has shown that using one's hands while talking can unlock something they call "lexical memory," helping people retrieve words from their long-term memory storage. Even pantomiming an activity can help retrieve the memory of the activity and data or learning associated with it. Also, physical movement releases acetylcholine, a brain chemical associated with communication.

We have known for years that gestures can be a language themselves, such as American Sign Language (ASL) used by handicapped students. In fact, many world language teachers currently using the Comprehensive Input (CI), methods such as Accelerative Integrated Method (AIM) or Total Physical Response Storytelling (TPRS), report that they use ASL gestures while telling a story in the TL, which enhances students' comprehension and retrieval of the vocabulary.

Begley (1998) shows that gesture is like a key to unlock a door in the brain, especially for words that connect easily with spatial ideas or movement, for example, the word *castanets*. Researchers attached electrodes to people's arms, and found that people who didn't even think they were gesturing were actually activating their muscles in response to words (for instance, a "clench" movement for the word *castanets*.) Doctors also notice that people whose memory is impaired after a stroke also tend to gesture more.

This makes sense: the more associations, especially using the senses, we can link to a word, the more accessible it becomes. I often use gestures to practice reflexive verbs such as wake up, hurry, get dressed, comb hair, brush teeth, as well as the less spatially obvious ones like remember, be nervous, have fun, and other emotions. I have my students decide which gestures we will use (this is important as if they feel they created/voted for the action, they learn it better.) As we begin to practice them, I'll say, "this one was Mark's verb" to prompt them, and they all nod and do the action as they say the verb) and we rehearse using gestures: first, as I say the word, they do the gesture, and later I gesture and they say the word, and then they do the same with a partner. Later, individually, I will see many of them gesture, nod, and write. It really seems to help.

Not only does using gestures help retrieve items from long-term memory, the ownership of thinking of the gestures, as well as the extra sensory stimulation of doing them, makes the material more likely to go from the working memory into the long-term memory. In one study done at the University of North Carolina at Greensboro, subjects had to hold on to a bar so they were unable to use their hands. These subjects often failed to learn the vocabulary, or took longer to do so, than a group who were allowed to use their hands.

In conclusion, students should be encouraged to think in spatial terms for any vocabulary. Even abstract concepts like "freedom" may be linked to some sort of physical idea that would be easy to make into a gesture, and this will enable students to learn it more easily, and to retrieve it again more quickly.

Increasing Transfer

Transfer is the ability to learn something in a certain situation, and then apply it to other situations. Transfer is involved in problem solving, creative thinking, artistic endeavors, and other higher-level mental activities.

As new material is introduced to the working memory, it searches through the long-term storage for similar material. We have probably all experienced hearing a song that brings with it a flood of old memories associated with it. This is another example of how emotion attached to information guarantees its storage in long-term memory. It is also an example of transfer in action. Specifics on using music to aid memory are in Chapter 2.

But studies show that students are generally not good at recognizing how things learned in school apply to life outside school (Perkins and Salomon, 1992). Teachers should help them look for two things when new information is introduced in order to maximize transfer: similarities and differences.

Similarities means linking the past to the present: showing students how one verb tense resembles one they already know, or how the Spanish/French use of the preterit and imperfect is similar to how it is used in English. It could be things like talking about the ways Japanese food is similar to what they can get at the Chinese restaurant in town. Discovering similarities helps students' brains decide what material already in long-term storage this new material fits with, and can be stored with ("chunking"). Positive transfer is especially easy when the two skills (new and old) are similar: learning one Romance language makes learning a second one easier, for example. When similarities exist with "old" material, the brain simply adds the new to the old, and stores it as a chunk of information.

Metaphors, analogies, and similes are especially effective ways to promote positive transfer. For example, telling students that conjugating a verb is like smoking a cigar: first, the tip is clipped off, which is like dropping off the –en, –ar, –ir, or whatever ending is on the verb as it is found in the dictionary. Then, a match is needed (matching the new ending with the subject pronoun) and then, as the end of the cigar changes appearance as it is transformed into ash, a new ending appears on the part of the verb that was left when the end was clipped off. Or, for compound tenses, compare fixing a sandwich with conjugating a verb: trim off the crust/endings, put in some filling (helping verb, adverbs, negatives, and pronouns) and so on … Any colorful comparisons such as these, especially if accompanied by a poster or drawing containing this same image (for the visual learners), will positively affect students' ability to remember the material.

Students also need help linking the present to the future. While material is filed in long-term storage by its similarity, it is retrieved by its differences, called "critical attributes." An example from everyday life would be finding a friend in a crowd of people. To find your friend, you need to think about what about him or her is different from everyone else, and look for those attributes. Here again is a place where the teacher can guide students to discover what the critical attributes of the new information are, so they can find it when they need it again. If material is very similar, it will be hard to learn.

Another way to link the present to the future is to provide students with an activity in which they will have to use the current information to communicate: a simulation. Simulations are discussed in depth in Chapter 2.

Providing Variety

Variety is the key to learning, but be careful! Too much variety is as bad as too little. Sousa (2016) warns us not to overload students with symbols, images, and input—the working memory in older students can only hold *seven* items at a time (see chart in Figure 1.4).

Students must have time to process, select, and file information before more is added. However, since students are usually either verbal or visual learners, providing information in both modes will not overload anyone, as a verbal student's working memory will retain verbal

Figure 1.4 Changes in Working Memory with Age

Age range	Minimum no. of items	Maximum no. of items	Average
Less than 5	1	3	2
5 to 14	3	7	5
14 and older	5	9	7

information, while a visual student will process what is taught verbally. Use graphic organizers (i.e., diagrams) to talk about relationships between subject and object pronouns, masculine and feminine adjectives, or other concepts that are easy to organize into groupings. Show the smallest possible portion of a video, then stop it and discuss what was shown.

Here is a possible visual representation activity: after reading a story, have students draw a stick person and attach their notes to it. Have them write the character's ideas and draw a line to the brain, his hopes and dreams with a line to the eyes, words to the mouth, actions to the hands, feelings to the heart, movements to the feet, and so on.

Diagram the plot of the story like a mountain: the causes on the left (upward) slope, the effects on the right (downward) slope, and the conclusions (theme/message/moral) at the base.

Appealing to Upper-Level Thinking Skills

Using Bloom's taxonomy scale (see Figure 1.5), let's examine the types of thinking skills you can ask students to do. The bottom level, Knowledge, is just rote recitation ("What is the word for 'cat'?") The Comprehension level asks students to summarize, or convert the information to a new form ("Why is Cecile's cat important in the story?") The Application level has the student use the information in a new situation ("If Cecile brought her cat to your house, what would you do?") The Analysis level and above are where you want to concentrate the majority of your classroom activity. At this level, students will be actively using the language to communicate more than just basic necessities. They may also notice a gap between what they want to say and what they are able to say, test hypotheses about the TL, and also retain more of the language they were successful in using. For example, an Analysis question would ask, "What happened in this story that is typically French?" or ". . . that could really happen?" A Synthesis activity is one that results in a product, such as having them retell the story from another viewpoint, or adding Cecile's brother, or a dog. An Evaluation activity asks students to make a judgment based on given criteria: "Was it right for Cecile's cat to eat her sandwich?"

Another scale based on educational research is that of William Glasser. His scale shows the outcomes of various teaching strategies in terms of the amount of information that is put into long-term storage. Figure 1.2 showed Glasser's learning scale, which I have posted on my classroom wall. It is easy to see that watching a video on how to make croissants only engages

Figure 1.5 Bloom's Taxonomy Scale

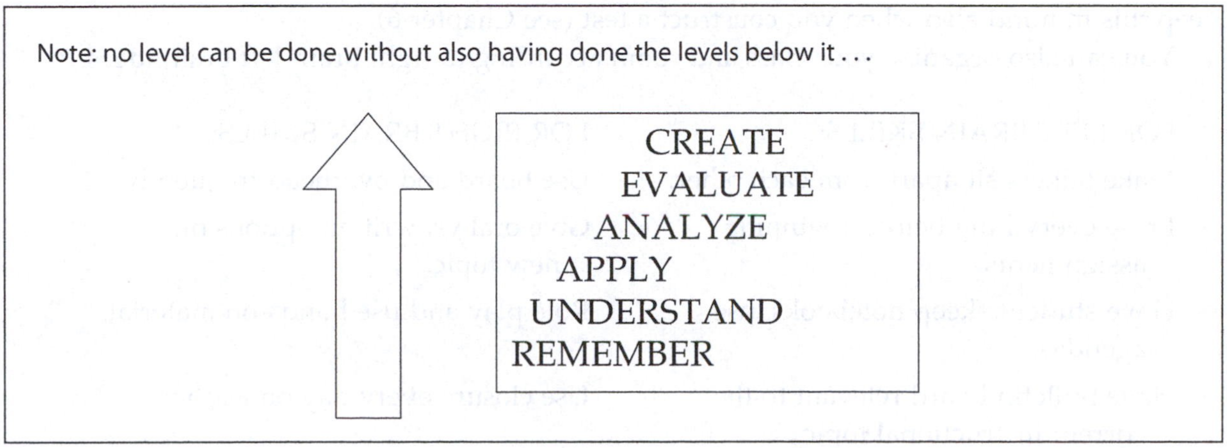

Note: no level can be done without also having done the levels below it . . .

CREATE
EVALUATE
ANALYZE
APPLY
UNDERSTAND
REMEMBER

students through eyes and ears, but taking them to actually make and eat them offers feel, smell, taste, and a lively discussion as well as an enjoyable activity and interactions with class-mates. Again, we can reach the same conclusion: students working with the language on a personal, individual level (whether with a partner, a group, or one-on-one with the teacher) are learning the most.

Right Brain/Left Brain Learning

Right brain/left brain research and information tells us that girls tend to be more left brained, and boys more right brained. Whatever your beliefs about this aspect, it should be obvious that this is yet another reason to include as much variety as possible in your lesson to accom-modate the different learning styles of your students. To briefly summarize in terms of foreign language learning, the left brain processes "text," coding information verbally, and the right brain handles "context," nonverbal, visual information. The right brain is superior, according to Danesi, in processing new information and stimuli.

For foreign language and ESL teachers, it is *very important* to begin instruction following a right-to-left hemisphere sequence of strategies (Danesi, 1990). This means that you should initi-ally teach students using brainstorming and concrete visual strategies, only later moving on to more organizational and formal types of instruction such as drill, translation, dictation, etc.

Do not rely heavily on grammar or vocabulary memorization during the early stages of instruction. Do more with contextual activities, incorporating trial and error, brainstorming of meaning, visual activities, and role-playing/simulations such as TPR and TPRS (all examples of active learning), giving the right hemisphere time to establish the context of the activity. The right brain uses verbal and nonverbal cues to adapt speech to a specific person or social context, and enables students to use grammatical forms (i.e., usted vs. tu, vous vs. tu, Sie vs. du–type) in context.

After the right brain has the context it needs to grasp meaning and nuance, then apply left brain-type activities (vocabulary memorization and grammar drills). This approach benefits left brain learners as well as right, since it increases the role their right brain plays in their language competence. The left brain does the analytical and sequential processing of infor-mation necessary for vocabulary, rules of punctuation, word formation, and sentence structure.

Conversational competence involves both hemispheres, says research, in order to combine form and thought into something coherent. The analytic ability of the left brain generates the grammatical features, while the right brain synthesizes them into meaningful, coherent wholes. Keep this in mind also when you construct a test (see Chapter 6).

You can also organize your class and room according to right brain-left brain ideas.

FOR LEFT BRAIN SKILLS:	FOR RIGHT BRAIN SKILLS:
Make talkers sit apart from each other.	Use board and overhead frequently.
Erase everything before beginning assignments.	Give oral vs. written options on new topic.
Have students keep notebooks, use agendas.	Role play and use hands-on material.
Have bulletin board relevant to the current instructional topic.	Use closure every day on lessons.

Both types will benefit from lots of metaphor and simile-creation activities, or "what if" questions, such as "how is this verb tense like (other verb tense)" or "What if we tried to draw a picture based on this poem? What would it look like?"

Metamemory Techniques

Metamemory is the area of study that deals with people's understanding how their own memory functions, and using that to their own benefit. Students will often tell us how hard they studied, yet they perform poorly on tests. Teaching them some basic metamemory knowledge about themselves may help them study more efficiently. Memory is based upon three sets of variables: personal, task, and strategy variables.

To discover what your personal variables are, ask yourself what you remember best. Is it the words to songs (things set to music)? Things that rhyme? Things stated like a formula? Things you hear, say, or see? If, for instance, you remember musical things, then put whatever you have to memorize to music. Sing it to a familiar tune, such as a commercial jingle, or a nursery song such as "Twinkle, Twinkle Little Star." Another type of important personal variable is discovering what time of day is best: are you a morning person? A night owl? And what mood you need to be in to study well. Then, arrange your schedule as much as possible to make use of that time and that mood. If you study best late at night when the family is asleep, take a nap before or after dinner so that you can use the late-night hours without falling asleep in school. If you need to be in a relaxed mood, discover music that relaxes you and play it softly in the background.

Task variables that affect learning are things such as the amount of information involved, essay tests versus objective ones, and the different approaches taken by different instructors. If you learn small amounts of information (i.e., chapter tests) better than large ones such as exams, plan to study a chapter a night until the exam rather than cramming the night before. Since objective tests require more knowledge of detail, a person good at trivia/details might want to ask for an objective test, while a person who likes to understand the "big picture" would prefer an essay format. Some teachers provide choices in test format. Often, in bigger schools, students also have a choice of teachers. If they have found one whose teaching style seems to suit their learning style, they should request that teacher for future classes, if possible.

Finally, strategy variables are important. Mnemonics are one strategy that works for almost everyone. For example, "Caroline" contains all the letters that are doubled in Spanish. This could really help when, for example, spelling *gato* (cat)—since there are no "t"s in Caroline, the "t" in *gato* cannot be doubled. A variation of mnemonics is to make a silly sentence using the first letter in a string of words to memorize. Another Spanish example is to list the Spanish-speaking countries in South America (Venezuela, Colombia, etc.) as the sentence Victoria Can't Eat Peas, Beets, Carrots, and Uncooked Potatoes. Let the students, however, make up their own sentences, or have a class contest to do so, and they'll remember them better. The word "Careful" is useful in French, as it contains the letters that are pronounced at the end of words; in most cases, all other letters are silent. I still remember inventing (and drawing a caterpillar-like monster) the "Be-ent-er-ver-zer" (one syllable on each section of the monster) in order to remember some verbs with inseparable prefixes for a German lesson. The name contained the beginnings of all the verbs I needed to remember.

Education Abroad

Japanese students traditionally score higher than American students on tests, and social psychologists have been studying their educational system and techniques to determine what differences there are. They hope to apply these to education here in America; the University of Michigan in particular is investigating and promoting the Japanese approach to learning.

The major differences lie in students doing less drill and seatwork, and less repetitive practice during class time. Instead, whole class discussions and PBL are initiated that encourage students to find solutions and strategies, explaining their thought processes. Students are encouraged to give feedback to each other. Japanese texts also purposely use real-life situations to show the relevance of what is being taught, along with eye-catching pictures, and many short story-type presentations of data such as vocabulary or grammar ideas.

The countries (including Japan) whose students score better than ours do basically use the following ideas:

- More is not better. In-depth learning is preferable to quantity of material covered.
- Conceptual thinking is used much more often than rote memorization and drill.
- Problem solving and sharing strategies and concepts are the best strategy.
- The person leading the discussion should not supply the answer right away, so all can participate.
- Learning should be made meaningful for students.

I find it interesting that the above five strategies are some that not only are sound according to the principles of the latest brain research, but that teachers on block schedules also often emphasize. When teachers worry about "getting the material covered," perhaps they are overlooking the benefits of in-depth coverage. Learning that goes into long-term storage is the goal of educators, rather than a "spray and pray" approach.

The conceptual idea can easily be applied to language learning by using methods I observed in math classes. When a teacher asks a student to write on the board, the teacher afterward asks the student to explain why he or she wrote it in that way. Walking mentally back through the thought processes that were used, such as "I decided to use the imperfect tense because this was description, and so I dropped X from the verb, and added Y," will more firmly fix the process necessary in that student's memory. It will also embed the idea in classmates' minds, due to the frequency of hearing others go through the same processes that they themselves used, or perhaps hearing an approach they had not yet considered. Taking the class time to do this is important, and should show good results.

Using Concept Attainment and deduction strategies (based on scientific observation of data, drawing conclusions from it, and forming a hypothesis or vice versa) fits perfectly with the active learning, through discussion of learning.

Concept Attainment

This activity, which begins on the individual level, proceeds to pairs work, and ends as a group activity. It is used to introduce new material, replacing the traditional lecture method. Prior to beginning the activity, the teacher selects the concept to introduce, and also chooses and organizes the examples that contain characteristics of this concept. At least 20 pairs are needed, especially for more complex concepts. Few texts provide such lists, so it will involve a bit of work and thought. Concept Attainment works well for introducing concepts like masculine/feminine/neuter endings, teaching students to identify a particular style of art or that of a particular artist, or learning how to form a new verb tense.

In Phase One of the activity, in class the teacher lists several examples, labeled as positive (good/"yes") examples of the concept or attribute, or as negative (bad/"no") examples. The teacher asks the students to contrast the positive examples with the negative (to themselves, not out loud), and to take notes on those differences. (Note: this would be a good sponge activity.) If he/she wants, the teacher could underline portions of the example in order to call attention to the important portion to examine. Then the teacher adds a few more examples, asking students to make a hypothesis about what the difference is between the positive and negative ones. Then, a few more examples are given, to test the hypothesis and refine it. Then, a new step: unlabeled examples are presented, and students are asked to (still working on their own, and not out loud) guess, using their hypothesis, if they are positive or negative. (Students love this approach: it is challenging, yet game-like.)

Phase Two begins when it looks like most of the students have a workable hypothesis. (Use body language to identify this: nodding heads, smiles, etc.) Pair the students and have them share hypotheses with their partner and then test these new, combined/synthesized hypotheses with a few more unlabeled examples. The final step is to share these as a whole class discussion. At this time, the teacher confirms the correct hypotheses, refining how they are stated if necessary, and supplies the name of the concept (i.e., "This is called the future tense, and you have correctly identified how it is different"). Finally, the student pairs generate their own examples of this concept.

Concept Attainment is also an excellent review tool or evaluation tool if you want to check to see if some material you covered previously has been mastered: by giving good and bad examples of the concept, you will determine the students' depth of knowledge by how quickly they catch on, and also reinforce their understanding of this concept.

Concept Development

There are three basic steps in this method, which was first used in scientific investigation:

First, a set of data on the topic is created, either by the students or by the teacher; second, the data elements are grouped into categories based on similarities observed; and third, these categories are labeled, or named. When students identify the similarities, they are using many higher-level thinking skills (interpreting, inferring, generalizing) that lead to a greater ability to manipulate the category and apply it to new situations, so this strategy is very often used to teach basic grammatical concepts such as how an adjective, adverb, phrase, or clause functions and how it is different from other parts of speech, *without* having to teach the concept in English, or use grammatical terms. Students, for example, provided with sentences with all the adverbs underlined, would group them into categories such as location, time, or description, and then you could discuss, still using the sample sentences, how any words that would fit these categories are placed in a typical sentence (i.e., immediately after the verb) without having to use the word "adverb."

A couple of warnings: the more examples the better, and, even more important, the simpler the better. Beware of "false decoys" such as sentences some with noun subjects and some with pronouns, or alternating adverb clauses with simple adverbs. Make sure the only element that varies is the adverb, or whatever concept you are presenting. Use the words in a sentence, so the students learn to handle them in context.

I like to use the Concept Development method in French for the simple –ir verbs (dormir, partir, servir, sortir, etc.), which are rather confusing for my students when simply presented separately in the book. A similarly useful activity is to present students with sets of irregular verbs whose nous/vous forms closely resemble the infinitive (vouloir and pouvoir, followed by aller, boire, and devoir) and have students discover this pattern for themselves, using Concept Development), and then apply it to new verbs.

One small variation is to have the students create their own data file (Step One), perhaps by looking at a page in a text, and making a list of what they see/read. For example, in French, by making a list of fruits, they might discover that most fruits listed are feminine in gender, and end in –e, a useful generalization.

Making it Meaningful

There are three lesson-planning strategies that also directly involve active learning. Each could (and probably does) have a book written about it alone, so I will only summarize these below:

Thematic Units

The emphasis on teaching foreign languages is on relevance. The National Standards' Communication, Communities, Culture, and the other two Cs all promote student involvement with the language, which in turn, according to brain research, will make that material more likely to go from the working memory to long-term storage. Interdisciplinary learning, another new trend, also aids students in making a lot of connections between material learned and material previously learned in other classes, making the material much more easy to retrieve from where it is stored in the brain.

Integrated Performance Assessments

An IPA is a perfect way to introduce active learning (and spiraling) as well as culturally authentic material and tasks (the great strength of this method) into a unit, perfectly correlated to the ACTFL National Standard #1: Communication. An IPA involves at least three tasks involving only one theme or concept (whether vocab, grammar, or cultural), one for each of the three modes—interpretive, interpersonal, and presentational. While the interpretive mode isn't usually very active, the other two modes are great examples of active learning.

An interpretive task usually involves having students listen to, view, or read something aligned to the learner's proficiency level (novice, intermediate, or advanced). Ideally it would be an authentic resource. Students are asked questions about it written on two levels: literal and interpretive. A literal-level question when reading a recipe might be "What word means 'potato'?" or "How many vegetables are listed?" An interpretive question might be "What meal would this dish be appropriate for?" or "What American dish might this be compared to?" or "What other ingredient could be added to make this even better?"

An interpersonal task generally involves speaking with another person in an unrehearsed and negotiated manner. Unrehearsed means learners need to "think on their feet," not memorize or read from notes. Negotiated means they must listen to the other person and react to what that person says. Staying with the food unit idea, I might have students plan aloud what they need to buy for a dinner party, how much to buy, and how it should be prepared. I could also set up a shopkeeper/shopper situation where one says the dish they want to make and the other recommends ingredients.

A presentational task is an oral or written performance done before an audience. This must be a "polished" product and so the preparation, practice, and revision process are important parts of the task; evaluation is done on all those, just not the final one. For a food unit, a video or live performance where a student prepares a culturally authentic dish is both high interest and enjoyable for the audience, as students love to sample food.

It doesn't matter at all which activity you do first, second, or third. Rubrics for evaluating IPAs are easily found online. An IPA may be done as a formative (practice) activity or one or more of the elements can be a summative grade for the theme or unit.

If you are a French teacher, I have a public IPA Resources Symbaloo online at this address: www.symbaloo.com/mix/frenchiparesources.

Project-Based Learning

Project-Based Learning (PBL) is also currently in vogue. It is just what the name says: learners are assigned a project involving a theme, topic, or skill, with a performance-based product. Projects allow and require for students to engage in real-life communication, in context, with real people, often across the globe. There are several requirements regarding the projects:

1　A need to know (involving student interests or a real-life application).
2　A driving question ("driving" is loaded with action!) A driving question should engage students to solve an authentic problem in a creative, standards-based way.
3　Student voice and choice: students may modify the project or choose their own groups or design the final assessment and/or rubric for the project, for example.
4　Twenty-first century skills (especially collaboration, communication, and critical thinking).
5　Innovation: Learners must not be able to use Google to find something to use without modification.
6　Feedback and revision: As for an IPA, there must be practice presentations and modifications to the original.
7　A product presented to an audience other than the teacher.

Again for a food unit, I would combine PBL with a study of a variety of different TL-speaking countries' cultures to create an ethnic restaurant here, representing the food from a chosen TL country. They would name the restaurant, develop a menu (complete with descriptions of the dishes), and also develop a logo, Twitter account, and website for it, consistent with authentic ones found on the Internet. To incorporate speaking, students would either do a recorded advertisement or a live pitch as the owners, wanting the audience (local or global) to come to their restaurant. To incorporate a global aspect, they might survey people in their chosen TL country online about their favorite foods and restaurants or post their final presentation for comments from them.

One final observation: If active learning works so well, why don't more teachers use it?

● We tend to teach the way we were taught. Try to think of what is best for the students!
● We know and love our subject matter and love helping others by explaining. But, just watch the energy in the room while you guide and encourage learners to explore actively. This can be much more enjoyable (and less work), and the feedback you'll get is very informative.

2

Research-Based
Active Learning Practices

In today's world, educational initiatives are expected to result in increased student achievement as measured by systematic, empirical research. This chapter will discuss the two most internationally known, scientifically researched, teacher-tested, and accepted learning methods, Gardner's multiple intelligences, and Marzano's best practices, with many active learning applications for each.

Gardner's Eight Intelligences, and Their Applications

In 1983, Howard Gardner proposed his Theory of Multiple Intelligences, which is accepted and taught widely today. He defines intelligences as "the capacity to solve problems or to fashion products that are valued in one or more cultural settings" (Gardner and Hatch, 1989). His theory is based on biological and cultural research, and expands the traditional outlook on intelligence from just two: verbal and computational, to involve also music, spatial relations, physical activity, and interpersonal and intrapersonal relations, as well.

Gardner's eight intelligences have several effects on classroom teachers as well as curriculum. His theory states that all eight intelligences: linguistic, logical-mathematical, visual-spatial, musical, bodily-kinesthetic, interpersonal, intrapersonal, and naturalist, are needed to function productively in society, and must be considered, therefore, of equal importance. Therefore, teachers need to use more variety when teaching to appeal to a broader range of talents and skills, to engage most or all of those intelligences.

This need for variety when teaching is one foreign language teachers have recognized for years, but perhaps have not implemented as effectively as we could. During one grading period, we perhaps did something musical, something active, something communicative, something artistic, and so on, but not during one unit, or one lesson. This chapter will suggest types of activities for you to choose from, for each type of intelligence. A varied presentation of material will not only excite students about learning, but will lead to a deeper understanding of the material because it reinforces the same topic in a variety of ways.

Using Multiple Intelligences in the Foreign Language Classroom

All students come into your classroom with different sets of developed intelligences. The fact that they all have strengths and weaknesses is not a new concept at all, but the fact that you, the teacher, need to appeal to many is perhaps newly emphasized. One way to do this is to modify assignments to accommodate more learning styles. For example, last time I gave an assignment that had previously only been one option—to write a short story—I offered two or three options: short story, poem, cartoon, postcard, song or rap, video, or PowerPoint. Not only did I get a wider variety of output, but also the general quality was better, more students completed their work, and test scores improved, as well.

Of course, it is foolish, and quite impractical, to appeal to every learning style in every lesson, but a little effort to offer more variety will pay great dividends, both in student engagement and performance and in their satisfaction with you and the language you teach. An awareness of your students' learning styles will also help you show them how to become better learners. For example, you could suggest that an especially musically intelligent student learn verb endings by making up a song about them, or a kinesthetic student should associate each subject-verb ending with a different gesture or movement. Teaching students how to use their more developed intelligences to learn material outside the classroom will also free you from having to appeal to every intelligence every time, instead working to strengthen their weaker learning styles.

Assessments need to be changed, as well. As you will see, the linguistic intelligence involves listening, reading, writing, and speaking a language—everything we do in a foreign language class. It's no surprise, then, that most standardized foreign language tests only appeal to this one intelligence. Assessments are needed that allow students to explain the material in their own ways using the different intelligences: student portfolios, projects, journals, performance assessments, and creative tasks. The ACTFL National Standards' emphasis on five aspects of foreign language teaching: Communication, Cultures, Connections, Comparisons, and Community, is evidence of our recognition for a need for variety in foreign language education. (Note: In this book, all activities suggested will be accompanied by notations showing what Common Core (CCSS), ACTFL, Bloom's (B) and Depth of Knowledge (DOK) standards and levels they incorporate.)

Especially interesting is that Gardner's research (2006) argues that culture plays a large role in the development of intelligence, and that different cultures will value different types of intelligence. The cultural value placed upon the ability to perform certain tasks provides the motivation to become skilled in that area. We, as foreign language teachers, should teach our students to look for these cultural differences, and understand them better.

Linguistic Intelligence

Linguistic intelligence, according to Gardner (2011), consists of the ability to read, write, and speak a language to express and appreciate complex meanings. It also involves the ability to use language in order to remember information (reading for understanding as well as taking notes). Linguistic intelligence-influenced teaching and testing dominates most Western educational systems (Lazear, 1999).

LISTENING

The first skill that is part of linguistic intelligence, and the first that foreign language students are asked to use, is listening. From the very first day of class, students will listen to the teacher

Figure 2.1 Gardner's Eight Intelligences

Linguistic
Listening, speaking, reading, and writing.

Logical-Mathemtical
Using deduction, induction, patterning, interpreting graphs, and sequencing ideas.

Visual-Spatial
Using three-dimensional ways to perceive imagery, navigate, produce, and decode information.

Musical
Using rhythm, tone, melody, and pitch.

Bodily-kinesthetic
Using the mind to control bodily movements and manipulate objects.

Interpersonal
Communicating and collaborating with others.

Intrapersonal
Maintaining self-esteem, setting goals for oneself, and acquiring values.

Naturalist
Sensing patterns in and making connections with elements in nature.

speak in the TL (ACTFL prescribes 90 percent usage of the TL). Listening is much more important than you may think. Postovsky (1981) found that focusing on training students in listening comprehension early in the first level had a much greater effect on the students' foreign language skills than did an initial focus on oral use of the language.

What many teachers do not realize about listening is that this activity inherently involves a huge time lag that students rarely take advantage of: a speaker can only speak about 200 words per minute, but a listener can hear and process from 300–500 words per minute (Campbell et al., 2004). Students need to learn how to make use of that extra time.

One easy way is to encourage the student to repeat, aloud or silently, all or part of what was heard. Repetition of passages appears to improve listening comprehension more than other technique (Berne, 1995).

Taking Notes. Teach your students to take notes, especially to identify the main purpose or main point the speaker is trying to make. When taking notes, also underlining the most important ideas supporting the main point, learners should place an asterisk (*) next to unclear concepts and/or particularly interesting items, as well as write questions. See Figure 2.2 for an example of a form given to teach note-taking as well as elicit multicultural observations. It was used as a part of a learning center, where students listened to a conversation in which two students planned their evening activities: where to go, what time to meet, and who to invite with them.

> CCSS: SL 2, 3
> ACTFL: 1.2, 2.1, 3.2, 4.1, 4.2, 5.1
> B: Understand
> DOK 2

Figure 2.2 Conversational Record

Conversational Record: Learning Station 3

Name _____

Date _____

Who is speaking?   _____

To whom?   _____

Where are they?   _____

What is the purpose of this conversation? _____

List the topics discussed:

   1 _____

   2 _____

   3 _____

   4 _____

What was their final decision? _____

Did this increase or decrease your stereotype(s) of French students? Explain.

List any questions you may have about this conversation (vocabulary words not understood, cultural ideas, places named, and so on):

What was the most interesting thing about this conversation?

Other things you could ask students about such a conversation, especially beginners, are: How many people are talking? How many male/female? Are they arguing or friendly? What do you think their relationship is? Doing this sort of activity early will reassure students that they are not expected to know everything they hear, and that they do understand more than they think they did. Confidence in listening abilities is an important attitude to instill in your students.

Authenticity. An important aspect of *any* TL activity is the need for two things: variety in the type of activity presented and authenticity. Foreign language students are usually asked to listen to conversations, to stories read aloud, and to lectures via the Internet or the teacher. These may be presented live, or on video or audio, by native speakers with a variety of accents, or by non-native speakers such as the teacher or classmates. Research on listening points to the increased benefits of video listening as opposed to audio only (Bal-Gezegin, 2014): remember the 30 percent better retention rate for "see and hear" vs. just "hear" (reviewed below).

Authenticity is also a strong factor in the quality of learning. There are strong arguments for using technology to provide a wide variety of listening activities through TL films on DVD or the Internet, as well as native speakers and music. The more different types of sources, different types of listening passages, and different modes of presentation, the better the language is learned (Rost, 1991).

Finally, it is possible to teach your student to be a better listener, but you might be surprised which approaches seem to work best. One way that research says has little benefit is providing students with a list of vocabulary as a pre-listening activity. Instead, they say it is much better for students to be either provided with a short synopsis of the listening passage, or allowed to preview comprehension questions that will be used afterward (Berne, 1995). Why make a secret of where the activity is headed? Real-life conversations always take place in a context. Too often listening activities lack this aspect and students waste valuable time listening for the setting and purpose of a conversation pulled out of context.

Longer Listening Activities. It is important to remember to keep listening activities short. A student is like a glass of water. Even the strongest student (biggest glass?) will overflow if you continue to pour in information without giving him or her time to process it. In fact, even the best student cannot absorb more than about 10 minutes' input all at once. Think of that the next time you lecture for more than 10 minutes. Do you have to stop lecturing? Of course not, just structure your lecture to include time to summarize and/or discuss what has been said.

Here is how to have students handle a longer listening activity, ideally:

Before, have students write down:

- everything they already know about the topic;
- questions they have about the topic; or
- how they feel about listening to this talk (A KWL works well for this).

> CCSS: W2, W9, SL1, 3, 4
> ACTFL: 1.2, 1.3, 4.2
> DOK 1, 2, 3

During the activity, have them list the main points you or the speaker make, but stop every 5 minutes or so, and have them process what they've heard by doing at least two of these:

- underlining the most important thing written so far;
- putting a star next to the most interesting thing;
- reading someone else's notes and having a brief discussion (agree/paraphrase, etc.);
- looking back at the list of questions written before the lecture, and checking off any that have been answered.

While students do these, there will be valuable feedback for the instructor on what the students have or have not comprehended.

Afterward, ideally within the next 8 hours, for maximum learning to take place, have students jot down, or tell someone else (a classmate, or even a parent):

- what they heard that was new to them;
- how what they heard relates to what they had already known;
- the relevance of the information in the lecture to their own life.

Students love to be read aloud to, or told stories, even high school seniors. Most of us have collected little children's books in our foreign language, and may use them to teach colors or numbers, illustrate verb tenses, or cultural things such as familiar fairy tales. However, since, according to Glasser's scale (see Chapter 1), students only remember 20 percent of what they hear, you need to involve them more. Present visuals during the story (students remember 50 percent of what they see and hear), or have students discuss something during a break in the reading (70 percent on Glasser's scale), act out what they have just heard (80 percent for personal experience)—even if it's just something such as "show me with your face how this character feels," or, at the upper levels of foreign languages, have the students take turns reading to each other (95 percent retention of what we teach to someone else.)

The addition of visuals will also appeal to the students' spatial intelligence, acting will appeal to the kinesthetic, discussion to the interpersonal, and reading to each other to the intrapersonal—you can easily see how you could use one activity, modified slightly, to provide more variety and to appeal to different students' strengths. The TPRS method (see more about this under Kinesthetic Intelligence) uses many props and visuals.

Figure 2.3 Eight Steps to Better Listening

For better listening:	Weak listeners:	Strong listeners:
1 Find areas of interest.	Tune out "dry" subjects.	Ask "what's in it for me?"
2 Work at listening.	Fake attention; easily distracted.	Concentrate and show active listening posture and gestures.
3 Listen for ideas.	Listen for facts.	Listen for themes.
4 Judge content, not delivery.	Tune out if delivery is poor.	Judge content; skip delivery errors.
5 Hold your fire.	Give up if listening becomes difficult.	Listen for possible clues or answers later in a sentence.
6 Be flexible.	Take intensive notes using only one system.	Take fewer notes and use four different systems.
7 Keep your mind open.	Agree with information only if it supports your ideas.	Consider all points of view before forming opinions.
8 Use a graphic organizer.	Get off task easily unless the task is well defined.	Listen for key words.

SPEAKING

Speaking may be formal or informal in nature, humorous or not, presenting brief data, or storytelling, but in a foreign language class, in the context of linguistic intelligence, it does not mean short replies to a teacher's questions, or repeating aloud what was heard. Speaking means producing communicative responses to a given situation, and, of course, Communication is one of the five goals in the ACTFL National Standards. Therefore, students need to be asked to explore as many different types of communication as possible. Speaking usually takes one of the following forms:

- conversation/discussion
- circumlocution (description)
- memorized speech
- oral reports
- interviews.

Q and A (Conversation/Discussion). The simplest form of conversation is the question-and-answer format. I have a game we play called "Hot Seat," in which students prepare a set of questions to ask classmates. One at a time, they take a turn in the Hot Seat (a high chair set in front of the class) and answer ten different questions put to them by ten different classmates. In addition to taking a turn in the seat, each student is required to ask ten questions. Note: make sure that these questions are not yes/no or either/or questions, and are not totally obvious (such as, "What color is your hair?"). To make it a bit more conversational, let the person in the Hot Seat ask questions of the questioner, either asking them to explain the question a little more, or adding something such as, "And how about you?" to their answer.

> CCSS: SL1, 6
> ACTFL: 1.1, 1.2, 5.1
> B: Apply
> DOK 2

Another question-and-answer game is called "20 Questions." Have students think of famous people, places, or even just vocabulary words, and then have students ask them questions, in the TL, and try to guess. For example, if the topic is food vocabulary, students might ask questions like, "Are you a fruit or a vegetable?" "Are you large or small?" "Are you eaten for breakfast?" and so on. The student who correctly guesses the word takes over the chair, and a new round begins.

> CCSS: SL 1, 3
> ACTFL: 1.1, 1.2
> DOK 3

Another question-and-answer game is called, "Botticelli": for upper-level classes only.

The person who is "it" pretends to be a well-known person, either living or dead, and tells the other players the first letter of his or her last name. The others ask yes-or-no questions to

> CCSS: SL 1, 3, 4
> ACTFL: 1.1, 1.2, 2.1, 2.2,
> 3.1, 3.2, 4.2, 5.2
> DOK 3

discover who "it" is. However, to earn the right to ask a yes-or-no question, the person must first ask "it" a question they cannot answer. For example, the questioner might ask, "Did you invade England in 1066?" If "it" answers, "No, I am not William the Conqueror," then the questioner may not ask another question. If, however, "it" is stumped by the question, and the questioner tells "it" the correct answer, then the questioner may ask a yes-or-no question about the person "it" is impersonating, such as "Are you male?" or "Are you alive?" If the questioner asks a question about the person "it" has chosen to be, "it" answers, "Yes, I am

Mad King Ludwig" and the round is finished, and the person who asked the question is the next "it."

CCSS: SL1, 4, 6
ACTFL: 1.1, 5.1
B: Apply
DOK 2

The next level of conversation is one in which additional information is given, which is not asked for. This may be in the form of introducing a new topic, or just expanding on an old one. My upper-level classes often do an activity I call "Elaborations" in which a question is asked which is a yes-no question, but to which students are not allowed to simply answer yes or no. Instead, they must provide at least one more item of information. For example, if asked if they like pizza, they could say that they indeed like pizza, and prefer a certain brand, or tell what their favorite toppings are, or when and where or with whom they last ate pizza. More advanced classes could do longer appropriate dialogues, for example, "Say, Paul, how are the slopes? Great! I'm going back up right now. Is the snow good? Yes, it's deep."

CCSS: SL1, 4
ACTFL: 1.1, 1.3
B: Understand or Apply
DOK 2

Conversation Stimulators. If you have a group that is reluctant to talk, try one of these ideas:

- Hand around a bowl of M&Ms, Skittles, or other small edibles to the class, instructing them to take a few and place them on the desk to await further instructions. After everyone has taken a few, tell them that they owe the class one sentence for every one they took, on (name a topic—their summer vacation, their likes and dislikes, or something relevant to the chapter you are on). Note: once you've done this, they'll take just a few, so next time, tell them to subtract their number from a bigger number and do that amount. Specifically, if one only took 3, and 20 is chosen to subtract from, he'd have to do 17 but if another took 12, he'd do 8.

- A less expensive version, but which high school students think is hilarious, is to hand around a roll of toilet paper, asking each student to take some. Again, for each square of toilet paper, they owe one sentence. It's fun to watch them move their fingers slowly down a strip of toilet paper from square to square as they speak. If you want, have them tear off the squares as they complete them, tossing them into the air.

- Yet another enjoyable way to limit/force speaking is to give the student a jar of bubble liquid, and a topic to speak upon. Have the student wave the wand, and then he must speak until the last bubble has broken. If students don't produce enough bubbles and don't speak for as long as you would like, pair them and have them make bubbles for their partner.

- Take a ball of yarn or string. Tell something about yourself and, holding the end, throw it to someone else. They tell something and, keeping hold of the yarn, throw the ball to someone else, until everyone has one. Then, reverse the direction, with the class trying to remember what each person has said, aloud, winding the yarn back onto the ball as you go. This tests listening and speaking skills, and is a good team-building activity as well.

- If one person monopolizes conversations, consider using "talk tokens." Before the discussion, give each person the same number of tokens. Each time a person speaks, they must put one token in a container. When they are out of tokens, they may not speak. You could also designate an item (a stuffed animal or realia item, for example) that the speaker must hold, and only someone holding that item may speak.

Think/Pair/Share (T/P/S). This is a very good activity to use in almost any classroom situation in which you would like to begin a conversation or discussion. First, ask a question of the class, telling them to think silently for a minute or so. Then pair them with another, and have them exchange opinions. If there is disagreement, they must explain further, until they reach an agreement. If you want the paired students then to share their opinion orally with others, there are several options. One is to combine the original set of partners with one other set and have them interact once more (usually called Think/Pair/Square or TPS). This is really beneficial if they are practicing a structure or vocabulary that will come up on a test. The more times they must say it, the more firmly it will be embedded in their minds, and the more different versions of it they hear from others, the more likely one will stick in their minds.

> CCSS: SL1, 3, 4, 6
> ACTFL: 1.1, 1.2, 1.3
> B: Apply (speak),
>   Analyze (discuss)
> DOK 2

Another way to have them share with others is to call on selected students to say theirs. This could be done randomly by the teacher (or perhaps based on good ones heard while walking around during the sharing sessions), or have each team pick their favorite to speak, or using the draw-a-name-from-the-jar method. However, my favorite way to have the whole class share is to ask the students to stand up when they have finished sharing with their partner. Not only can the teacher see clearly who is still working (or needs help) and go to that area, it is one more chance for students to get out of their seats, student movement which is built into the lesson plans. Once everyone is standing, there is another benefit: the teacher will pick one student at random to say the phrase for the class. When he/she is done, and sits down, the teacher asks everyone else with that answer to sit, also. The whole class will look to see who has the same answer, and a little bit of "bonding" occurs, based on similar interests. The teacher will also get a very good idea of how similarly the class feels on that topic, and, by writing on the board what each person/group answers, will have a nice list for review (or for visual learners) by the time everyone is seated.

Some possible T/P/S topics might be: Why did you take this class? What would you most like to learn this year? What sport is the most interesting? What is your favorite holiday, and why? What is your stereotype of a Spanish/French/German/Japanese person? What city would you most like to visit and why? If you had a million dollars, what would you do? These generally are short-answer questions, and a TPS activity doesn't take very long to do. According to Glasser's scale, discussion has a high retention of material, and so these are very worthwhile to do. The "think" portion is also a very good activity to use at the beginning of a class period, or as a transition activity (as students change seats, or hand in papers, etc.).

Telephone Use. If you have school voice mail, a free Google Voice account, or use a Padlet or other online platform where a recording may be made/uploaded, you have a valuable conversational accessory. Assign your students to make telephone calls to you on various topics. Be very specific. Tell them they must greet you, identify themselves, and then tell you

> CCSS: SL1, 5, 6, L1
> ACTFL: 1.1, 2.1, 2.2
> B: Apply
> DOK 2

something, ask you something, and then say goodbye. Here are some things I have asked my students to do:

1   Name three things they saw at a local store and want to buy. Ask me to lend them money.
2   Tell me they saw another classmate, where he was and what he was doing. Ask me to call them back, and tell me what number to call.(uses imperfect, preterit, and commands)
3   Pretend they are at a restaurant in (city). Tell me the name of the restaurant and what they are eating. Ask me a question about a monument or museum in (city): a review of food and culture. [adds ACTFL: 2.1, 2.2]
4   Phone in a response to a note they got. (I wrote each student a short note asking him or her to do something with me.) They were to tell me that they could not accept, and why.
5   Call and ask me to do something with them: tell me what we would do, when to meet, when we would get home, and at least one reason why I would want to do this with them.

With very little thought, it should be easy to come up with a phone call topic for every unit. (Note: this could also be used as a writing prompt for a note or a text message as well.)

CCSS: SL1, 3, 4, L1
ACTFL: 1.1, 1.2, 1.3
B: Apply, Analyze, Evaluate
DOK 3 for guessers, 4 for speaker

Circumlocution Activities. Circumlocution is a longer form of discussion. It involves talking about something without specifically naming it. An easy circumlocution listening activity involves the use of pictures from the text, numbered and displayed to students. The teacher would say something like, "I see an animal that likes to eat birds. It has green eyes, a long tail, and claws. It says, Meow." As the teacher speaks, the students note which picture is being spoken about. To change this to a speaking activity, you would put students in groups. Each group would have a smaller set of pictures. Students would take turns: Student A would describe one of the pictures in a similar way (without using the vocabulary word). When Student A is done, the other students say the vocabulary word. If the majority of the group identify the picture from Student A's description, Student A gets to take the picture. If not, the picture remains there for someone else to describe. The student with the most pictures wins.

Another easy way to incorporate circumlocution in a lesson is to use it for a "show and tell" type situation. Have students bring in something to describe, and describe it for the class without showing it. The others guess what it is, and when it is guessed correctly, the student may show the object. For example, I like to have students bring in something someone in their family has made, when we do a unit on families. Then, while telling about it, we not only use descriptive words and verbs, but the family unit vocabulary also.

CCSS: SL 1, 4, 5 L 1
ACTFL: 1.1, 1.2, 1.3
B: Apply
DOK varies by difficulty

Buzz Groups. Buzz groups are cooperative student groupings designed to facilitate discussion, in the form of group brainstorming, followed by evaluation and selection of the best idea. This is a good activity for students to fill in open-ended statements ("I wish . . .") using key structures or phrases being practiced, and that have many possible answers. It is also a good anticipatory activity before assigning a project or a paper.

One of my favorite buzz group activities involves a prop: a plastic key. I purchased keys, originally hooked together as a combination rattle/teether for babies. After separating the keys, I gave one to each student, and, as homework, asked them what this key opened for them. The next day, they sat in buzz groups and discussed. (Incidentally, the buzz groups found each other by the color of their keys, an easy way for them to sit together quickly in small groups.)

Each buzz group usually has a recorder/reporter for the group. As each person speaks, the recorder writes down his or her opinions or ideas. Sometimes all the teacher does is collect these; other times the group must choose the best one to report back to the class.

Inside-Outside Circle. This activity can be used almost daily for any type of communicative exercise. First, divide the students into two groups. Have half stand or sit, forming a circle facing outward. Have the others stand or sit around them, facing inward, each with one of the inner circle students as a partner. Explain the activity: each should tell the other his/her favorite sport/greet each other appropriately (Level 1), tell what

> CCSS: SL1, 4, L1, 2
> ACTFL: 1.1, 1.2
> B: Apply
> DOK 2

he was doing at 7 o'clock the previous evening, or what he would like his parents to give him for his birthday, or whatever concept you are working on at the time. After about 30 seconds, the teacher will interrupt, and instruct one or both circles to turn, move over two or three places, and do the same activity again with a different partner. In several minutes, a student will have had four or five different partners, at which point the activity is finished, or the teacher assigns a different topic of conversation.

Compare the efficiency of this to the traditional method of questioning each student individually, going up and down rows until each has answered: in Inside-Outside Circle, each student speaks many times (and will be gently corrected by classmates if there are any errors) rather than only once. Each student is actively involved at all times. The student must learn the phrase, sentence, or pattern being practiced more completely, in order to use it many times with partners whose answers may vary. Finally, physical movement is involved, which helps keep students active and alert.

Here are some other Inside-Outside Circle topics I have used and liked:

1 For a beginning-level class: find out your partner's name, age, and hobbies.
2 The inner student runs into (literally) another, apologizes, and introduces a friend.
3 The inner student calls the outer to ask about a homework problem. The outer helps and then is thanked politely.
4 The inner student is a clerk in a (type of store) and the outer is shopping for a party/picnic/new outfit/birthday present.
5 The outer is walking down the street and meets the inner, who asks him/her to do something that evening. The outer declines, explaining that he/she has a test, and says goodbye.
6 The outer is a salesman selling dictionaries (or whatever). He/she introduces him/herself to the inner student, and tries to sell them something. The inner person doesn't want one, as he/she already has one. They, of course, stay polite, and end the conversation.
7 The inner person calls the home of a friend to tell him or her something important. The outer person answers as a parent, to say that the friend is not home, and to take a message.

8 This may also be used to review vocabulary. Have students prepare a card, listing several vocabulary words in the TL on one side, and the same words in English on the other. Each will quiz his or her partner, TL-to-English, or English-to-TL, giving hints in the TL if the partner doesn't know the vocabulary.

9 Another way to review vocabulary, which involves more discussion, is to arrange for student to pair vocabulary words in a logical fashion. For example, the inner circle is given cards with the name of a room in a house. After stating what room they were in, the outside circle asked them if they saw a (certain item, found in a house) to which they would answer positively or negatively, using complete sentences, depending on whether or not it was logical.

10 Grammar can also be practiced using Inside-Outside Circle. The inner circle has a card with a situation on it (sort of a Dear Abby type), while the outer circle advised with a phrase such as "I think that you . . ." or "In my opinion . . ." that they were required to use to begin their answer (which in French requires the subjunctive). Again, both students and cards rotated, and the advice was sometimes silly and sometimes serious, but a very high-interest activity.

11 Figure 2.4 is another circumlocution activity my students enjoyed, and which was suggested by a foreign exchange student. Each student would have a list of some typically American things. Taking turns, each student had to explain one item from the list to the partner in the TL, and the partner would guess what the idea being explained was. When they were done explaining, they compared lists to see how well they had done.

Figure 2.4 Topics for Circumlocution Activities

Partner A	**Partner B**
1 yo-yo	1 Barbie doll
2 cheesecake	2 Jell-O
3 cheerleader	3 pep rally
4 detention	4 field trip
5 flip-flops	5 braces
6 pajama party/sleepover/lock-in	6 garage sale

More ideas:

workshop—pun—learner's permit (for driving)—white out—penalty box—play offs—gang violence—fender bender—convenience store—bagel—CD (bank)—pom-pom—derby (horses)—chain gang—marshmallow—doggie bag—raccoon—sequins—to drop off—Mr. Potato Head—sprinkles (on ice cream, etc.)—double agent—hard hat—squeegee—Plymouth Rock—charades—apron—Drano—piñata—strings attached—Oscar—polar bear—lunch box—hot air balloon—pretzel—hay ride—Christian music—Prom—Homecoming—Groundhog Day—Thanksgiving.

12 Inside-Outside Circle is just great for doing skits. Put the skit pairs facing another pair. Pair A does their skit, then Pair B, then they each rotate one space and repeat. If the teacher stands in one spot, in a class of 24, after six rotations, the teacher has heard every skit; every

student has done the skit six times instead of once (more practice speaking AND receiving gentle peer advice/correction/encouragement). This is much less stressful for shy students AND it saves a lot of class time:

- if each team did a 3-minute skit, plus a minute to get up from and return to seats, and a minute of teacher feedback, that would be 12 skits/5 minutes each = 60 minutes;
- using Inside-Outside Circle, two 3-minute skits plus feedback times, six rotations = 42 to 45 minutes, enough time saved to do another activity or two.

And, if the teacher doesn't need to hear every single skit, there is no need for six rotations; two or three are sufficient practice, so let's say this activity now takes 25 minutes, less than half the time, and students were active all the time, either performing or listening, and they have repeated their performance three times, with peer feedback.

Kagan (2009) says that requiring the students who listened to provide feedback (praise or correction) after each performance is perhaps the most valuable aspect of this activity, so don't skimp on that portion. I have been known to give my whole class grades based on how perfect the skits were. If I heard serious errors that their partners should have caught and corrected, then the partners lost points on the activity. This is an excellent way to teach and promote social language.

Memorization. Memorizing and saying aloud phrases, poems, and other short bits of a foreign language is highly recommended. Not only do they gain a small bit of "cultural literacy" that will stay with them, but also they will practice the pacing, rhythm, and flow of the TL, with an authentic resource. Poems, especially ones like Mother Goose rhymes, not only provide practice speaking the language, and have high appeal to students, but also can point out some cultural differences (or

> CCSS: SL4, L2
> ACTFL: 1.1, 1.3, 2.1, 4.2, 5.2
> B: Understand
> DOK 2

similarities) when translated. There are some very good sources for children's rhymes to be found on the Internet. It's not authentic, but my morning students all learn the Pledge of Allegiance in the TL as our state requires it to be recited every morning.

For vocabulary, have students learn a new word every day, in class as well as over the holidays or weekends, and then practice them in conversation. There are two types of mnemonics (memorization methods) that work best: rhymes and reductions. Rhymes and jingles, especially ones that teach a concept, are worth a dozen lectures. They are easier to memorize if they rhyme, and even easier if they are set to music. (See Musical Intelligence for several suggestions.) For students who are oral learners, record the rhyme and play it back. For visual learners, provide a written copy. For kinesthetic learners, add gestures.

Reduction mnemonics are also a method of memorizing, in which information is clustered or chunked for the students by reducing a lot of information to a shorter form, with one letter to represent each shortened piece, making it easier to handle and remember. In French, we use BANGS to remember the rules on adjective order. Most adjectives follow the nouns they modify; the exceptions are the ones to do with Beauty, Age, Numbers, Goodness, and Size. Spanish can teach the subjunctive by using the words WEDDING and DISHES (see Chapter 5 on teaching the subjunctive). The French subjunctive can be taught using UWEIRDO, similarly to Spanish. Reductions can also be in sentence form. For example, the descending order of metric prefixes—kilo, hecto, deca, (measure), deci, centi, and milli—become the sentence "King Henry Doesn't Mind Drinking Cold Milk."

> CCSS: SL4, L1
> ACTFL: 1.1, 1.3, 2.1, 2.2,
> 4.2 if cultural
> DOK 2

Oral Reports. Public speaking is usually required in any class, but consider using Inside-Outside Circle (see the previous section of this chapter) for this type of activity, as it encourages active participation at all times, as well as decreasing the fright factor for shy students, as they don't have to face an entire room of people all at once.

However, there are some very rewarding activities to evaluate student learning and progress orally. Here are some tips for a successful oral presentation:

- Try to make reports more interesting by varying the setting. For a report on ecology or the environment, go outdoors. If the students are reading a poem or performing part of a play, go to the auditorium. Instead of a plain report in front of the blackboard, make a backdrop: for example, a café scene for a report on food, or a TV news set for an activity like the next one.

- Try the talk show format, complete with authentic touches like backdrop, costumes, and even commercials. Make the report a "special broadcast": a famous person has just passed away, and the student will recap that person's life for the class (who take notes, of course.) Or arrange for one student, or a panel, to interview another student who would pretend to be a famous person, or an expert on something like the environment, a sport, movies, or politics. Do the talk show live or on video, and assign another group to do the commercials on products typical for that type of program or that country or time period.

- If possible, structure presentations so the student is not presenting alone. For example, in a unit about movies, do a "thumbs-up, thumbs-down"-type presentation as an oral report. Each student would give his or her opinion about the same movie, agreeing or disagreeing about various aspects. Let them show a short clip of the movie, and your classes will beg to do this activity again.

- Make the report a debate or a panel discussion. For example, have two students argue whose food item is healthier, whose hobby is more interesting, which sport/city/holiday is better, and why.

- Incorporate props whenever possible. Posters are OK to use, but everyday items are more interesting. For example, students speaking on a city/region/country/holiday could have a suitcase, and as they pull items from it, explain what each would be used for: suntan lotion for the many beaches, a menu of typical foods, a charcoal briquette for the coal mined in the area, and so on. If a student is talking about himself or herself, have each person bring in three items that show something about him or herself. A student might bring car keys, an award, a picture of their horse/pet/family, and so on. Not only do these items jog the memories of the presenter(s), but also they take a bit of the focus off the person giving the report, helping shyer people, and again, more directly involving the audience.

- Make oral reports more interesting by audience participation. Have students prepare a list of questions about a city/region/country/event/holiday or custom they have researched, and distribute these questions to their classmates. If the order of questions is important, they should number these questions. Then, have students ask these questions, which the reporter will answer. This is much more relaxing (and entertaining) than the standard speech.

- Have the audience participate by reviewing the speaker—but don't make it negative. Have your students list the things they liked best about the report. Don't let them criticize, except perhaps to have a listing such as "I wish you had told more about . . ."

Interviews and Surveys. An interview can also be a great *short* communicative opportunity. Students love to learn more about each other. Pair students, and have them interview each other. You may give them a set of prepared questions on a topic such as: family members and pets, food likes and/or dislikes, sports and hobbies, vacation plans, future plans (college, career, family), what makes them angry/happy/sad, chores they have to do at home. Most topics lend themselves to this format.

> CCSS: SL1, L1
> ACTFL: 1.1, 1.2
> B: Remember
> DOK 1

However, many students prefer not to talk about themselves. If you have a class like this:

- Have the partner take good notes, verifying what is written with the interviewee (writing AND reading practice) and then report on their partner's responses to another person or pair. This would practice changing the verbs from the "I" form of the interviewee to the "he/she" form for reporting, as well as changing any possessive adjectives ("me/mine" to "him/her/his/hers"), so I highly recommend it.
- Have students write questions and then interview native speakers of the language who work in the school (students, teachers, other staff and employees) or who live in your area, and/or people who have traveled to an area that speaks your TL: where they are originally from, how/when/where they came to the United States/foreign country, their initial reaction, cultural surprises, and so on.
- Give your students the option of presenting live, or on video.

Since there is usually no whole class presentation made, unless you need to grade these, you will simply need to eavesdrop a bit. If possible, take notes and, the next day, provide your students with a list entitled "Find a Classmate Who . . ." and have them locate the person described, and ask the person referred to in that item to sign or initial that space. Reward the first few who complete the activity, or all who get every blank signed correctly. Here are some examples.

Find a classmate who:

1   plays football;
2   hates oranges;
3   lived in New York;
4   wants to be a teacher;
5   has a grandma who speaks Spanish;
6   spent last summer cooking at (local restaurant).

This is a good "mixer" activity in an intermediate or advanced class.

Story Sequencing. Using a storyboard (such as those available online at Makebeliefscomix, www.makebeliefscomix.com/Printables/), or drawn by your students, cut the cells apart, and give one to each student in a group. Without showing them to each other, they take turns describing theirs, and decide what the logical order would be.

> CCSS: SL 1, 4, L1
> ACTFL: 1.1, 1.2, 1.3, 4.2
> B: Analyze
> DOK 2 or 3

Socratic Seminar. Unless this is done in English, I use this primarily in my upper-level classes, as it is best suited for discussions of literature, opinions on things such as global warming or cats vs. dogs, historical events such as World War II, and abstract topics such as "What is beauty?" (an AP topic). It is, however, a highly effective way to get meaningful discussion going in your classroom, so I'd like to include it here.

> CCSS: RL 1, SL1, 3, 4, 6, L1
> ACTFL: 1.1, 1.2
> B: Analyze
> DOK 3

When speaking, students need freedom to speak freely, to feel that their ideas will be accepted. They also need to feel some control over the discussion, as well as to have fun while doing it. Guidelines for a Socratic seminar:

- Sit in a circle.
- Everyone must have previously read/viewed/learned the material to participate.
- Quiet is not bad; allow students to formulate their thoughts. The greatest skill being developed in the Socratic seminar is critical thinking.
- Allow the discussion to move on its own.
- Always make students give specifics to support the opinion (usually based upon something previously read). This is the best way to make sure discussion doesn't stray too far from the seminar topic.
- It's important that the facilitator allow only one student to speak at a time. A Socratic seminar is not a debate.

The trickiest part of organizing a Socratic seminar is writing the questions. Here are my suggestions:

Focus on the goal:	The goal is to enlarge understanding by exploring ideas and issues, NOT to establish facts. There is usually not just one possible answer.
Use open-ended questions:	Avoid yes/no questions and factual questions.
Keep questions value-free:	Participants make judgments and connections. You remain neutral.
Use questions with depth:	Can the group explore this for 15–20 minutes? Does it prompt thinking beyond the obvious? It should not be answerable without knowledge from what was assigned. Questions should be based upon experiences, events, and vocabulary that are common to all participants.
Use questions in order:	Begin with an opening question, then two to five core questions, and a closing question.

Follow-up questions: Questions should be asked of speakers to clarify and probe. These are not planned ahead, but should include things such as:

"Are you saying that . . .?"
"Where in the text do you find support for that?"
"What do you mean by . . .?"
"What is your point?"
"Would someone take issue with . . .?"

Figure 2.5 is a sample sheet of questions I have used for one of my Socratic discussions. The usual follow-up to this discussion would be for them to write/draw/sing/rap (my assignments always have options for different learning styles) a fable of their own.

Figure 2.5 Fables of La Fontaine

1 A fable is a story in which animals have human characteristics. Why?

2 What types of animals were used?

3 The fox is in every poem. Describe him.

4 What behaviors or characteristics were portrayed as positive/good?

5 What behaviors or characteristics were portrayed as negative?

6 Were "good" animals rewarded, and "bad" animals punished? Give examples.

7 Each poem has a moral, which can be stated as advice ("Do this" or "Don't do that"). What was the advice contained in your poem?

8 What does this advice tell us about life during La Fontaine's time?

9 Why were La Fontaine's fables popular?

I have rather strict rules for Socratic seminar participants:

1   You are NOT allowed to simply give your opinion on the question you read aloud. Rather, lead others to your opinion by dropping hints, using quotes, asking for more varied opinions from other students, and so on.
2   No one needs to raise their hand. Simply allow the speaker to finish, and then state your opinion.
3   If you are called on by the teacher or a member in the group, and you do not want to answer at that time, you can PASS.
4   Respect all participants. If you disagree with what someone has said, don't moan and groan or roll your eyes. Wait for them to finish, then say that you don't agree with them. Improper body language will result in being sent from the room with an alternate assignment.
5   Be honest about your opinions. If you are playing Devil's Advocate, announce that you are doing this.

Figure 2.6 Differences between Socratic Seminar and Class Discussion

Socratic	Class Discussions
Students and teacher in circle. All have eye contact; teacher is on same level.	Students are in rows. Teacher is set apart and often higher, on stool or behind podium.
97 percent student talk; students know teacher won't comment, just help with vocab.	97 percent teacher talk, even if many questions are asked. Teacher elaborates and answers.
Average response for students is 8–12 seconds.	Average response for students is 2–3 seconds.
No verbal or nonverbal approval or disapproval is present. Affirming feedback by the teacher is taboo; only students provide feedback.	Teacher affirmation of correctness is critical. Sustaining feedback for incorrectness is critical.
Thinking, backed up with textual evidence, is required. There is not just one answer.	Rightness is key; thinking ends as soon as one is right.
Students listen primarily to peers.	Students listen primarily to teacher, who has the answer.
Students have ownership for much of the flow.	Teachers have ownership for most of the flow.
Students are held accountable for contributions based upon pre-established criteria.	Students see discussion as a frill, a "participation grade." If you miss class, you didn't miss much.

READING

The third aspect of linguistic intelligence is reading. Reading in a foreign language is difficult, and often is not presented in a way that is active so help your students by building in the following steps for *any* reading assignment, no matter how short:

> Step 1—Pre-reading/prediction
> Step 2—Skimming/scanning
> Step 3—Careful reading
> Step 4—Applying what is read

Step 1: Pre-Reading/Prediction. Have students inventory their knowledge prior to reading a selection—vocabulary they expect to encounter, cultural aspects they are likely to find, attitudes or stereotypes they hold. For example, before reading an article on clothing, you could have students do one of the following:

CCSS: W2, 4, L2
ACTFL: 1.3
DOK 1

- Board Race: review all the clothing vocabulary they know.
- Graffiti: on large sheets of paper on the wall or whiteboards, students write all the clothing-related vocabulary they remember (prizes for those who remember the most in a pre-set period of time).

- Think/Pair/Share: think of your stereotype of a Mexican/ French/German/Roman/Japanese person. With a partner, draw the person. Label as many items on your picture as possible. Share your picture with another pair (or the class, lined up on the front chalk rail to see how many common items there are).

> CCSS: W 2, 4. L2
> ACTFL: 1.1, 1.3, 2.1, 2.2,
> 4.1, 4.2
> DOK 2

- Sponge: Look at the title and picture accompanying today's reading selection, and share your prediction of the content and vocabulary that will be in the selection (written, oral, or online).

> CCSS: RL 1, L1
> ACTFL: 1.2, 2.1, 4.2
> B: APPLY
> DOK 2

Step 2: Skimming/Scanning. Have students, in pairs to make it more interactive, scan the selection quickly for additional information. Perhaps they could underline all the words they find easily recognizable. They should always be told to look for *cognates* (words similar to English words). [CCSS: RL1, L4; ACTFL 4.1] After they skim the selection, have them revisit the prediction they made in Step 1, modifying it if they found additional information while skimming. You could also have them run up and write the cognates they find on the board if you have one, or post them online [adds ACTFL 1.3], and look for *false cognates* (words that look like English ones, but have different meanings) [adds ACTFL 2.1, 4.1].

If the selection is very difficult or long, I sometimes have students underline or highlight unfamiliar words, and we brainstorm what they might mean, based on their context: how is the word used in the sentence—description? Action? [adds ACTFL 1.2, 3.1] If reading time is limited, I give them each three words to look up prior to reading the selection, and also have them make a nametag with "their" three words so they can be the authority to consult if anyone needs to know what that word means.

Another way to use skim/scan and make upper-level students more accountable is to first provide them with several title-synopsis combinations, and ask them, by skimming, to match these to the actual article, poem or story. This is a great method to use for an IPA reading.

After checking their results, have each group then choose a story, article, or poem to read.

Step 3: Careful Reading. Doing the two steps previously described will have equipped students with a frame of reference as well as some confidence in their ability to handle the material. Students who get bogged down by unfamiliar vocabulary and quit should guess at what a word or phrase means, or skip it and see if the sentence or paragraph still makes sense.

> The axtlzbn is worn primarily by meebs for the blurvle ceremony each kipto. It consists of a wlomb made of cygde and tied with a qorf. It is decorated with many hujas.

For example, in the above selection, the "axtlzbn" is obviously an article of clothing worn for a special purpose. There is a very good chance that that unfamiliar word will be explained later in the selection, or in an illustration, or may not be necessary for comprehension in the rest of the selection.

Step 4: Applying What is Read. After reading, do NOT have students answer simple questions, or do cloze exercises. Go back to the boxed selection above, and see if you can do these:

Describe the axtlzbn. _____

Who wears an axtlzbn? _____

What ceremony is it worn for? _____

Fill in the blanks: The _____ is worn by _____ for the _____.

Of course, you were able to answer these—but did you have to understand any of the new vocabulary words? No!

A good application is one that uses creativity, higher-level thinking skills, and active learning. Have learners:

- Draw a picture of what they think an *axtlzbn* or a *blurvle* ceremony looks like if none is in the book. [CCSS: RL 10; ACTFL 1.3, 2.1 or 2.2, 4.2]
- Write a comparison between an *axtlzbn* and what they are wearing that day. [CCSS: RL 3 and 10; ACTFL 4.1, 4.2]
- Tell you why or why not they'd be willing to wear one, or show you with their faces/bodies how an *axtlzbn* wearer feels. [CCSS: RL 1, 10; ACTFL: 1.3, 2.1, 4.2]
- Look online or in a different book or magazine, to find more examples of the clothing, the ceremony, or whatever else was in that selection. [CCSS: L6, RL 7; ACTFL: 1.2, 3.2, 4.2, 5.1]
- Rewrite the selection from the viewpoint of a *meeb* getting ready for the ceremony. [CCSS: RL 1, 4, 6, 10 and L 1, 2; ACTFL: 1.1, 2.1, 4.2]
- Write quiz questions over the selection, and quiz each other. CCSS: SL 1, 4; ACTFL: 1.1, 2.1, 2.2, 4.1, 4.2]
- Create a postcard to tell the folks back home about the ceremony they saw (using various past tenses). [CCSS: RL 1, 2, 4, 5, 10 and L1, 2, 3; ACTFL: 1.1, 2.1, 2.2, 4.1, 4.2]
- Create a one-sided telephone conversation about the reading selection. [CCSS: SL 4, 5, 6; ACTFL: 1.1, 2.1, 2.2, 4.1, 4.2]

I'd suggest giving the class two or three options of equal difficulty, so they can choose one to suit their own strengths. Careful: too many options bogs them down deciding which one to do. Creative applications like these test knowledge, and require students to demonstrate their understanding of what was read.

A good online resource for creative reading strategies in Spanish is: www.creativelanguage-class.com/30ira/ (as of August 2017).

Using Newspapers, Magazines, and Infographics. Newspapers and magazines are great resources (print or online) for reading selections. In addition to newspapers and magazines, don't forget that catalogs or telephone books, which also have ads and information that must be read, and are also available online, are wonderful resources. An infographic is a sort of chart or diagram with information, easy to read even for brand-new learners. To find them, just search online using the word "infographic" in the TL: infographique (French), Infografisch

(German), infografica (Italian) infográfico (Spanish). It might explain the difference between tu and vous/usted, how to tell if you're a hipster, what the most popular video game is, and many more things.

Either print or online, why not have a scavenger hunt? Set up teams of students, and give them lists, written in the TL, and a time limit. Have them cut out (or copy-and-paste) the items when they find them, and glue them to sections of the answer sheet or a Padlet online. Items on the list could be things like "a picture of a man wearing a tie" or "an ad for a one-bedroom apartment" (vocabulary), "a verb in the third person singular preterit" or "a feminine plural adjective" (grammar), "an ad for a bullfight" or "an ad for a New Year's party" (culture). In a telephone book, they could look for: rates for calls to a particular city at a certain time, an area code for a city, an emergency number, the phone number of the "fifth Smith" in the book, or some sort of comparison with our own phone books, such as "what color are the Yellow Pages?" (in France, they *are* yellow!)

First-year students can usually read ads for restaurants, hotels, concerts, movies, etc. and tell you who/what/where/when information. Second-year students can read more complex documents like apartments for rent, obituaries and wedding announcements, and news articles. Then have them do activities such as:

- question each other on information from the article; [CCSS: RL 1, 2, 4, 7, 10; ACTFL: 1.1, 1.2, 2.2, 3.2, 4.1, 4.2]
- in small groups, rate the items read as to: most interesting, most useful, most specific, most confusing, most unusual, most amusing, etc.; [CCSS: RL 2, 4, 6, 7, 10; ACTFL: 1.1, 1.2, 2.2, 3.2, 4.1, 4.2]
- role play the event described, each from a different perspective. For instance, for a birth announcement, from the viewpoints of: a journalist, the new mother or father, a grandparent, the baby, a big sister or brother. [CCSS: RL 1, 4, 6, SL 6; ACTFL:1.1, 1.2, 1.3, 2.2, 4.1, 4.2]

Role-Playing and Dramatization. Role-playing is a good way to test for comprehension of a reading selection. The obvious sort of role-playing is for each student to become a character in the story, and act it out. Dramatization involves rewriting a story into a play or choral reading, creating more dialogue than the original story, and also modifying verbs from the third

> CCSS: RL2, 5, SL4, L1
> ACTFL: 1.1, 1.3, 5.2
> DOK 4

person to the first person. Again, the end result would be to perform it. For upper-level classes, you could take a longer selection, and give groups each a different section to present to the class. If you would like to do something a bit less obvious, have students try some of the following:

- producing a puppet play version of the story;
- inventing and inserting a new character in the story. This could be to see if the class notices that this has been done, or it could be incredibly obvious, like putting a movie star or other famous person in;
- drawing the events in the story in cartoon form for the whole class to read/critique;
- making a storybook version and reading it to the class, perhaps changing the ending, or inserting errors in order to have the class correct them.

Remember also, role-playing does not have to be done live. Any of the above could be done in video form or using an online presentation method such as VoiceThread, ScreenCastify, and others.

Fairy Tales, Folk Tales, and Children's Books.
These are good for any level of language study, due to their repetitive nature. They can be read aloud (active), or used for pleasure reading (not active). They provide background on cultural traditions, and are usually heavily illustrated. Fairy tales' plots are usually already known to the students, who listen and look for familiar parts, quickly learning the key words ("bears," "porridge," etc.) and chiming in quickly on refrains such as the "Fee, fi fo fum" or "The sky is falling!" Here are two more active ways to do these:

> CCSS: RL2, 5, SL4, L1
> ACTFL: 1.1, 1.3, 5.2
> DOK 4

- Use props to retell the story—but with mistakes they must correct. For upper levels, give students the props, and have them re-enact the story as you or a classmate tell it, encouraging humorous variations which the students with props must hear, understand, or attempt to act out.
- Have students write and illustrate their own. Let them alter real ones (i.e., a male Cinderella) or combine two (Sleeping Beauty and the Beast) or do their own entirely. On the day they are due, bring in milk and cookies, pillows, blankets, etc. and relive story time from kindergarten days as they read each other their stories.

Jokes and Humor. Because cultural references and values heavily influence them, jokes are the most difficult things for students to read and understand. Comic strips are equally short and lacking redundancy, but have the advantage of visuals to go with the story. Few of either will be funny to your TL learners, but don't overlook trying them anyway. The occasional one that works will have enormous payoff in terms of interest, and as we saw in Chapter 1, that means that an awful lot of learning is taking place, and it will "stick" better due to the humor. They aren't authentic French ones but I use some of Sue Fenton's terrible puns about France from her book *The Wit of Madame Fifi* as well as those I find online, and have heard Spanish teachers discuss the *chistes* from El Gancho and other sources. Have students research to find a favorite one to bring into class and share!

Riddles, Puzzles, and Folk Sayings.

> CCSS: RL 1, 4, 6, L1
> ACTFL: 1.1, 1.2, 1.3, 4.1,
>   5.2
> DOK 2

Riddles and verbal puzzles especially interest students. Find a source in the TL, preferably authentic ones (try the Internet), or translate riddles into the TL for your students to read. There are easy riddles: "Marco is my father's brother-in-law. What is he to me?" or story riddles. Riddles can be spelling-based ones, such as "My first letter is in book but not in look . . ." They can be ancient ones such as the "In the morning, I walk on four feet; at noon on two, and in the evening on three—what am I?" (The answer is a man: as a baby, he crawls; as an adult, walks; and as an older person, walks with a cane.) They can be modern ones such as "I walked into the living room and Romeo and Juliet lay dead on the carpet. I didn't call the police, and no one will be charged with murder, yet they did not kill themselves. What happened?" (Romeo and Juliet are goldfish and something knocked over their bowl.) Students love these, and they may be used as sponges for early finishers, as extra credit assignments, or as group reading/ discussion/writing exercises. Have advanced students write riddles for the lower-level classes and post them; you'll find many rushing into class to get a head start on a solution.

Small-Group Discussions about Reading. Group discussions about reading combine both the benefits of reading, as well as practice speaking and listening (and sometimes writing), so here are some activities you may wish to use:

> CCSS: SL 12, 3, 4,6, L1
> ACTFL 1.1, 1.2, 1.3
> DOK 2

BEGINNING-LEVEL CLASSES

Correct errors in written or spoken statements.

Fill out a bio sheet for characters in the story.

Answer either/or questions about the story.

Given a list of adjectives and characters' names; determine who the adjectives refer to.

Line up incidents from the story in chronological order: these may be written on strips of paper, or in picture form to be numbered. When done, retell the story to each other.

Complete a close summary of the selection.

Find recurring words, and discuss why they are repeated.

Graffiti a list of keywords from the selection.

Given an answer card (card with written answer) respond aloud when the teacher asks the question to which they hold the answer.

Bring in a picture that represents something in the selection.

Share these, and discuss them.

Collaborate to report on setting, plot, theme(s), literary devices, author's life, characters from the selection.

ADVANCED-LEVEL CLASSES

Paraphrase/retell the story to each other.

Present a page/scene/chapter the test of the class hasn't read.

Identify which character made a given statement, and in what circumstances.

Create a new title for the selection.

Personalize: "If I were in X's situation . . . If I met X, I'd tell him . . . I like/ dislike X because . . ."

Substitute synonyms for underlined words in the selection.

Choose and justify a color to associate with each character.

Do TV or radio coverage of the story: either a newscast, or a talk show where the characters are interviewed.

Conduct a trial of one character in the selection.

Given a movie review, decide if the writer liked the movie, and agree or disagree with the writer.

Make an ad for the selection read.

WRITING

Reading is, of course, closely associated with writing, so I will continue the above list of activities to do after reading, adding written activities, listed here in approximate order of how much creativity is required (from low to high levels of DOK):

- List as many facts as possible about the selection.
- Given three columns of vocabulary, combine one element from each column to make statements about the reading selection.
- Replace nonsense words inserted in the text with appropriate vocabulary, or delete extraneous words inserted in the text.
- Given a paragraph written as one long word, separate it into component words, adding punctuation and accent marks as needed.
- Write a summary of the selection.
- Write a review/critique of the selection.
- Write a letter to a character in the reading selection.
- Change the story, adding class members as characters in it.
- Write an epitaph, obituary, or wedding announcement for the main characters.
- Create a dialogue that could have taken place in the reading selection.
- Create a new ending for the story.
- Create a sequel for the selection.

The easiest way to encourage writing is to make it short, and personal. I like to make the writing portion of each test require students to write about themselves, and also include an extra credit question about the student, or the student's opinion, on a topic of my choice. Topics might include an old question from a previous unit as review, an attitude survey, something about current events, or even something on a topic in the new unit we are about to begin, which would test their ability to guess meanings based on context.

> CCSS: SL 1, 3, 4, 6, L1, L2,
>   W2, 3, 4, 5, 7, 8, 9
> ACTFL: 1.1, 1.2, 1.3, 3.1,
>   5.1
> DOK 3

News Writing. Students find it easy to read news articles, and writing them is good practice, too. Have your class write a weekly or monthly column for the school paper or the local paper. They could report on national, local or school events, write puzzles or riddles, poems or stories. They love to see their names in print, and it is great PR for your program. Interviews with students, staff, or community members are of high interest to both those writing and those reading them, and your students will undoubtedly be asked to translate/read the articles to friends or family who are not taking your language classes.

In fact, why not have them publish their own paper, especially as an end-of-the-year project? Underclassmen could tell of travel or work plans, and seniors can "will" their belongings, lockers, or bits of wisdom to underclassmen, or use the superlative to name each other the "best" at something or "most likely to . . ."

Upper-level classes can report on the fun things they did, as well as give advice to lower-level students (again, good recruitment possibilities for those upper-level classes). If your school has daily televised announcements, write something short for selected students to do live, once a week (telejournalism practice).

> CCSS: W3, 4, L2
> ACTFL: 1.1, 1.3
> DOK 4

Story Writing. Short stories, because they are generally not illustrated and often have little dialogue, should probably be reserved for more advanced classes. Anecdotes are the easiest to begin with: a typical day's activities, a hobby or collection, a real or imagined meeting with someone famous, an accident or illness they had, their best/worst birthday or holiday. For writing fiction, put students in groups for more success. I like groups of three: a secretary, a dictionary researcher, and a leader. Before beginning, I strongly recommend also that you have the students help you prepare a rubric (see the chapter on assessment in this book) that spells out clearly what elements a good story should have, and how much of the grade each should be. Then, group-brainstorm to develop a list of key vocabulary, and get the bones of the story ready ahead of time (a good homework assignment). Students should also fill out and attach a checklist like the one in Figure 2.7 before handing their story draft to another group for peer editing using a response sheet like the one in Figure 2.8 overleaf. After receiving peer feedback and making necessary adjustments, the story is then submitted to the teacher. This process usually results in an interesting story with all the required elements, requiring much less correction (for the teacher *and* students), and a better grade for students, building confidence in their ability and resulting in higher satisfaction with the class.

Figure 2.7 Composition Checklist

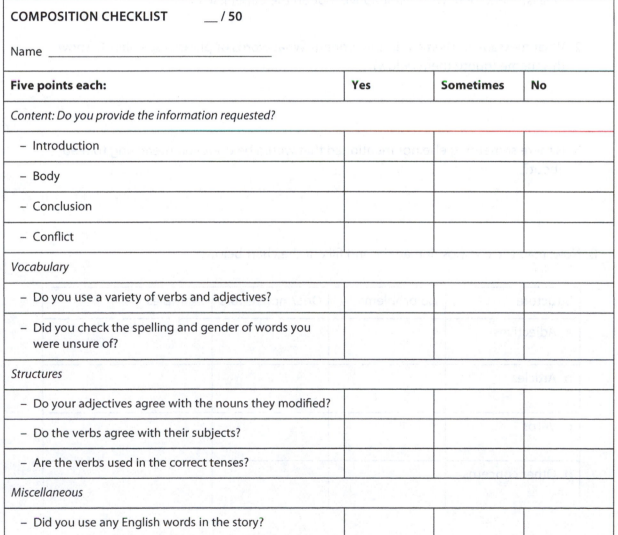

COMPOSITION CHECKLIST __ / 50			
Name _____			
Five points each:	**Yes**	**Sometimes**	**No**
Content: Do you provide the information requested?			
– Introduction			
– Body			
– Conclusion			
– Conflict			
Vocabulary			
– Do you use a variety of verbs and adjectives?			
– Did you check the spelling and gender of words you were unsure of?			
Structures			
– Do your adjectives agree with the nouns they modified?			
– Do the verbs agree with their subjects?			
– Are the verbs used in the correct tenses?			
Miscellaneous			
– Did you use any English words in the story?			

Figure 2.8 Peer Editing Sheet

PEER EDITING SHEET **Name** _____

A. Exchange compositions. Read the composition through once and answer the following questions:

   1. What is the main idea of each paragraph? List them below:

     Paragraph 1 _____

     Paragraph 2 _____

     Paragraph 3 _____

     Are there any paragraphs where you have difficulty trying to decide what the main idea is? Mark them with a star above (not on the paper itself!)

   2. What message or theme is in this writing? What words or phrases specifically show this theme (quote them below):

   3. Is there something else not mentioned that would be useful or interesting to read about?

B. Now, read the composition again, and fill out the chart below:

Structure	No problems	One/more errors	Examples
a Adjectives			
b Articles			
c Verbs			
d Other concerns			

As I wrote earlier, folk tales and fables are always rich in cultural traditions and may be studied on that basis alone. After reading several, develop a "formula" such as (1) an animal (2) with a personality flaw like greed or gullibility (3) who has an adventure in which (4) it is tricked by another animal and (5) his appearance is altered. Then, assign a similar story using that formula, or have them rewrite one they read with a human subject instead of the animal, or have students update a story to the present (i.e., the Tortoise gets run over while crossing a superhighway, or the Hare takes steroids).

> CCSS: RL1, 3, 4, 6, W3, 4,
> L1, 2, SL4
> ACTFL: 1.1, 1.2, 1.3
> DOK 2, 3

As a follow-up activity, take one or more of the student products and read or perform them for the elementary or middle school students—speaking practice, feedback, and it could recruit many more students for your foreign language program. [CCSS SL 4, L1; ACTFL 1.3; DOK 2]

Here's a fun writing activity called "Fortunately, unfortunately." The first writer comes up with the situation: "Once there was a little girl who loved to eat truffles." The next person adds a sentence beginning with "Unfortunately . . ." as in "Unfortunately, her truffle pig Maurice went on strike" and the next person makes a sentence about a positive event beginning with "Fortunately . . .": "Fortunately, she got famous on YouTube" and this alternates until the story ends, happily or not. Note: if it is a big class, do this Round-Robin (a paper is passed in small groups, each person adding a sentence). [CCSS: W 3, 4, L2; ACTFL 1.1, 1.2, 1.3]

Games for Linguistic Intelligence. Any games that encourage reading, writing, and speaking such as crosswords, word searches, word jumbles, as well as any sort of role-playing games use primarily the linguistic intelligence. Scrabble, Hangman, HedBanz, Password, Apples-to-Apples, and Pictionary are good examples of commercial games that emphasize verbal/linguistic skills.

Logical-Mathematical Intelligence

Logical-mathematical students are able to detect patterns, reason deductively, and think logically. It also can be stated as the ability to calculate, quantify, and consider hypotheses. This "scientific reasoning" is most often associated with sciences or mathematics, but may be quite effective when applied to a foreign language, as well. Note: all activities listed here will be DOK level 2.

STORY PROBLEMS

Performing calculations is a basic skill that can be and is practiced briefly in most foreign language classrooms when teaching numbers (see Chapter 3 for some more unusual ones). Make them more authentic by converting them into simulation-style activities: The T-shirt costs 100 pesos/francs/marks/yen, and you give the salesperson 200; how much change do you get? Have students take turns ordering off a menu from each other, adding the costs, paying, and calculating change. Do a metric measurements unit: their height, shoe size, and many other things is metric in most countries they could visit.

Story problems are another good way to practice numbers and vocabulary. At the first or second-year level, keep them in the present tense, and structure them to practice the vocabulary for the unit in progress: Paco has one cousin, and Maria has three; how many do both Paco and Maria have all together? You can even work in a little cultural information: If Hans and Peter are going to Berlin, driving on the Autobahn at 100 miles an hour, how long will it take them to get from Trier to Berlin? Then have the class tell you what to add, subtract, and so on.

Have students make up number series like 2, 4, 6, 8, 10 or 1, 1, 2, 3, 5, 8 and see if their classmates can figure out the sequencing pattern (of course, the numbers are either said aloud, or written as words rather than as numerals.) At higher levels, teach some basic algebra in the TL, or tricks like how to see if a number is divisible by three (add the integers, and see if the sum is divisible by three. For example, given the number 1,083, show them $1 + 0 + 8 + 3 = 12$, and $1 + 2 = 3$, so it is divisible).

Higher-level classes' story problems could also demonstrate a bigger variety of verb tenses, especially the conditional (If Marcus had ten apples, if he would give two to Julia, how many would he have?) or the subjunctive.

Other story problems could be as complex as "brain teasers": There are five students. Pierre is not afraid of anything alive, or the dark. Anne and Antoine live in the Alps and love it, and they also love stories about haunted houses. Marie likes "things that go bump in the night." David likes to climb mountains at night.

Use the following chart to indicate who is afraid of what:

Table 2.1 Each Person has One Fear

	Spiders	Dark	Ghosts	Heights	Snakes
Pierre					
Anne					
Antoine					
Marie					
David					

(Note that this also has students chart the results, also a logical/mathematical as well as a good visual intelligence task.)

GRAPHS

Graphs appeal to right brain students, as we saw in Chapter 1, and they also are perfect for students whose logical-mathematical intelligence is strongest. Whenever it is possible to use a graph or chart, for example, to show preferences in music or food, attitudes toward different issues, the rise and fall of intonation in a spoken sentence, verb endings from singular to plural, or whatever, use the visual method, and as early as possible in the lesson. Add color to reach even more learning styles.

Students can also make graphs. Have them survey their classmates on various topics and show the results in graph form, with a verbal explanation of the graph. Topics for a survey can range from easy ones like how many have a cat or a dog, or ate breakfast or made their bed on that day, or drive to school regularly, to the more complex opinion surveys on vacation likes and dislikes, thoughts about capital punishment, and so on.

CCSS: SL1, 4
ACTFL: 1.1, 1.2, 1.3
DOK 2

DEDUCTION

There are three basic steps in this method which was first used in scientific investigation: first, a set of data on the topic are created, either by the students or by the teacher; second, these are grouped into categories based on similarities observed; and third, these categories are labeled, or named. When students identify the similarities, they are using many higher-level thinking skills (interpreting, inferring, generalizing) which lead to a greater ability to manipulate the category and apply it to new situations, so this strategy is very often used to teach basic grammatical concepts: without having to teach the concept in English, or use grammatical terms, students will discover, like Sherlock Holmes, that the power of deduction will lead them to the truth. Students, for example, provided with sentences with all the adverbs underlined, would group them into categories such as location, time, or description, and then you could discuss, still using the sample sentences, where words that fit these categories are in a typical sentence (i.e., immediately after the verb) without having to use the word "adverb."

A couple of warnings: the more examples the better, and, even more important, the simpler the better. Make sure the only element that varies is the concept you are presenting. Use the concepts in sentences, so the students learn to handle them in context. Another application might be to present students with sets of irregular verbs and have students discover the patterns for forming them, using deduction (sometimes called Concept Development), and then apply it to new verbs.

Let's try some deduction, using French adjectives:

MASCULINE	FEMININE
africain	africaine
japonais	japonaise
chinois	chinoise
allemand	allemande
anglais	anglaise

Now, try to formulate a rule to explain how to change from the masculine to the feminine form. Got one? Look at some more:

russe	russe
danois	danoise
belge	belge
espagnol	espagnole
canadien	canadienne

Look at your rule again. Does anything about it need changing? Now, try to make feminine forms for the following:

siamois
français
américain
australien

At this point, I would check the answers, (Step 3: application) and then debrief the class, asking volunteers to state the rule, refining it to everyone's liking, and having them verbalize their discovery process (Step 4): what did you first notice, and then what, and so on. This last step is *very* important for retention of the concept they have discovered, so don't skip it. Deduction has cut the time I need to teach some units practically in half, with much fewer practice activities needed. Since students found the rule by themselves instead of my just telling them, even though more time was spent discovering than if I had just told it to them, their ownership of the concept is much more permanent.

Most books (i.e., Kagan, 2009) state that this method is the most effective when done in a whole class setting, as the more input there is, the better, but I find that Steps 1 and Two are good pair or team activities, with a Roam Around the Room and then a time for revising categories before the class unites to list these categories and make our final Steps Three and Four discoveries about the concept. One small variation is to have the students create their own data file (Step 1), perhaps by looking at a page in a text, and making a list of what they see/read. For example, in French, by making a list of fruits, they might discover that most fruits listed are feminine in gender, and end in –e, a useful generalization.

SYLLOGISMS

Syllogisms are another form of deductive reasoning. Students must use/devise these to apply the rules of grammar to new words. A syllogism is a logical argument with two premises and a conclusion. A categorical syllogism helps fit items into a category: for example, "All feminine words end in –a. This word ends in –a. Therefore, this word is feminine," is a syllogism.

Statements such as "*aller*'s past tense form will be *allé*, because it ends in –er" is actually the result of a syllogism: All –er verbs change to –é; *aller* ends in –er, therefore *aller* changes to *allé*.

Other types of syllogisms seem to be easier to use for cultural items. A hypothetical syllogism has at least one hypothetical ("If . . .") portion. Example: "If a city is in Germany, it has a Rathaus. If Bonn is in Germany, it has a Rathaus. Bonn *is* in Germany, so it has a Rathaus."

A disjunctive syllogism has at least one "either/or" statement: Either soccer or baseball is the most popular sport in the world. Soccer has the most TV viewers, therefore soccer is the most popular.

For visual-spatial students, draw the syllogisms with a big circle for the main category, and a smaller circle for the subset within that category. This will fix the syllogisms more firmly in students' minds.

INDUCTION (OR CONCEPT ATTAINMENT)

Induction is another method to use to introduce new material, replacing the traditional lecture method with a more active one. First the teacher selects the concept to introduce, and also chooses and organizes the examples that contain characteristics of this concept. At least 20 pairs of examples are needed, especially for more complex concepts. Few texts provide such lists, so it will involve a bit of work and thought. This method of reasoning works well for introducing concepts like masculine/feminine/neuter endings, teaching students to identify a particular style of art or that of a particular artist, or learning how to form a new verb tense.

In Phase One of the activity, in class the teacher lists several examples, either on the board, on an overhead, or on a handout. The examples are labeled as positive (good/"yes") examples of the concept or attribute, or as negative (bad/"no") examples. The teacher asks the students to contrast the positive examples with the negative (to themselves, not out loud), and to take notes on those differences. (Note: this would be a good sponge activity.) The teacher could underline portions of the example in order to call attention to the important portion. Then the teacher adds a few more examples, asking students to make a hypothesis about what the difference is between the positive and negative ones. Then, a few more examples are given, to test the hypothesis and refine it. Then, a new step: unlabeled examples are presented, and students are asked to (still working on their own, and not out loud) guess, using their hypothesis, if they are positive or negative. Students love this approach: it is challenging, yet game-like.

Phase Two begins when it seems that most of the students have a workable hypothesis. (Use body language to judge: nodding heads, smiles, etc., or use signaling—cards, tap on desk, a tech survey app like Poll Everywhere, etc.—for feedback on who has a good idea/hypothesis.) Pair the students and have them share hypotheses. Test these new, combined/synthesized hypotheses with a few more unlabeled examples, and then ask groups to share their methods with another pair, and then the class. At this time, the teacher confirms the correct hypotheses, refining how they are stated if necessary, and supplies the name of the concept (i.e., "This is called the future tense, and you have correctly identified how it is different.") Now, have the students, in small groups, perhaps using Round-Robin, generate their own examples of this concept, or assign this as homework.

Phase Three is to check these new examples for accuracy, and to have students describe what thoughts went through their minds as they attempted to identify the concept: what did they concentrate on first, and reject; how did they modify their hypothesis based on additional examples? This is very important to voice, either to the entire class, or within their groups, because it more firmly fixes the concept by reviewing the steps they went through to find it. Concept Attainment is also an excellent review tool or evaluation tool if you want to check to see if some material you covered previously has been mastered. By giving good and bad examples of the concept, you will determine the students' depth of knowledge by how quickly they catch on, and also reinforce their understanding of this concept.

PATTERNING AND SEQUENCING ACTIVITIES

Discerning relationships and connections between objects or facts is another facet of logical/mathematical learning:

> CCSS: SL1, 3, 4, 6, L1;
>   (written instructions)
>   RL1, 3, 4, 6; (spoken)
>   SL1, 3, 4, 6
> ACTFL: 1.1, 1.2, 1.3, 3.1
> DOK 1, 2

- Assign students to bring an object to class that they don't usually bring, or provide each student with an object you have randomly gathered, and put them into groups. Have each group organize their objects by any method they wish, and then "show and tell" their collection of objects and method of organization. When teaching comparative adjectives or ordinal numbers, concepts like shape, color, size, or use are a few of the ways to categorize objects.

- Do any project involving step-by-step directions: build something simple, cook, do origami or some other activity where steps clearly must occur in a certain order, using command forms of verbs.

- "Postcards"—students will use their prior knowledge to fill in missing elements on a "postcard" in which words have been wholly or partially blotted out by "rain," reconstructing the message. An example:

Dear Paul,

I am very h_____y to be coming to your c_____y next week. I can't wait to meet your _____ and say _____ to them. My plane arrives at n_____ o'clock. Will you meet me at the _____?

Obviously, some of these blanks have more than one correct answer. "C_____y" could be country or city. Others, like "h_____y" could be "hungry" or "happy" (or other words) but from the context, "happy" seems to be best. Filling in blanks using clues and context is a logical skill.

- Have students assemble a puzzle, using only the TL, preferably a puzzle with a scene of a country or a building studied in class. When it is completed, talk about the picture.
- Have students list objects based on common characteristics rather than categories. For example, they could list anything that is triangular, or shiny, soft, curved, and so on. For "soft" they could list a kitten, a sock, a marshmallow, lips, sand, and anything else they can think of, using only words they know, or are currently studying in the TL. Have them illustrate their list to involve visual intelligence, as well as labeling the pictures in the TL, and share the results.
- Use pattern blocks or task cards to teach or learn things. A pattern card is one that is cut down the center in an irregular pattern, much like a puzzle piece: each card has only one other card that is its "match." Use these cards to pair a verb with its subject, a question and its answer, a numeral and its number (written as a word), a word in Spanish with its translation in English, a country with its capital, or any other obvious pairs. This is also a good way to "pair" students before a partner activity: have each take one, and find their partner.
- Puzzles are, according to research, the application that uses the most logical-mathematical intelligence.

GAMES FOR LOGICAL-MATHEMATICAL INTELLIGENCE

Any sort of game that involves calculations or logic would be appropriate. Calculation games would include card games like Mille Bornes, or board games like Monopoly. Logic games would include Clue, Battleship, Stratego, Connect 4, chess, or checkers. These games practice not only logic, but vocabulary such as prepositions of location. Battleship is also good for practicing almost any concept, if the student must answer a question before finding out if the space is a "hit" (and there are online templates to make these for your students).

Visual-Spatial Intelligence

Even though the name refers to the sense of sight, blind children also have visual-spatial intelligence. This is the ability to visualize, manipulate, and create mental images in order to solve problems. People with visual-spatial intelligence think in three-dimensional ways, and are able to recreate, transform, or modify these thoughts and perceptions, as well as to navigate and both produce and decode graphic information.

DISPLAY AREAS

One of the easiest and most commonly used ways to appeal to visual/spatial learners is to have a classroom display area with information (photos, articles, posters, projects) posted and which can be handled, read, and so on. However, it is very important that this be changed regularly *and* that students be encouraged to check it by:

- scavenger hunts whose answers are/were on display;
- display of high-interest items such as classmates' work;
- extra credit questions on tests based on displayed material.

Besides getting posters from going to conferences or buying them online, I have gotten some beautiful ones by writing consulates and asking, as well as having online cartoons, menus, pictures, etc. enlarged at the local printing place.

ROTATING SEATING

Another easy step to take is to change students' seating fairly often. A move from the back to the front, or right to left, will change a student's perspective on the items displayed in the classroom. Visual/spatially oriented students will benefit from the change in perspective, and it will give everyone a change of pace to have new neighbors.

NONVERBAL COMMUNICATION

Any use of nonverbal communication techniques or activities appeals to, and practices, visual/spatial intelligence skills.

- Have students perform actions (i.e., walk, dance) the way someone happy would do it, then try doing the same way if sad, bored, excited, and so on.
- Have them show you nonverbally how a character in a story feels, or a person of a particular nationality, an animal, a food, a piece of furniture, or whatever else you are studying.
- Have students mime activities, while classmates guess what they are acting out. If you are doing this like a game, prepare two lists of words, expressions, or sentences to be acted out. Teams should take turns. Keep track of how much total time the teams take to guess the items; the lowest total time wins.
- You can also give nonverbal signals. For example, have a signal to call for students to be quiet and listen, or a praise signal (such as Carol Burnett's earlobe tug, for example).
- If possible, teach some typical gestures used when speaking the TL, like the French shoulder shrug, or Italian gesture of disbelief, the European method of counting where raising the index finger indicated you want two of something, not one, and so on.

IMAGE MANIPULATION

Image manipulation is a great assist to visual/spatial skills. Writing items on different colors of cards or paper, or with different colors of ink, provides strong visual cues, like highlighting sections of an activity or notes, as any college student knows. For example, when the vocabulary involves a lot of nouns, put feminine words in pink, masculine blue, and neuter yellow. I guarantee you will hear students say something like, "No, that's a *pink* word!" Make action verbs green, and linking verbs red. Varying the sizes of letters in a word to emphasize unpronounced letters, or commonly misspelled portions helps fix the correct spelling in a visual/spatial learner's mind (Examples in English: recEive, Aisle, cloTHes.)

Dellawanna Bard, on the FL-TEACH list (see Resources listed in the Bibliography section) gave me this idea that works for her: have students think of some sort of dress, look or behavior that just screams "masculine" or "feminine" (for neuter, think of drab clothing and color). Then, every time you learn a noun, picture it wearing/doing that thing. The example she gave was a butterfly, which to most people is a very feminine thing, but in German is masculine. So, picture a butterfly, badly in need of a shave, walking around in boxer shorts, smoking a cigar (her masculine stereotype). Perhaps the feminine stereotype is a pink tutu . . . so picture an apple in a pink tutu. Then, picture all the masculine words at a party, or all the feminine ones doing a Rockettes-style number, like the hippos in "Fantasia." This sort of active-imagination visualization should be quite successful for the visually-oriented students in your classes.

Another image manipulation activity is the old standard party game I call "Word Search." I give my students a fairly long word, and have them compete to see who can make the most shorter words using only the letters found in the base word.

A form of image manipulation that teachers should use is to be very aware of how items are listed on handouts, chalkboard, and so on. If the items are of equal importance, they should be listed horizontally:

> CCSS: RL1, 3, 4, 6
> ACTFL: 1.1, 1.2, 1.3
> DOK 2

_____ _____ _____ _____

Items that are of varying importance should be written vertically, with the most important at the top.

VISUAL ARTS

Any sort of visual arts are the most common and most necessary aspect of visual/spatial intelligence to incorporate into a lesson plan, as well as what many students will remember and enjoy most. However, doing a craft must be done in the TL, and students working on the craft should be encouraged to converse *only* in that language, or else the craft should be done as homework instead of wasting class time on an activity done in English. My students usually remember vividly vocabulary (paper, scissors, glue) that we used when doing a craft in class. A well-designed craft activity can be a perfect way to provide input, imitation, assimilation, and invention as kids work to meet their needs in the activity. Visual arts would include all of the following, and more:

> CCSS: RL1, 3, 4, 6, W9, L2
> ACTFL: 1.1, 1.2, 1.3
> DOK 2

- Draw: yourself, a map, a house plan (fully furnished), your favorite meal . . .
- Create a calendar, using student artwork.
- Create slide show (or PowerPoint), and narrate it.
- Start with a supplied shape such as a triangle, and create something.
- Design T-shirts for the pétanque or foreign language club, or Foreign Language Week.
- Illustrate proverbs
- Translate, or invent, sayings for bumper stickers.
- Make posters to recruit foreign language students, advertise a fictional product or restaurant, or show mastery of a concept.
- Construct dioramas of volcanoes, marketplaces, or typical shops, starting with an old shoebox.
- Also using shoeboxes, make mini cultural floats to take through the halls/classrooms or cafeteria during Foreign Language Week.
- Make edible maps of countries being studied, using pudding, peanut butter, candies, marshmallows, etc.
- Sculpt your feelings, or typical people from a certain region of the globe that speaks your language.
- Make mosaics out of scraps of torn paper, beans, rice, bead, and so on. For a Latin class, use mythology as the subject for the mosaic.

- Draw murals for inside or outside the classroom: life-size outlines of students, with body parts or clothing labeled, graffiti walls of world from the TL that we also use in English, a typical city scene from Madrid/Paris/Munich/Kyoto/Roma, a backdrop of a news studio for "broadcasts" of the news.
- Sew or paint quilt squares or tiles with items representing bits of cultural information.
- Make puppets of famous people, and take turns guessing who they are, and/or having them perform.
- Draw storyboards or scrolls, and read them to each other.
- Make felt banners for the classroom, with phrases or cultural items on them.
- Map out a complex, interesting scavenger hunt for each other.
- Cut and paste collages on themes or ideas of interest/being studied. Use foreign language magazines as the resource for the collage, if possible.
- Use clay, paint, storyboards, or felt-tip markers to express a feeling or emotion (hungry, sad, sleepy).
- Make block prints of vocabulary, cities or symbols using old inner tubes and blocks of wood, and an ink pad. Cut the design from the tube, glue it to the block, and stamp away!
- Sew simple traditional clothing items: a Basque apron, a Roman toga, a bib attachment to turn shorts into "Lederhosen."
- Make cultural artworks such as: God's eyes (Ojos de Dio), piñatas, origami, sculptures, Scherenschnitte (paper cutting), Mardi Gras masks (or for Dia de los Muertes, or Fasching), "santons"(traditional Christmas dolls for a French manger scene), a Chinese character "chop" and prints, models of Roman temples, Gothic cathedrals or Renaissance castles, or of devices such as a guillotine, plus any other crafts you make know.
- Write "rebus stories" in which pictures replace words, and read them to each other.

PICTORIAL REPRESENTATION

Visual-spatial learners need to see *everything* represented visually, and visuals such as flow charts, mind maps, and concept maps help them organize and make sense of information. Concept mapping comes in many forms, with many names:

mindmapping or mindscaping	webbing	visual brainstorming
topic mapping	bubbling	graphic organizing
semantic mapping	clustering	flow charts
story mapping	chalk talk	Venn diagram
	hierarchy	

Many of the above names are synonymous. They are all ways to visually represent and organize the content of a story, a discussion, or students' own thoughts on an issue.

To use this method for vocabulary, I like to use my whiteboards (see Chapter 3 for more activities with those), on which I have my students write the topic in the center, such as "My Favorite Animals" and then quick-draw pictures of their favorite animals in a circle around the topic, with lines attaching the drawings to the center. Then they should label this spider-like design. After you check them for accuracy, erase the labels, redistribute them to different people, and have them identify and label the animals as drawn. The same method could be used for a story: students could, as a group, list the key elements of a story they either read, or heard the teacher read aloud. After putting the title of the story in the center, for each element they name, they draw a picture, labeling it.

Story Map. A story map is a more advanced way to represent the content of a story. It looks a bit more like a family tree. The title goes at the top, and the themes or key elements are below it. Below each element are examples or evidence of that element. Pictures may be used if desired, but usually words are used—quotations from the story, brief descriptions of the plot, and so on. The visual aspect of this is that each branch is a main point, with the supporting information visibly attached to it. Seeing these connections more firmly fixes the information in the brain. See Figure 2.9 for a simple visual representation of this method.

Figure 2.9 Story Map

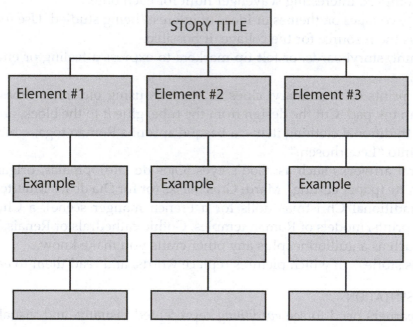

This method works really well for grammar, also. I use it to list when to use the various past tenses, especially the imperfect. We use it for the various uses of the subjunctive, also. A visual representation of mnemonics like BANGS, a way to memorize which adjective in French precede the noun: those dealing with Beauty, Age, Number, Goodness, and Size; or DISHES, a way to memorize the Spanish verbs with irregular subjunctive forms—dar, ir, saber, haber, estar and ser—and others would be good to do in this way, also, for the visual-spatial learners in your classes.

Flow Charts. Flow charts or chain maps are used for activities or ideas that must occur in a certain order. In these, students draw pictures, marking the order they are to be read or looked at by numbering the pictures, or drawing arrows from one to the next. We use these a lot when doing a food unit and cooking. Get an illustrated recipe, and cut apart the pictures. Have students reassemble the pictures in the correct order. THEN, prepare the recipe. You will find the students make a lot fewer mistakes, and accomplish the task in less time. It also doubles as a logical activity. This works equally well for simple construction projects (we build simple things using Lego blocks to practice the prepositions of location), learning coding online, or sewing projects.

Hierarchy. A hierarchy is used to show relationships between objects. The most important goes on top, with the subordinate portions below. A family tree is a good example of this type of visual representation, and similar cultural items are what are best suited to this type of chart. A hierarchy would be good for showing the relative levels of the eight different forms of "you" used by the Japanese (for example, one is used between equals, another from a superior to subordinate, from a subordinate to a superior, and so on). Structures like the feudal system or the food pyramid are routinely drawn using the hierarchy system.

Line-Ups. A continuum scale is one that lists items based on where they fit between two extremes. These are great for practicing vocabulary. Give your students cards with the names of sports, and have them line up according to where their sport fits in the following situations: most violent to least, most difficult to least, outdoor to indoor, cold weather to hot weather, requiring special gear to requiring none, or team to individual. Of course, you require them to discuss who belongs where in the TL, even if they sound like Tarzan: "Me, more." And if you want to complicate matters a bit, at the end of each line-up have them hand their card to the person to their left or right; then give a different set of parameters for the line-up.

Line-up sentences are also great to do. Give students cards, each with a word on it. Put colored dots on the back of the cards, and first have them locate other students with the same color. Then, have them line up to make an intelligible, grammatical sentence. Have the groups take turns reading each other's sentences, and translating them. Have people holding nouns come to you and exchange their noun cards for pronouns. Point out where an adverb goes in the sentence. This makes students very aware of sentence structure.

Line-ups have also proven quite valuable when doing a unit on history. Students often have difficulty placing events in the proper perspective: which came first, second, and so on. I give cards to students doing a history unit with the names of events, people, or ideas. First, I have the events find their people (i.e., the Battle of Hastings finds William the Conqueror and Harold of England) and then they line up. Then the "ideas" find their people (i.e., "patriotism" finds Joan of Arc). Then, in chronological order, each person steps forward and says who they are, and a little about themselves, hands me their card, and is seated. This is great review right before a test, and just takes a couple of minutes. Last year, I also got a big piece of butcher paper and drew a huge time line on it. As we studied history, the students recorded the events on the time line, and were encouraged to add events they studied in other classes. They added mathematicians and scientific advances they learned about, when pieces of music (i.e., Handel's *Messiah*) were published, a bit of American history and literature, and several of their own birthdays (claiming they'd be famous some day). It was an interesting chart and a high-interest display for the classroom, as students would check to see if anything new had been added.

Other Pictorials. Venn diagrams (discussed previously, as well as below in the Marzano's best practices section) are good for visual-spatial learners. They help students relate new material to familiar, writing characteristics of each into a circle, but characteristics they both share into the space where the circles overlap. I use these to compare verb tenses, to compare stress pronouns with subject pronouns, but mostly I use this with literature, like when I have them compare the title character of the French book *The Little Prince* to the Bible's Jesus, making the many similarities between the two not only visible, but memorable. (I do give non-Christian students the option of comparing the Prince to another religious or historical figure if they wish, but the activity focuses on what critics perceive as an intended comparison, the writer of the book being Catholic.) We used Venn diagrams around Valentine's Day for a sometimes humorous comparison between two people to see if they had enough in common to be a "couple" (see Chapter 4).

The final chart I often use is called a "K-W-L," also mentioned in the linguistic intelligence section. Before we begin a new chapter, video, or unit, we do an inventory of what we already know (K is for Know) about the topic. Then we think about what we want to know (W is for Want to Know), writing questions we want to have answered. Each day, for closure, we examine this chart, adding anything we learned to the L portion (L is for Learned), until all the questions have answers.

GAMES FOR VISUAL-SPATIAL INTELLIGENCE

Games for this intelligence would include many board games like Scrabble, Monopoly, Cluedo, Bingo/Lotería (especially picture bingos like Lingo, available from the UNICEF catalog, as well as others found in many teacher supply catalogs), Twister, or Pictionary, as well as playing charades. Adding pictures to online games like Quizlet, Kahoot, and Quizizz is suggested as well. Almost all card games use this intelligence, especially ones of the "Go Fish" type where students' cards show clock faces, or other pictures representing vocabulary words.

A great way to "discover" visuals is to use a free jigsaw-creating app like www.jigsawplanet.com/ and visuals of a city, a country, or some art and let the kids, online, solve the puzzle (I recommend no more than 45 piece puzzles).

Musical Intelligence

This intelligence is defined as the ability to recognize and compose musical pitches, tones, and rhythms. Deaf students would be handicapped in this area, but still able to master rhythm. Every foreign language teacher knows how important pitch, tone, and rhythm are to languages.

Willis and Mason (1994) discuss the use of popular music in the TL as a tool in language instruction. They argue that not only are TL songs more relevant to the students' experiences than textbook material, but that songs, in addition to providing authentic use of the TL, also are a good source of exposure to the TL culture. Music naturally transmits and reflects the culture in which it was created.

I personally find that songs are also a good way to teach vocabulary and grammar structures, and give examples in Chapter 5 on teaching difficult concepts through music. Many students will learn a particular form of a verb, or key vocabulary by learning a song that uses that word or tense repetitively. The web site Lyricstraining, http://lyricstraining.com, has thousands of songs in many languages (and you can add more with a free account), where learners do a gap-fill activity involving the song's lyrics. Students can compete with each other to see who can get the best score. It boosts confidence, and many of mine do it at home as well as in school.

However, listening to music or watching a video are not good for long-term retention (remember Glasser's Learning Scale, Figure 1.2: hear = 20 percent and see = 30 percent). Music needs to be actively assessed; seven of Gardner's intelligences are addressed when teaching using music:

Kinesthetic (clapping, dance, body movement, percussion).
Musical (listening, singing, playing, distinguishing sounds).

Linguistic (lyrics: reading or listening).

Logical/mathematical (music is mathematical by nature, especially rhythm and pitch).

Interpersonal (chorus, dance, cooperative learning with lyrics).

Visual-spatial (video, dramatization, illustrations).

Intrapersonal (personal connections, enjoyment).

LISTENING TO MUSIC

Show a music video. Play it several times, interrupting it frequently to say the words loudly and clearly, explaining the meaning. Then encourage the students to sing along. The best sorts of songs for this would be those that are highly repetitive, and those that can be acted out (like *Sur le Pont d 'Avignon*, the *Hokey Pokey*, the *Chicken Dance*, and others) or those that have

CCSS: SL 1, 3, 4, 6
ACTFL 1.1, 1.2, 1.3
DOK 1, 2

special steps, like the Macarena or movements to go with the animals in *Le Poussin Piou*. Songs with an interesting message or visual will be favorites of your students.

Another way to get students to listen and appreciate is to do one of the following:

- Have them keep a tally of how many times they hear a phrase you tell them to listen for.
- Give each student a card with a word from the song. If they hear their word, they should stand up.
- Have students listen for a particular verb tense, and signal when they hear it.
- Give students the song, cut into strips of one line each, and have them figure out what order they think they are in. Then listen to the song, and let them see how close they were.
- Give each student half the lines to the song, and one piece of paper. Each takes turns reading their line to the other, who writes it down.
- Have students create a cover for the song. It should include the title, singer's name, and at least three items representing themes/ideas/things mentioned in the song. This is good as it involves several other intelligences, as well as creativity, and you end up with a visual you can display to jog their memories.
- Give students the words to the song, with key words missing (which they should already know). Have students fill in the blanks while listening to the song.

Good music to use for the above activities is popular music in the TL. Spanish music is fairly easy to find: Selena, Shakira, Daddy Yankee, J. Balvin, Wisin, and many others may be purchased via the Internet, or in many popular music stores. For French, try to find some Stromae, Zaz, Corneille, or Shy'm. For German, Tokio Hotel and Rammstein are popular. YouTube is, of course, a great resource, but why not have students ask their penpals for and give their recommendations? Writing a music review would be a great authentic use of the TL, as well as authentic culture.

MUSIC AS MOTIVATION

Use music as background while students are writing. Warning: teenagers especially are very closed-minded about music, so for this purpose, don't use "theirs," or let them provide the music. Instead, play classical music, or music of the folk/ethnic variety in the TL, preferably some that is unknown to the students. The object is to play something that will *not* distract them from the task at hand or encourage them to sing along, comment on whether they like it or not, and so on. It is to serve as a sort of subliminal motivator. For example, music with a fast beat will speed completion of an assignment. Music sung in the TL's rhythms will help jog memories for vocabulary. Mood music like *Clair de Lune* by Debussy will influence the setting and characters of the story they are writing, or the content of the poem. Others, like Saint-Saens' *Danse Macabre* may be used to jumpstart creative writing; it is a musical representation of the dead, witches, etc. rising and riding about the night, only to fall back asleep at the rooster's call announcing dawn. Tell this to the students, and let their imagination run wild as they listen.

Music can also provide a topic for conversation. Music with a message about the environment, human rights, or love can be used to introduce a discussion of those topics. You can also bring in examples of several different styles. Play a little of each type, and have students identify the style: techno, emo, pop, alternative, folk, and so on. Talk with them about the possible use, audience, popularity, etc. of each type. Correlate music with how fans might dress.

Music, used correctly, will help focus students' attention and relax them or invigorate them (for example, after something very lively, or a fire drill or some other interruption, soothe them with soft, slow music). It can also provide transitions: some teachers use certain music to signal when a regular activity begins or ends, and playing that music tells the students to close their books and get into their groups, or whatever. Music will definitely jumpstart creativity.

SONGS THAT TEACH CURRICULUM

Sometimes we are lucky, and a good, traditional song exists for teaching material. For example, *Alouette* is good for teaching body parts, as you sing about plucking feathers off various parts of a bird (or *Jean Petit qui Danse*). *Il était une bergère* is good for introducing the passé simple. Two of Selena's songs, *No Me Queda Mas* and *Si Una Vez* mix the present, preterit, and imperfect, and are perfect for a verb unit. Other songs can be translated; I use *Head, Shoulders, Knees and Toes* in my French classes when we study body parts or for a "brain break" when they look like they need a change of pace. A fabulous resource for French is this site: http:// platea.pntic.mec.es/cvera/hotpot/chansons/or the AATF wiki. For Spanish I'd recommend www.songsforteaching.com/spanishsongs.htm.

The best songs for teaching are the simplest. Take material from a chapter, especially more difficult things, and put it to familiar childhood tunes like *Twinkle Twinkle Little Star* or *Jingle Bells*, or some more modern ones, like *We Will Rock You* or *Royals* (look on a karaoke list). I have some wonderful vocab songs created in this way (my current favorite is the days of the week to the Flintstones theme) as well as grammar songs that I have gotten from other teachers. Some of my favorite verb songs are in Chapter 5. Here is a sample song, involving the possessive adjectives in French, sung to the tune of *Jingle Bells*:

mon ma mes,
ton ta tes,
son sa ses, voilà!
Notre, nos
Votre, vos
Leur et leurs, c'est ça!

I also like to involve my students in making up their own songs; not only are they proud of making up a song (or a rap) but they have learned the material it covers, "accidentally." We have "verb operas" when students are challenged to make songs conjugating difficult verbs.

If you are not feeling creative, the "Sing, Dance, and Eat Tacos/Quiche" CDs (some songs are on YouTube) have lots of songs set to nursery rhymes. I also have CDs by Etienne (Stephen Langlois, alias DJ Delf, a very creative Canadian who writes materials to teach French and Spanish grammar and vocabulary through music).

DANCE

Dance belongs in musical intelligence because of its reliance on rhythm. There are many dances you can teach your classes, and dancing to a song makes you appreciate music even more. Is there a flamenco society in your area? They may sponsor classes, or at least come demonstrate the castanets and steps for you. Find a video on YouTube on how to play castanets, or of folk dances, or show something silly like the German dance from the movie *National Lampoon's European Vacation*, or the can-can from Check out ballroom dancing opportunities: the cha-cha, rhumba, tango, mambo, and merengue are fairly easy to learn. Many of the calls in square dancing are in French: "Promenade" (promener = to walk), "do-si-do, or dos à dos" (back to back), and so on, and many of the steps are in traditional French dances

CHORAL READINGS

Choral reading are included under this intelligence because, in order to read together, pause together, and so on, they must really learn the rhythm and tones of the language—where to accent syllables, what sounds the vowels make, and many other aspects of the sound of the language; they do not necessarily have to know what the poem they are reading is about, but they must feel the beat, rhymes, and mood in order to read it well. For this reason, it can be a wonderful change of pace activity in the beginning classroom as well as in an advanced class. Have a program of readings of love poems right before Valentine's!

MAKING MUSICAL INSTRUMENTS

Are any of your students musically talented? Have them bring in the guitar, get them a piano, or whatever. For the rest, why not make them the rhythm section? Making simple rhythm instruments is the easiest, and involves the Kinesthetic Intelligence as well. Easy instruments kids love to make are rain sticks and maracas. To make a rain stick, take a cardboard tube (mailing tubes are more durable) and nails that are almost as long as the tube is wide (but not quite). Nail them right next to each other in a spiral pattern down the tube. Cover one end of the tube with masking tape, tissue paper, or papier-mâché (don't use anything slick) and pour in some dry rice, lentils, popcorn, or really small pebbles. Cover the other end, paint and decorate the outside. When you tip the stick, it makes a sound like raindrops on leaves.

For small maracas, use a paper plate and decorate on one side. Cut it in half, folding each half in half and putting some dry popcorn kernels inside. Staple or tape it shut, attaching a piece of dowel or a craft stick as a handle, and you have two small, triangle-shaped maracas that are cheap to make. For larger ones, use a plastic bottle, partially filled with dry rice or popcorn. Use duct tape or package strapping tape to firmly tape a wood dowel in the mouth of the bottle. Wrap with paper (crepe, construction, tissue), decorate, and use. Another way to make maracas is to cover old light bulbs with papier-mâché, and then break the bulb (that's what rattles inside), then paint and decorate.

CCSS: If listening: SL1, 3, 4, 6; if reading RL1, 3, 4, 6; writing W3, 4, 5
ACTFL: 1.1, 1.2, 1.3, 5.1, 5.2
DOK 2

Bodily-Kinesthetic Intelligence

This intelligence challenges the commonly held belief that mental and physical activities are unrelated. Kinesthetically talented people use their mental abilities to coordinate their bodily movements and to manipulate objects. Kinesthetic activities are easy to incorporate: daily exercise, walks, and dance as well as gestures (see Chapter 1) are examples. Play a "Simon Says" game with built-in content: Point to the north/south/left/right/up/down. Have students move around the room touching objects in the colors named, in the order they are named. Use ball-toss games for review, storytelling, or talking about themselves.

Movement can raise blood pressure and epinephrine levels in sleepy kids, reduce restlessness, and reinforce content. Recent research has found that physical activity enhances memory to a large extent for *any* learner; the mind-body connection definitely exists.

LEARNING ENVIRONMENT

How your classroom is set up physically is very important for kinesthetic reasons. Kinesthetic learners must have movement. An easy way to provide this is to organize the classroom into areas designated for seatwork, performances (skits), crafts, computer or language lab work, and conversations, as well as having a clearly defined entry, library, and storage place. Mark an area on the floor to designate: the only place it is OK to speak English, or where to leave backpacks so movement in the classroom is easier.

This can be done visually by using different colors of paper, tape in different colors, or strategic placement of desks, file cabinets, etc. The purpose of these areas is to have students move about the classroom during the course of a day's lesson. Unfortunately, many of us have large enrollments and full classrooms, but by rearranging seating for different activities, it is still possible to provide for movement. For lecture and class discussion, a "fishbone" formation is good: short rows, facing each other, around a wide central aisle (useful as a stage, for line-ups, etc.):

```
XX   XX   XX   XX   XX   XX   XX
XX   XX   XX   XX   XX   XX   XX
```

XX = one desk This setup seats 28.

```
XX   XX   XX   XX   XX   XX   XX
XX   XX   XX   XX   XX   XX   XX
```

For conversations or group work, set up "pods" of three to five chairs pushed together into one large unit:

```
XXXX        XXXX        XXXX        XXXX
XXXX        XXXX        XXXX        XXXX
```

This also seats 28.

```
   XXXX        XXXX        XXXX
   XXXX        XXXX        XXXX
```

DRAMA

To make any topic a kinesthetic activity, turn it into a play. Write a script and make costumes. Choreograph a poem, dance to one of the grammar songs, memorize and lip synch a tape (music or conversation). Have a puppet show version of the dialogue in the chapter. The more senses you can involve (sight, sound, hearing, touch) the more they will remember the material.

RUNNING DICTATION

Post a story on the wall; Partner A will run up to it, memorize as much as possible, and then run back to Partner B and tell it to B. B will write it down, A will correct it, and then run back for more. Halfway through the story, they will switch roles.

SIMULATIONS

Simulations are probably what foreign languages have always done best: how you make students see that the vocabulary and behaviors you are teaching them are really useful. Most kids know that movies are not real life, so videos have some but not significant impact on their perceiving grammar or vocabulary as relevant. But, put them in a situation where they must actually perform, using the language, in a life-like "reality" situation, and they suddenly see the relevance of what they have been learning, as well as get feedback on how well they have mastered these communications skills.

In short, simulations are the "meat" of foreign language teaching. A good simulation has several different parts. When choosing a simulation, a teacher makes several decisions, based on time available, what classroom resources are needed (and finances), how to assign teams (small groups of no more than five are best, says the research; I prefer even smaller ones), and, especially, how to distribute the high-status roles in a manner the students will perceive as fair. The teacher must also decide if this activity will be graded, and if so, how this will be done. Of course, a simulation usually follows extensive preparation by the students (learning vocabulary and practicing skits and conversational skills), and preparation of the students by the teacher, by explaining the goal or goals and the rules of the simulation, as well as assigning the students to teams, modeling the correct behavior, and giving the students a small practice session before beginning the actual simulation.

Some good, easy short simulations would be:

Ask directions	Buy tickets	Shop: for food, clothing, toiletries, etc.
Make a phone call	Bargain for a taxi	Complain: at a restaurant or a hotel.

A good example would be when, after practicing vocabulary and culture, I have my students check into my "hotel." As they enter my classroom, singly or in small groups, they ask for a room, specify the type of bed and bathroom facilities they want, ask the price, whether or not breakfast is included, and any other information they need. I hand them a room key, and they fill out a form like those used in most hotels, with passport number and other relevant information, which they return to the desk, picking up a sheet with vocabulary about a standard hotel room, and which, at the bottom, tells them that there is a problem with their room, and they must complain to the desk clerk. My check sheet for this activity looks like this:

Table 2.2 Hotel Simulation

CHECK-IN	Began conversation	Yes	No
Name _____	Answered questions	Y	N
	Asked price	Y	N
	Asked/breakfast	Y	N
	Said thank you	Y	N
	Form turned in to clerk	Y	N
	"Filled out correctly"	Y	N
	Complaint made	Y	N
	Understandable	Y	N
	Polite	Y	N

Each *Yes* is worth one point.

A good, longer simulation has two characteristics: it is like real life (authentic), and it involves an ongoing process, or series of necessary behaviors. In a game called *El Mercado/ Le Marché/Das Kaufhaus*, students go shopping. First they study vocabulary on clothing, which is sold at the market, as well as the tradition of bargaining ("too expensive," "three for 10 euros"), which is in the text and videos, if possible. Then the students are divided into teams. Some are the store owners, and their aim is to sell as many items for as much money as possible. Other teams are shoppers, who want to buy clothing "outfits" (what good is a shirt if it doesn't go with anything else?) for as little as possible. Stores are given identical sets of cards with clothing items pictured, and money for making change. Shoppers are given money to spend. After a brief planning period when stores set prices and shoppers plan strategy, the teacher must explain a few more rules. As I have done this simulation over the years, the rules get longer: I now add "No armed robbery" and "No shoplifting" to my usual "No English" rule (smile), and also explain the scoring system.

After handling any questions, the stores open and shopping begins. During this time, the teacher has two roles: Referee, to see that rules are followed, and Coach, to give advice in a supportive way, while still allowing the students to make mistakes. Since most stores close for a noon break, or a siesta, a closing bell is rung after about 20 minutes, and shoppers finish their current buying and everyone regroups. The teacher can use this time to highlight common errors observed, the stores to mark down prices, and the shoppers to lay out their outfits and see what is still needed. Then, shopping begins again. When time is called, the exercise is over, scoring is done, and the winning stores and shoppers are rewarded.

Then comes the most important portion of a simulation: debriefing. How closely did this exercise resemble the real world? What difficulties did shoppers encounter, and what solutions did they find? What cultural differences did they observe? What would they do differently next time? What additional vocabulary did they need? What gestures did they use? Students need time to analyze what happened, compare it to their previous experiences, and appraise their performance, planning how to redesign it for future simulations, or, hopefully, during a real trip to that country.

Grading a simulation is up to the teacher. It could be a simple participation grade: 4 points for participating fully in the TL/3 if used English/2 if had to be encouraged to participate/

1 if breaks rules, based on the teacher's observations while circulating. The activity could culminate in a written exercise that could be collected, or you could have a check sheet similar to the one I showed above for the hotel activity. I have written three multiweek simulations (a murder mystery, an action adventure, and a soap opera) and have used them in my classes for more than 20 years.

There are many, many different ways to use simulations. Wish you could find a guest speaker, but don't have one? Simulate one: have students write questions they would like to ask a guest speaker, and then research the answers. For example, have students prepare questions for a German/French/Spanish exchange student, and then, using encyclopedias, letters to embassies, or the Internet, try to find answers.

Elaborations. Simulations do NOT have to have a lot of props, and a good simulation need not even involve a lot of preparation, because in real-life situations, the outcome of a conversation or situation will depend on the other person's reactions and responses. It is this unknown factor that is both a little scary and a little exciting for the students. Simulations can be simply setting up conversational situations. I have several of these I like to do primarily with upper-level classes. One is called Elaborating. In it, students are not allowed to simply answer *yes* or *no* to *yes/no* questions; they must Make It Juicy. My definition of Juicy is "one or more of these: With Whom, What, Where, When, Why or How elements." For example, if asked if they live in town, they may reply *yes*, but then they must volunteer more: how long they have lived there, or what color their house is, or what street they live on, and then they must turn the question around on the interviewer: do you live in town? Do you like living in town? I usually provide question cards for this type of activity, based on whatever topic we are studying: where to shop, driving cars, studies, or whatever.

Another variation on Elaborating is Multiple Responses, where students are asked to provide a variety of responses. In La Aduana (customs), to the inspector's statement "Su pasaporte, por favor," give as many appropriate responses as possible: (it is fun to play this in teams) "Como no," "Claro," "Aquí tiene Ud. mi pasaporte," "Un minuto, por favor. Está en mi maleta." Translations: Why not? Of course. Here's my passport. Just a minute please; it's in my suitcase. See how creative your students can get!

Another variation is called Reactions. After reading or hearing a description of a situation, students are asked to play the roles of different people, and react to the event:

Example: Ein junger Arzt, der eben aus dem Krankhaus gekommen ist, läuft über die enge Strasse, die mit den vielen Wagen des Hauptverkehrszeit verstopft ist, ein unvorsichtiges Benehmen. (A young doctor has just left the hospital, running across a narrow street that is full of rush-hour traffic, very careless behavior.)

Roles to assign for this would be accompanied by a suggestion as to what type of reaction is desired: ein Politzist/Frage (a policeman/ask a question, such as "what do you think you are doing, young man?"). The policeman could also exclaim, or could question another person. Other roles would include such people as ein Kind zu seiner Mutter/Frage, Bemerkung (child to his/her mother/question or observation), the child's mother/reply, a bus driver/exclamation (Ausruf), the doctor's wife, a pedestrian, an elderly woman to the child/negative question, a merchant at the door to his shop, and so on.

Elizabeth D. Morie, in her chapter in *Teaching in the Block* (Canady and Rettig, 1996), lists the following advantages to using simulations:

1 Student interest and enthusiasm, "for the content, the teacher, greater motivation for learning in general" (Canady and Rettig, 1996, p. 155).
2 Better attitudinal changes. Students are more empathetic and tolerant. Increased peer and student-teacher interaction. A more relaxed, open classroom.
3 Skills enhancement: improved coping and decision making, bargaining, and persuasive skills.
4 Factual learning. Simulations make knowledge more relevant and understandable, leading to more transfer and long-term retention of material.
5 Variety and change of pace, since the activity's outcome is unpredictable, and since simulations are not done as often. It is an opportunity for movement, also.
6 Responsive environment. Students get immediate feedback, and know how well they are doing.
7 Safety. A perception that it is OK to make errors, and keep going.

MANIPULATIVES

Even if full-body movement isn't always possible, involve students physically through manipulatives, things they can do with their hands. The "signal" sponge listed in Chapter 1 is designed specifically for kinesthetic learners. Manipulatives can be as simple as using different colored pencils to write a sentence (black for nouns, red for verbs, blue for other) or vocabulary (one color for each gender). Total Physical Response (TPR) activities are good, too: give commands to the students to put their paper on their head, stack different colored blocks. Clocks with movable hands when telling time are typical manipulatives. Have students assemble things: Lego structures, an origami bird. Here is a long list of manipulative activities:

- Bring in dolls or stuffed animals that can be dressed, introduced to each other, placed in various regions of a map marked on the floor with tape, seated in various rooms of a "house" drawn on butcher paper.
- Using toy cars and a large map, or a model of a city you have built, have students take turns driving the cars according to their partner's instructions. This could practice learning places on a map, as well as prepositions and command forms of verbs. Even more fun is to have someone bring in a remote-controlled toy car to drive. The student could drive the car, describing what he or she is doing, or asking for advice such as whether to turn left or right.
- Use play money to shop or purchase food during a simulation. Make change.
- Teach students a magic trick in the TL, and assign them to teach it to a friend, parent, or sibling as homework.
- Living mannequin: arrange students in various positions, and have them guess what vocabulary word they are.
- Get a book of string games like Cat's Cradle and Jacob's Ladder and you will be able to see easily who is listening and following directions.
- Have students bring in a toy or hobby and demonstrate it, or pick a skill they'd like to teach the class.
- Eating a meal is different from country to country—how forks and knives are held, how to get food (serve yourself or ask people to pass it), how to use spices and sauces. Set up

typical table settings, and have students eat a meal according to the etiquette of another country (especially fun when it involves chopsticks or eating with your hands).

- See Chapter 3 for mention of Cootie Catchers and an extensive list of creative flashcard activities.
- Foldables templates are easy to find online. Make cardstock into a row of shops, a family, and many more things. Mine made "verb snowflakes" last winter.

GAMES

Table games are the least physical, but anything using dice or cards will appeal to a kinesthetic learner. Board races also are good for students who need movement.

Have scavenger hunts (inside or outside the classroom). Play kinesthetically oriented games like Simon Says, Mother May I?, Charades, Jenga (Chapter 3), or Twister. Draw or masking tape a hopscotch path on the floor, with vocabulary words or verbs in each square, and have students define or conjugate the word they land on. Do exercise routines in the TL (practices body parts, commands, numbers, and adverbial expressions). Tai chi is good for Japanese or Chinese culture as well as the kinesthetic value.

Mark off the floor into squares that have letters and numbers and then tell yourself to walk, hop, run, crawl, skip, jump, walk backward, walk on your knees, etc. to a particular square. Ask students to volunteer to participate when they feel comfortable. When you get a larger number of volunteers, put them in teams and see which team can follow more of your orders correctly. The next day, repeat, but direct students toward classroom objects like the desk, chair, door, flag, wastebasket, pencil sharpener, and other locations.

Although it is technically not a game, palm reading is an entertaining activity that generates a high level of student interest. It also practices the future tense, and students can observe and comment on the similarities and differences between their "fortunes" and those of classmates. Books on palm reading are available at many libraries, or you can just pretend, and make up a fortune.

Outdoors, demonstrate (in the TL) and then have them practice skipping rope to rhymes used in another country. Play a game of softball, soccer, or pétanque (boules, bocci) using only the TL (practice appropriate things to say first, of course). Arrange for contests of strength, speed or agility, and have students encourage each other, measure the results, record and compare the performances, in the TL. Begin an exercise program, and have students keep track of their progress, and report on it.

COOKING

Once again, cooking is best done in the TL. I try to have metric measuring cups, as well as recipes with photos. If possible, I have a local chef demonstrate how to make an omelet or a crepe; if not, I demonstrate, in the TL (and a lot of nonverbal communication). Then, I turn the kids loose, and we make and eat the food. Here are some good recipes:

Quesadillas

Start with prepared flour or corn tortillas (one per student or serving). Put slices of cheese on half, fold the top over, and heat until the cheese melts. Enjoy with salsa, beans, and other traditional accompaniments.

Flour tortillas (also an easy dessert)

Cut into strips, deep fry briefly (they will puff up) and sprinkle with cinnamon sugar.

Sangria (a traditional Spanish fruit beverage)

- one 12-oz can frozen grape juice concentrate
- one 12-oz can frozen pink lemonade
- one 2-liter (or 2 quarts) ginger ale
- orange, apple, banana slices

Mix the first three ingredients in a large pitcher. Pour into cups filled with ice. Put an orange slice in each (apples and bananas for those who want them or hate oranges.) Serves 25.

Crepes (French pancakes)

- three eggs
- one 1/2 cup milk
- three cup flour
- two tbsp. sugar

Mix the above at least 6 hours before preparing crepes. Heat a small empty frying pan until it is quite hot (a drop of water will dance or sizzle). If the pan is not nonstick, oil it lightly. Take about 1/4 cup (or a bit less) of batter, and pour it all at once into the pan, quickly tilting the pan to spread the batter as thinly as possible. When the crepe is cooked on one side, check it to make sure it is loose, and flip it into the air to turn it (it's a lot easier than it looks). When done, place on a plate, fill with honey, cinnamon sugar, jam, or Nutella (chocolate spread) or melt in a little Swiss cheese, or cheese and ham. Other less traditional fillings could be to use canned pie filling or pudding. Roll up and eat with your fingers. Makes eight to ten crepes. We have the traditional crepe race afterward: make two "racing crepes" (thicker than usual) and have volunteers run from one point to another, flipping the crepes as they run.

Kartoffelpuffer (German potato pancakes)

- two large potatoes, grated (approx. two 1/2 cups)
- water with lemon juice
- one boiled potato, mashed
- two tbsp. milk
- one egg, beaten
- 1/2 tsp. salt
- fat for frying (about 1/2 stick margarine or butter)

Put the grated potatoes in the water, then drain, squeezing out any liquid. Add the rest of the ingredients, and drop batter for three or four pancakes at a time into the fat. Brown on both sides and serve with applesauce or sour cream. Makes enough for 3 or 4 people for a meal; more for students to just have a taste.

There are many, many other ethnic foods to fix; I just listed some very easy and inexpensive ones above as examples. Churros and chocolate, quiche lorraine or croque-monsieur, Apfel-strudel or Sauerkraut . . . the list of possibilities is endless.

My French club, outside regular school hours, has baked, assembled, and decorated a gingerbread replica of a French Renaissance castle, and entered it in the local gingerbread house contest. For several years, we have won a prize and spent the money for a DVD, t-shirts, or a party or meal that the students want. For many of my students, it is the first time they have ever done anything this creative, and we use our French, study architecture, and get to eat all the leftover candy.

FIELD TRIPS

Field trips are traditionally a kinesthetic experience, and if you have a museum, ethnic restaurant, a traveling theater company performing, or other worthwhile site to visit, or feel that a change of scenery would inspire your students' creativity, by all means give your students that opportunity. I would, however, venture that most field trips would be best done outside regular school hours; interested students could still attend, and class time could usually be used more productively.

Interpersonal Intelligence

The ability to communicate one's feelings to others as well as to understand their feelings and intentions is highly valued in our society today. Anything interactive will use this intelligence, which relies upon all the other intelligences. To improve or strengthen this intelligence, teach your students relational skills: give students opportunities to practice listening, encouraging others, and reaching consensus. The real goal is for students to learn to feel comfortable about personal abilities and characteristics, as well as acknowledge and respect the opinions, ideas, values, and characteristics of others.

> CCSS: SL1, 3, 4, 6;
> if speaking L1;
> if writing W2
> ACTFL: 1.1, 1.2, 1.3
> DOK 2, 3

COMMUNICATION AND EMPATHY

The first word in the definition of this intelligence is "communicate." Communication is both verbal and nonverbal. Begin with the nonverbal form:

- Have students use body language to express various emotions. Remind them to use gestures as well as sounds (but no words). Practice using body language to express encouragement and support for others. Point out, over the next few days or weeks, students exhibiting this body language, or ask the whole class to remember and show you this when they are inattentive.
- Practice people-watching. Show a video with the sound off. Evaluate the dress, gestures and facial expressions of the characters in the video, and speculate about what they are thinking, feeling, and saying. Then watch it again, with the sound on, to check for accuracy. (This is an integral part of the method called Movie Talk, part of CI teaching).

To foster verbal communication, have students draw something related to the unit you're on in the text, as homework: a person's face, a plate of food, a fully clothed person, a room in a house, a town map. The next day, pair two of them back to back, and have Student A draw while Student B describes his or her drawing. Neither can look at the other's paper, and no gestures or other nonverbal communication is allowed. Student A is allowed to ask any questions (in the TL, of course). When they are done, have them compare drawings, and discuss. Feedback is important.

INTERPERSONAL COMMUNICATION PROJECTS

Have students survey their classmates to find things they have or do that are unique (at least, for that particular class). For example, they might be the only ones who collect baseball cards, or have no siblings. They could also look for opposites to tell about: My dog is black and Henry has a white cat.

A standard project for interpersonal communication is some sort of "me project." This may take any form. Some teachers have students make a coat of arms, divided into four sections. One section is for family, one for hobbies and interests, one for the future, and one for school and studies. A student would then draw, or paste pictures in each section that represent things in his or her life. To present this, he or she would show the pictures and explain their meaning (in the TL, of course).

A similar project would be a collage of pictures and words that have meaning to the student. This would be presented to a partner, who should ask questions about the items in the collage, as well as commenting on items he or she likes or dislikes.

An interesting variation that I read about is the "me portrait" in which a face is drawn, with doors built into it: the forehead, eyelids, nose and mouth lift up to reveal pictures beneath them. These are usually posted in the classroom and students are asked to walk around, looking beneath the doors. Then, the class would hold a discussion about what was interesting, unusual, common, and so on.

I generally give my students several options of what sort of project they would like to do to help us know them better, but all projects must include the following:

1 some sort of audiovisual aid;
2 a one- or two-page summary of who they are (in the TL for second year and above, or at the end of the first year of Level 1);
3 an oral presentation that explains the project.

Another variation that I do the second day of school with my advanced classes is to tell students to bring in three items that "represent" them. They "show and tell" these (we use Inside-Outside Circle for this) to their classmates.

LISTENING INTERPERSONALLY

Verbal communication also means good listening skills. Have one student explain a typical day/a frightening or exciting experience/their last Christmas or birthday/a vacation taken as a child (or a similar topic). The listener should do the following:

1 Ask questions. Make a rule that, after making the initial statement, the initial speaker must wait for a question from the listener before speaking again. The speaker may, however, volunteer more information than the listener requests.
2 Make appropriate comments (see Figure 2.10).
3 Paraphrase to check for understanding, every other time he or she speaks.

Here's an example:

A: I went to Florida last summer.

B: What part? (Question)

A: My grandma lives in Miami. (Answer plus additional information)

B: Do you go to Miami often? (Paraphrase and question)

A: Yeah, it's very warm there even in winter. (Answer plus additional information)

B: I'll bet. Do you go to the beach? (Appropriate comment and question)

A: Every day. I get pretty tan. I like to body surf, too.

B: I can see the tan. Are you good at body-surfing? (Paraphrase, comment, and question)

Figure 2.10 Reaction Phrases to Use in Class

Español	Français	Deutsch
Sí.	Oui.	Ja.
Es verdad.	C'est vrai.	Wahr.
Es cierto.	Bien sur.	Jawohl.
Lo creo /Creo que si.	Je crois que oui.	Ich glaube das.
¡Qué bueno!	Très bien!	Sehr gut!
¡Qué fantástico!	Fantastique!	Phantastisch!
¡Qué interesante!	Très interessant!	Sehr interessant!
¡Qué formidable!	Formidable!	Wunderbar!
Espero que sí.	J'espère que oui.	Hoffentlich.
¿Verdad? / ¿De veras?	N'est-ce pas?/ C'est vrai?	Nicht wahr?/ Wirklich?
¿Es cierto?	Tu es sûr(e)?	Bist du sicher?
¿En serio?	Tu es sérieux/se?	Bist du ernst?
No estoy seguro/a.	Je ne suis pas sûr(e).	Ich bin nicht sicher.
A veces.	On verra.	Möglich.
No me importa(n).	Ça ne me fait rien.	Das macht nichts.
No.	Non.	Nein.
No es verdad.	Ce n'est pas vrai.	Das ist nicht wahr.
No lo creo/Creo que no.	Je ne te crois pas.	Das ist nicht glaubhaft.
¡Qué ridículo/ tontería!	C'est ridicule/bête!	Unglaublich!
¡Qué aburrido!	C'est absurde!	Unsinnig!
¡Pura mentira! / ¡Mentiroso/a!	Tu mens! Menteur/euse!	Du lügst! Lügner!

Empathizing. Interpersonal learners sense the perspective of others: mood, motivation, and intentions. In addition to the activity in which students watched a video with the sound off and guessed at character's feelings and motives, you could also have students look at a situation from someone else' point of view:

On Saturday night, what were the following people doing?
1. Your mother, 2. your Spanish teacher, 3. the bus driver.

The student could also be asked to look at himself through the eyes of others:

On Saturday night, what would the following people say that you were doing?
1. Your mother, 2. your Spanish teacher, 3. the bus driver.

Answers would be something like:
1. My mother would say, "She's cleaning her room."
2. My teacher would say, "She's studying for the quiz Monday."
3. The bus driver would say, "She's watching a movie."

COLLABORATIVE LEARNING/COOPERATIVE LEARNING

These two terms are often used interchangeably and are twenty-first century skills, but are actually different activities; however, both focus on peer interactions and promoting social skills. *Collaborative learning* is any situation when groups of students work together in small groups toward a common goal. Collaborative groups, with the teacher as a guide/resource, organize themselves and explore a significant question or create a meaningful project. It varies from the traditional student-teacher relationship because students are empowered and asked to do open-ended, more complex tasks such as collaborative writing, problem solving, debates, study teams, and other activities; students form their own groups and can even work with students overseas, mentors, and other people not in their class. Students in collaborative groups are assessed both individually and as a group. *Cooperative learning* is a type of collaborative learning in which the teacher is the authority and students work together in a situation usually involving previously learned material, with a students each having a specific role in the group. They have a common, highly structured goal or product that has a specific form or answer. Students in a cooperative group generally get an individual grade. PBL is a method where the problem/goal is introduced at the beginning of the unit and provides the context and motivation for all the learning that follows. It is always active and can be collaborative or cooperative.

Since 1898, over 700 studies have shown these methods offer the following benefits:

* higher achievement and greater productivity;
* greater retention of material learned;
* better, more supportive relationships, both among students and with the instructor; and
* greater self-esteem and better social skills on the part of the students.

There have been hundreds of textbooks written on cooperative learning activities. One of my favorites is by Spencer Kagan (see Bibliography), and I have a chapter on many different types of cooperative activities in my book, *Teaching Foreign Languages in the Block*. Students are often more willing to share their personal feelings in a small-group setting than when answering before the whole class.

Robert E. Slavin (1995) also found the following benefits: a greater liking for classmates, more acceptance for mainstreamed students, and a development of attitudes such as fondness for school, peer models who favor doing well academically, feelings of individual control over one's fate, and expressions of altruism, and these findings were true for high-, medium- and low-ability students. There are basically three different types: formal (the group stays together until a project is done), informal (extremely short-term activities such as checking with a partner), and base group (a long-term group whose goal is to provide peer support for each other as well as to be accountable in the long term for grades and participation/ performance).

Each student in the group must have one (or two) roles assigned to him or her. The Checker is the role every group must have. Rosenshine and Stevens (1986) found that checking frequently for comprehension was significantly correlated with higher levels of student learning and achievement. The Checker makes sure everyone knows whatever the essential learning is, because, to be successful, the group must have group goals (filling out the worksheet, etc.) but individual responsibility: each person must know everything.

Types of cooperative learning strategies would be: TPS, Pairs/Check, Pairs/Read, Pairs/Listen, Pair/Drill, Get the Picture, Graffiti, Inside-Outside Circle, Jigsaw, Round-Robin, Four Corners, Send-a-Problem, Team Test, and many others, most of which are found in this book as well as my previous book.

Perhaps, for interpersonal learning, students in a small cooperative group tell something about themselves that others don't know. After the group has learned each other's secrets, one person from the group picks a secret, tells it to the class, and the class guesses whose secret it is. Have the class vote whose was the most surprising, unusual, or interesting.

FOUR CORNERS

Four Corners is what it sounds like: the corners of the room are labeled and students go to the corner they prefer. As a regular activity, it is a good practice for conversation about vocabulary: I might, for example, label each corner something like "fruits, vegetables, meat, dessert" and have students go to their favorite, and name as many foods as they can in that category, or each tell their favorite. If I want something written, I have the people

> CCSS: SL1, 3, W2, 4, L1, L2
> ACTFL: 1.1, 1.2, 1.3
> DOK 2

in the corner record their list on the wall, each group in a different color, and then the groups rotate and compete to see which group can add the most words to other groups' lists. Other topics could be: what students did over the weekend, living situations (one parent, two, adopted, etc.), vacations taken to various places, favorite teams or sports. For more advanced classes, corners could represent characters from a novel, or from history, professions, types of cars, or even variations of one statement such as "The future is . . . bright, scary, what we make it, etc." Again, discussion in the TL would take place.

For interpersonal purposes, the last variation mentioned would be good, as the students would be discussing feelings. An even simpler and very effective use of Four Corners, however, is in team-building (as well as a valuable lesson about stereotypes). Have students, without staring or pointing or talking, choose someone else in the room that they feel they have little in common with. Then run them through five or six sets of "corners" such as pets they'd like to have, types of movies they like, and so on. Students will find some surprises each time they move, and that they have more in common with the student they picked at the beginning of the activity than they thought.

DETERMINING CLASS VALUES

Speaking of team-building, for good interpersonal communication, let your students have a say in the rules for the class. Ask them to think of at least five rules that the class should have, for example, "We will have fun/be creative/respectful of others" and so on. Use TPS to list the suggestions on the board, combining or condensing and discussing them as needed. Have the class vote on their three favorites, and then have them rank these in order of importance. This is good on several levels. You and they will be communicating expectations for the class. Students will feel the rules are theirs, rather than imposed upon them. They will also understand the rules better, and be more likely to follow them.

You may also want to discuss more controversial things, issues on which there will be many opinions: early vs. late marriage, large vs. small families, dress codes, public display of affection, social media, year-round school, politics, current events. List the issues on the board in the TL as students express them. Do a Line-Up. Have them write an essay, or do a drawing to show their viewpoint.

CCSS: W2, 3, 4, L2
ACTFL: 1.3
DOK 1 or 2

Have the students also share their hopes and fantasies. Choose a particular one, such as the perfect house, the perfect job, the perfect trip, the perfect day, the perfect date, the perfect mate, the "what would you do if you were given a million dollars," or "how would you spend the last day of your life" (a good way to practice the conditional tense!). Have the students write down their ideas and then share them. Make comments on how the fantasy might fit the student's personality.

ROLE-PLAYING FROM DIVERSE OR GLOBAL PERSPECTIVES

I like to check out the diversity within each class with the following activity: find out how many students do things in different ways. Examples are: when they brush their teeth, where they study, what they do when they have a headache, what injuries or operations they have had, types of watches or footwear or vehicles owned, what their favorite clothes are. (See Four Corners for more possibilities.) Point out the diversity you find, and ask them to imagine what the answers would be in a country where the TL is spoken. See if you can find out, using the Internet. For logical-mathematical, make a chart or graphic organizer of the results.

Barnga is an interesting card game that can be purchased online. In it, students are divided into groups and provided with a set of rules. In complete silence, the students read the rules, and begin playing the game. After several rounds, one student (with the lowest score) will rotate to another group, and begin to play with them, still in total silence. However, this new group did not have the same set of rules, and the new student will experience the "culture shock" of not understanding the rules, still without speaking, and the group will experience his frustration and puzzlement as he or she struggles to deal with them. These rotations continue until you judge that frustration has built up, some students are quitting, and so on, and then you debrief the class about what happened. In the discussion you should reach some truths about cultural differences and how to deal with them.

Another way to present cultural differences is to give students articles to read about current events, articles from other countries that have a different perspective. Viewpoints vary widely right now about the US's role in settling international disputes, women's issues, the environment, immigration, and many other topics. Reading a different viewpoint needs to be taught (different does not mean wrong), and cultural perspectives is one of the key ACTFL standards, so this is very worthwhile and can be eye-opening for some.

WORKING WITH AN ADULT

Students need to also work with adults as well as with their peers. Here are some things you could ask your students to do with an adult (and have the adult sign a paper as proof that it was done):

1   Read a story to the adult. Talk about what it means.
2   Teach an adult something you learned in class.
3   Cook an ethnic food together, and rate the new dish.
4   When current events are taking place in a country that speaks the TL, sit down and locate the country on a map. Talk about what is happening. Compare your points of view.
5   Interview: document a typical day in the life of the adult, find out what he or she does, or how s/he feels about an issue, ask about his/her past, etc.

> CCSS: SL 1, 4
> ACTFL: 1.1; 1.3
> DOK 2

VOLUNTEERING/SERVICE PROJECTS

Arrange for students to participate in several volunteer service projects during the year. Possibilities are things like tutoring Spanish or FL speakers in English through the local Literacy Coalition or raising a house with Habitat for Humanity. Outside the local area, have a bake sale or project to raise money for a humanitarian organization like Doctors Without Borders/ Médecins sans Frontières (provides medical care in war-torn areas internationally), Oxfam (Nobel-prize-winning group that feeds the hungry worldwide), UNICEF, Make A Wish, or other similar groups which, since they are international, could also provide you with classroom materials in the language you teach. My students make Christmas cards for shut-ins in Quebec (I send them to a church to distribute for me), and I started a chapter of Amnesty International (AI) at my school. AI is a Nobel-Prize-winning human rights movement, and we write monthly letters on behalf of people being tortured, imprisoned, or discriminated against. You can even ask to be given cases that involve only teens, or only in countries that speak the language you teach (and have students write in that language). We also, as part of our final exam, write about which projects we enjoyed most, and why: a good example of the next intelligence.

Intrapersonal Intelligence

The seventh intelligence is the ability to understand one's own feelings and motivations, and, in addition to use this self-perception to plan and direct one's own life. The teacher must provide an environment where the student feels free to express him or herself. If things are told to you in confidence, do not bring them up before the class. As in one of my favorite books, *Up the Down Staircase*, let students choose an alias at the beginning in order to feel free to express himself or herself (only the teacher will know who is who).

SELF-ESTEEM

Self-esteem is often based upon self-knowledge. Have students answer a "deep" question each day, keeping the answers in a journal. In the journal, they could write, paint, or draw feelings, ideas, insights, and important events. Questions help them get started; you might want to pick a question and require an answer, or simply provide one in case they are in need of inspiration for that week's writing. Questions could be:

Who is your hero/heroine?
If you had three wishes, what would they be?
What is one of your fears?
If you could change anything about yourself, what would it be?
What is your life motto?
When I am in school/at a dance/at home, I am . . .
Ideal parents are . . .
Teachers seldom are . . .
Agree or disagree: sports are very important.

They could also make lists: "Things I think are beautiful," "Things I want to finish," "People I know well," "Things I want to buy," "Things to do in my free time," for example.

In their journal, they could also keep a "mood graph" of their high and low points each day or week, noting the external events that contributed to these different moods. This would help them avoid situations that lower their mood, making them more aware of how their behavior or surroundings influence them (a skill many teenagers don't have).

> CCSS: SL 1, 3, 4, 6, L1, W2, 3, 4, L2
> ACTFL: 1.1, 1.2, 1.3
> DOK 1 or 2

Have students, with a partner, explore personal perceptions of themselves: have them talk about "Who I think I am," "Who you think I am," "Who you think you are," "Who I think you are" and so on. Then, in the journal, have them reflect on how their self-perception differs from the partner's perception of them.

Have students write a character sketch of themselves, using their fictitious name to protect their identity, since these will be shared with the rest of the class. They should use as many senses as possible to describe themselves, as well as describe their behaviors and why they do these, significant people in their lives, their own hopes and dreams for the future, and the impact they have on other students. Choose some to read and discuss in small groups, put them in a scrapbook for students who finish assignments early to read, or just post them in the display area for a high-interest bulletin board.

Have students write, draw, or compose a song or poem about an event that changed their lives and what they learned from that experience. Have students time-travel mentally into the far future, and view themselves as they are now from that distant perspective (an old person looking back at his/her youth). Have them write a future newspaper article about their achievement(s).

COMPLIMENT CIRCLES

Teach students to get and give compliments gracefully (I motivate mine by reminding them that these phrases are good to know when meeting someone, on a date, etc.). Have students write their name on a paper, and pass the papers around the room. Have everyone write something they like about a person on the paper. Collect them long enough to make sure everyone took this assignment seriously, and hand them out. I have had students tell me that this changed their whole life; perhaps someone wrote that they had a nice smile, so they made an effort to smile more, and people were nicer to them, and . . . good things happened to them. A variation on this is to sit in a circle and give compliments face-to-face, but I find teenagers aren't too comfortable with this. Once I taped papers on students' backs and they wrote compliments or suggestions on each other's papers (again, I read the papers before I removed them for the students to see). Another time, we made our compliments (after I approved them) into paper airplanes and flew them, with every student picking one up.

For National French Week each year, we write compliments on Post-Its and put one on every locker at school; they stayed up for 2 months or more last fall and were a major hit. French-speakers were in demand to translate what the note said for their friends, though we try to use cognates in our messages.

PEER SUPPORT

Choose a partner for each student, and, occasionally, give them time to meet. Their goal is to make a list of each other's strengths, and then plan how to use those strengths to achieve future goals. Each time they meet, they would report on their progress toward their goal(s). I usually have them set a goal for

CCSS: W2, 4, L2
ACTFL: 1.3, 3.1, 5.2
DOK 1

my class, a goal to accomplish before they graduate, and one other goal of their choice. Having a peer to report to, and who expects effort and progress from them, is a great motivator. Having a list of goals, with a written record of progress, is great for a student's self-esteem.

METACOGNITION

Another form of self-knowledge is to know how you learn best (metamemory). Asking students a list of questions will help them define how they will learn best: Do you learn best when you listen to music, or when it is quiet? Is it easier to memorize a list of opposites, or a list of similar words? When do you feel most like studying: right after school, or after dinner? Where can you go in your house with the least distractions?

What students believe about when, where and how they are most focused on learning influences whether they use that to learn more efficiently. If students are not aware of a strategy, or believe that it is not useful or necessary, they are very unlikely to apply it. A good learner has more "tools" with which to learn: he or she will think and plan first, and self-correct, for example. Many students believe that it is the teacher's responsibility to make them learn, or, if they know their learning style, they demand to use only that one. The more cognitive strategies and self-awareness they have, the more success they will see. To help them, use these six steps:

1 Provide explicit instruction in what the task is, what the objectives are, and how to assess progress or completion. For example, set time limits and clear expectations about how much should have been accomplished during that time.
2 Provide opportunities for the class to work cooperatively.
3 Suggest various strategies they might use, and provide practice.
4 Help students link newly acquired knowledge to previously learned knowledge. Remind them of rules previously learned.
5 Hold a discussion after the task to talk about what was learned and how, problems they ran into, and what strategies worked well to solve them, and how to avoid such problems in the future.
6 Model metacognitive behavior, using techniques such as thinking out loud during problem solving, explaining the process of deciding how to attack a problem or issue, doing some explicit self-monitoring for comprehension, checking the final answer, etc.

Students should be taught to plan how to study, select a strategy, self-monitor, self-question (i.e., "Is this all I need to do?" or "What does that mean?"), self-evaluate, and predict the answer. Cooperative learning will help them learn how, as other students voice their thought processes.

Here is a good strategy to use, and which few students know:

Memory Model. This method is good for learning new material as a group, but Memory Model is better for memorizing data such as names (both from novels and geography) and vocabulary lists. Memory Model is a form of mnemonics also called Link-Word, which attempts to make it easier for students to recall words by drawing from their own personal experience to form word associations. In Step One, the students select the terms they must know: by reading and then underlining or listing unfamiliar words, by choosing the key points in a story or speech they wish to memorize, or by looking at a list the teacher has given them.

Step Two is to link the unfamiliar material to something they know, by several methods. To make the image memorable, the new idea must be sensual (using the senses such as taste, smell, etc.), or motion-oriented, perhaps very colorful, or very exaggerated in size . . . in short, as creative as possible and as humorous, outrageous, absurd or downright silly as possible. Even if they are a bit off-color, let the students use whatever works. In Step Two, therefore, the students, in teams will look at the vocab list and try to make as many crazy connections as possible. My students have come up with things like, for haricots verts (green beans), the idea of "green haircuts" . . . a translation of one word, and a lookalike for the other.

Step Three: make it concrete. Draw a picture of this idea, making it visual, auditory, and as exaggerated as possible. My students took the above connection, and drew a picture of a punk with a bright green Mohawk, ring in nose, tattoos, etc.

Step Four is to practice the words, using the visuals with their associations, until they become familiar. Warning: No matter how silly, the students will only remember these associations well if they are the ones who thought of them, although occasionally a really good one will help anyone. Giving them a good one from last year's group will *not* be remembered as well as one they themselves did.

With Memory Model, you can present more vocabulary more often, with greater retention. Your students will experience more success, and will add this to their selection of strategies to use when studying.

ASSIGNMENT PLANNING AND REFLECTING

Encourage students to keep an agenda and list their assignments in it. Many foreign language teachers also require students to keep a notebook or portfolio of things learned, written, and so on. These will be discussed in more detail later in the book. Again, this strategy leads to self-awareness, which is intrapersonal intelligence.

EDUCATE FOR HUMAN VALUES

Help your students learn human values such as altruism, honesty, compassion, mercy, loyalty, courage, justice, enthusiasm, tolerance, helpfulness. Service projects will help fulfill some of these. Reading examples of these values (i.e., the George Washington/cherry tree story) will reinforce these values. Watch videos/movies like *Au revoir les enfants*, *The Rocket*, or *Schindler's List*. By seeing examples of these qualities modeled for them by people they admire, they will learn and perhaps emulate them, and enhance their self-esteem by adhering to them.

Naturalist Intelligence

This intelligence reflects, I think, a sort of global perspective together with the modern concern for the environment, yet undoubtedly our caveman ancestors also were keenly aware of their surroundings, as well as changes in their environment. It is this awareness that forms naturalist intelligence. A student with strong naturalist intelligence would observe and remember patterns and things from nature easily, loving animals, camping, hiking, and being outdoors. They would have keen sensory skills—sight, smell, sound, taste and touch, and this is probably the best way to appeal to them.

Since they so easily learn characteristics, names, categorizations and data about objects or species found in the natural world, try some of the following activities:

- Do an expanded unit on animals, not just the usual cat, dog, and bird. Learn the specialized vocabulary for animals: paw, claw, wing, beak, snout, hoof, mane, tail, nest, burrow, and so on. Have each student pick an animal (or create an imaginary animal that is a composite of several), and do a report on it, including two or more of the following items:

  > CCSS: W2, 7, 8, L2
  > ACTFL: 1.3
  > DOK 2

    - a full-body illustration, with body parts labeled;
    - a map showing where this animal may be found;
    - a description of the animal's habits: food, home, babies, life span;
    - a poem about the world, from the animal's point of view.

- For the upper-level classes, do an environmental unit, maybe even as an interdisciplinary unit with the biology or environmental studies class, plus a writing/composition class. A unit on endangered species could also involve a current events or even a government or history class (foreign policy, etc.) Most upper-level texts have a unit on the rain forest, or recycling. If yours does not, go on the Internet, where there are many resources.
- Take students various places around the building, and have them list things they see, smell, touch, taste, and hear at each spot. When you get to the classroom, have them list their words on separate pieces of butcher paper, and then group the students to make a poem or a poster about each place. Places could include: the parking lot, the football

  > CCSS: W2, 8, L2
  > ACTFL: 1.3
  > DOK 2

  field, the outdoor eating area, the school's greenhouse (if there is one), and for contrast, the boiler room, the kitchen or wood shop, or backstage in the auditorium. Make it a French/Spanish/German/Italian-only excursion. Take a short field trip to a nature preserve, forest, meadow, river, or park nearby. Have students do their choice of labeled drawings, poems, stories, an article for the "travel" section of a newspaper, a postcard or letter to a friend, or even just make a list of things for a potential scavenger hunt in that area, in the TL.
- Get a live pet for the classroom: a fish, gerbil, or maybe even just a plant. Have students take turns caring for it, have a contest to name it, make up stories about its many adventures "in the wild," make a video about it and its habits, get a book in the TL about it (or write your own). Keep a diary from the pet's perspective of what goes on in the classroom.
- Have students create collections, scrapbooks, logs, or journals about natural objects—written observations, drawings, pictures and photos, or specimens.

- Join an environmental group that is active in an area that speaks the TL, and can send you brochures, posters or pamphlets in that language (or offer to make some for them). Sometimes you can even find materials in unusual places: for example, the Cracker Barrel restaurants had a coloring book on the rain forest animals.
- Have students write companies that have locations in various countries, asking them about their environmental policies. They may also have posters or literature to send, but just getting a reply is thrilling to students.
- Subscribe to, or read online, a magazine that features nature such as http://planeta.com/ (in English), www.catorce6.com/ (in Spanish), and www.environnement-magazine.fr/ (in French).
- Watch a video or movies about nature, in the TL, or environmental issues in areas like South America, central Africa, or other places that speak the TL. Spanish teachers recommend movies like *Medicine Man*, with Sean Connery as a scientist fighting to save the rainforest, and filmed in Mexico, or the series "La Catrina," in which the use of harmful pesticides is a theme; we learn native African plants and animals from the animated *Kirikou et la Sorcière*.
- Music is a big motivator. Use a song like Mana's *Donde jugarán los niños* (Where will the children play?) or Cabrel's song about the inhumanity of bullfights to begin a discussion about naturalist issues.
- Take advantage of volunteer opportunities: adopt a section of highway, recycle cans, clean up a park, plant trees or flowers somewhere in town, paint signs or picnic table, or even decorate paper bags (if still used in your area) for a "Save the Earth" or "Support the Humane Society" day.

Some states such as Maryland now require students to volunteer a number of hours for community service.

Marzano's Nine Instructional Strategies for Effective Teaching and Learning

Researchers Robert J. Marzano, Debra Pickering, and Jane Pollock have identified nine instructional strategies that are most likely to improve student achievement across all content areas and across all grade levels. To do this, they collected all the relevant research done previously, grouped the findings to translate them into easily used strategies. Then they tested each with experimental classes (using a particular strategy) and control classes (not using the strategy), analyzing the results to track each instructional strategy's effectiveness in a variety of situations. I have included that result as a percentage gain in student learning, and listed them from most effective to least.

1 Identifying Similarities and Differences: 45 percent gain

CCSS: SL1, L2
ACTFL: 1.1, 1.2, 2.1, 2.2
DOK 1, 2

Venn diagrams are perfect for both logical-mathematical and visual-spatial intelligences, and some examples may be found earlier in this chapter and also in Chapter 4. Figure 2.11 shows a typical Venn diagram, which helps students organize the facts about two things, comparing and contrasting them by filling in the diagram with items generated during thought or conversation about the assigned topic. For example, a student might be asked to compare and contrast the US and a TL country on topics such as table manners, homes, clothing, schools, foods, etc. One circle would represent the TL country, and the other the US. If the student notices that only the TL country has an item, it goes in that circle; if only the US has it, it goes in the USA circle, but if both have it, it goes in the center. After visually organizing thoughts in this way, he is ready to speak or write about the topic. As a paired activity, two students would converse about a topic, listing things they don't agree about in their own personal circle, and things they both like or dislike in the center. Again, their opinions are organized and ready to talk or write about at the end of the activity. Venn diagrams are easy for even lower-performing students to use.

Venn diagrams can have more than two circles. More complex Venn diagrams are very good with beginning students to check reading comprehension of dialogues and readings, with each circle representing a different aspect or character from the dialogue, and listing the family member of each in the circle, or what each was going to buy, etc. depending on the subject of the dialogue. Or, the student could compare himself or herself and/or a partner with the main character in the reading, i.e., when a reading describes a typical day. The Venn diagram also becomes a good product for assessment purposes, or even to post on the bulletin board if the class is still getting to know one another.

Figure 2.11 Venn Diagram

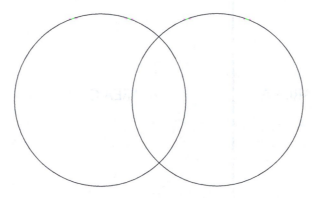

Creating Metaphors and Analogies

Metaphors and analogies also are a form of comparison, and help students make connections between previously learned and new material and contexts. After learning a topic, use an analogy to examine the similarities and differences between one system and another:

- How is Japanese food like ours? How is it different?
- Compare and contrast Napoleon and Hitler.
- With what the United State has learned about environmental issues, what advice can we give to Mexico?

Do these in the TL for upper-level classes. A good analogy easily can become a poem, as a creative writing assignment, or something artistic. To make it easier for logical/mathematical students to see the analogy, have them use a Venn diagram or some other form of visual representation.

2 Summarizing and Note-Taking: 34 percent gain

Cornell note-taking is a highly regarded and often-used method of taking notes.

CCSS: RL1, 3, 4, 6, L2, W9
ACTFL: 1.1, 1.2, 1.3
DOK 2

Area A is where students start, by taking notes; not exact words, but condensed to essential information, using whatever system you or they like. Area B, as soon as possible after the lecture, is where students write questions next to the notes in Area A. For example, next to notes on how to form the imperfect tense, they might write "How do you make the imperfect?" Finally, in Area C, they would write a summary, no more than three sentences long, of the material in Area A. Then, when you're ready to review the material, have them cover Areas A and C and try to answer the questions they wrote in Area B, in written or oral form.

Figure 2.12 Cornell Notes Form

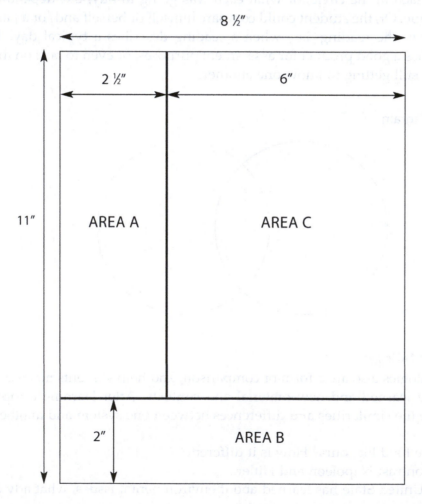

Other methods of note-taking are outlines, bulleted lists, graphic organizers to fill out, and even peer teaching or discussion (especially if you have students restate what the other just said).

3 Reinforcing Effort and Providing Recognition: 29 percent gain

Most teachers know this works, I think, because it involves posting students' finished products, encouraging students to share their work or express thoughts, creating a stress-free environment, giving high-fives, and many other methods. Note that recognition is more effective if it is contingent on achieving some specified standard, such as staying in the TL. Recognition could be individual (prizes or parent contacts) or whole class (rewards like a movie, a favorite music video, etc.)

4 Homework and Practice: 28 percent gain

Students and parents should be clearly informed of the goals and objectives, and due dates for the day and/or unit, but vary the methods to maximize effectiveness. (See comments on how to involve adults more in the Interpersonal Intelligence section).

Homework should be as authentic as possible, meaningful, and as enjoyable as possible, but it should focus on the more difficult concepts. Track homework by keeping a portfolio (see Chapter 6), or a reflective journal. Prompt feedback should be given for all homework assignments.

5 Nonlinguistic Representations: 27 percent gain

Using nonlinguistic (i.e., pictures) has recently been proven to stimulate and increase brain activity. In an ideal activity, students would view words and images together and use the relationship between them to store data in long-term memory.

Nonlinguistic, however, is more than just photos (see flashcard games in Chapter 3). It is manipulatives, graphic organizers, storyboards, and foldables, all discussed earlier in this chapter. It also includes using physical models and physical movement, as well as acting out situations to represent information. Many of these can be found in the kinetic intelligence section earlier in this chapter.

6 Cooperative Learning: 23 percent gain

Cooperative learning (discussed earlier in this chapter in Buzz Groups and the Interpersonal Intelligence section) is just what it sounds like: student work in small groups on well-structured activities, with assigned roles and responsibilities. Examples are: choral readings or readers' theater, plays, projects, debates, jigsaw work, and making a video, to name a few.

Jigsaw

I use the Jigsaw method for reviewing the previous year, the very first week of class for levels 2 and above.

- First, I ask students to list what they'd like to review.
- Then, I divide them into "expert" groups (one class chose four topics, so there were four groups of seven students each) and give them some instruction and some practice activities ... until I think they are fairly expert.
- Then I let them give me a teaching plan: how they'll introduce the topic, have students practice, etc. (I usually also require some sort of game or fun activity).
- After I approve that, they give me quiz questions over their topic, and I photocopy or post the teaching plan, practice sheets, etc. and then,
- I redivide them ... for the abovementioned class, there were be seven groups of four, containing one student expert for each of the four topics.

- Then they take turns teaching each other in the small-group format; the student expert grades the others' papers and gives feedback . . . and then the whole class takes a test made up of the questions the students wrote.

That's a very brief explanation. Divide things into small steps. Be very specific what their duties are. Brain research says the best retention comes from teaching others (that's why teachers know their subject so well!)

CCSS: SL1, 3, 4, 6, L2
ACTFL: 1.1, 1.2, 1.3
DOK 2

A nice way to watch a video is with Jigsaw. Divide the students into groups, and each takes notes on one aspect of a video featuring a city, region or country: one looks at architecture, another looks at food / dining, another at historical info, another at clothing, another at transportation, etc. As students watch the video, each takes notes on what he / she sees about the expert group topic. After the video, have the students compare notes . . . Then put the students in new groupings with one from each expert group, and have them each give a short report on their topic to their new group.

There are many ways to assess this type of activity. It could be something creative like a poster, a poem (or a rap) created by the group. You could have each student write a postcard from that area, showing what they have learned. You could have each group write a quiz over the video, and then have them take turns taking each other's quiz . . . the possibilities are endless.

7 Setting Objectives and Providing Feedback: 23 percent

Objectives should not be too specific and should be flexible, allowing some student choice. They should also involve authentic sources and topics, and be posted throughout the unit, with a review (and self-evaluation) done at the end of the unit.

"I Can" Statements

I use a table of "I can" statements and have students rate themselves: Well / Somewhat / Not at all, for each statement, before beginning a unit. Just before the final assessment, I have them re-rate themselves, and they (and I) can see what aspects they feel confident about, or confused about, and try to remedy that before the unit ends. It also helps the student set a goal: I need to learn more about X, or practice Y before the test (Note: I would not include the English in my table, just use the TL). Seeing themselves make progress is a great form of feedback, too.

Table 2.3 "I Can" Statement Sample

JE PEUX (I can) . . .	Plutôt bien (quite well)	Un peu (somewhat)	Pas du tout (not at all)
Dire l'alphabet (say the alphabet)			
Compter jusqu'à 20 (count to 20)			

Note: In October 2017 the ACTFL released a wonderful new Can-Do Statements document (see Bibliography).

Log

When students are working independently, especially on things like a genius project, I use a daily log to track progress, reward effort, and help students set a goal for the next day. It is quite simple:

Table 2.4 Activity Log

⇒ ACTIVITY LOG ⇐		
Student: _____		Project: _____
Date	**What did you do?**	**What will you do next?** **What help will you need?**

Feedback is only good if it is timely and as specific as possible. There is no such thing as too much positive feedback, but the method should vary. Rubrics and checklists are great (more about those in Chapter 6), but there are other ways: physical (a smile, nod, high-five) or word of praise all work well. Here is one that makes students active: before I give a final grade on a written task, I use a highlighter to signal errors, and ask them to try that word or phrase again. They can ask classmates for help (instead of asking me: I like the student-teaching-student dynamic on Glasser's scale, 90 percent retention). Hopefully, they will each thank or compliment the other.

8 Generating and Testing Hypotheses: 23 percent gain

To examine data and draw conclusions (i.e., looking for patterns in masculine/feminine/neuter nouns, or to find how a verb tense is formed), research shows that a deductive approach works best, but both inductive and deductive reasoning can help students understand and process material. In the logical-mathematical section of this chapter, examples of both are given. This method requires students to apply knowledge and use higher-order thinking skills.

It should be obvious that tasks like having students build something using limited resources i.e., an Eiffel tower with spaghetti and marshmallows (many examples in the Kinesthetic Intelligence section in this chapter) ask students to form, discuss, and test hypotheses about what may or may not work.

9 Cues, Questions, and Advanced Organizers: 22 percent gain

There are hundreds of ways to expose students to information before they learn it; I love the hooks in the *Teach Like a Pirate* book (2012), which are good examples. These are, of course, used before the lesson begins. I highly recommend using the Backward Design method of planning a unit, which includes a Driving Question, such as: How could I benefit from studying at a college in a Spanish-speaking country? or: Is it harder being black in a Francophone country or in the US? These, along with a graphic organizer, mind map, KWL, or manipulative (all discussed in this book), will activate prior knowledge and motivate students to add new things to it as they learn.

Asking questions should be done in the TL, and don't forget Wait Time: a brief pause so everyone has time to formulate an answer, instead of letting the fastest thinker to answer most of the time.

The next few chapters show more examples of variety, including the eight intelligences and Marzano-approved activities as well as right and left brain activities, applied to specific classroom situations.

3

Revitalizing the Basics

We all know students need a break from listen-drill-write monotony. Even crossword puzzles, word searches, board races, Pictionary, and Hangman, and online puzzles such as Kahoot, Quizlet Live, and Quizizz can get old, fast. I assume all those are already in your repertoire of activities. This chapter will attempt to give you a few new alternatives to practice basic groups of vocabulary taught in any language. And, of course, these will all be very active approaches, with the majority of these emphasizing speaking and reacting to spoken language. Try a few; your students will love you for these! Note: TL stands for Target Language in these activities.

Greetings

- For several days after teaching greetings, have students greet their teachers in the TL. Each day, you will arrange for a colleague to be a "Mystery Educator" who will put a note in your mailbox with the name of the first student who greeted him/her, for some sort of reward or privilege. Post that student's name. This is also a great excuse to teach the other teachers in the building how to reply back, in your language, and is good for promoting your TL. [CCSS: SL1, 6, L1, 2, 3, W2; ACTFL: 1.1, 1.2, 2.1, 5.1; DOK 1, 2]
- On Day One, once students have chosen a TL name, make nametags to wear (or stand-up ones to place on desks) for a few days. Have students sit in a circle, and snap their fingers twice (or clap their hands), slap their desk top twice, and then, as they snap or clap twice again, say their new name, and then the name of another. Snap, snap, slap, slap, snap-Marie, snap-Pierre! The student just named waits through the next four beats, and then replies with his name, and the name of another classmate. Snap, snap, slap, slap, snap-Pierre, snap-Marc! This is fast-paced, an easy to way for everyone to learn each other's

name, and also a pronunciation drill that they don't even realize is practice, it's so much fun! I play right along with the class, as I need to learn names, too. [CCSS: SL6, L2, W2; ACTFL: 1.1, 1.2; DOK 1]

- Props are great: students who don't wish to greet each other face-to-face seem quite willing to do so when both are provided with a toy cell phone. Puppets or other toys greeting each other are another way to get around the shyest student's reserve. [CCSS: SL 1, 6 and L1, 3; ACTFL: 1.1, 1.2; DOK 1]

- An authentic Spanish game to get to know each other: Sit or stand in a circle with one person in the center, and no empty chairs. The person in the center points at or approaches a classmate, and says in the TL, "I know you, (name), but I am better friends with (another name)." Immediately, all three people, the two named and the one who made the statement, get out of their seats/places, and change places. Since there are only two spots, the person remaining begins the next round. [CCSS: SL 1, 6 and L1, 3; ACTFL: 1.1, 1.2, 2.1; DOK 1]

- Make a recording of other non-foreign-language-department faculty members giving a greeting in the TL, and have the students guess who is speaking. [CCSS: SL 1; ACTFL: 1.2, 5.1; DOK 2]

123

Numbers (Juego de Números/Jeu de Numéros/Zahlenspiel)

First, present the numbers from zero to ten, using the TPR method, either using hand gestures or paper (flashcard) manipulatives. The method I use was found on FL-TEACH and is called Pam's Random Numbers Activity—don't teach them to count in sequence!

Show them a number of your fingers, or a flashcard, saying that number in the TL: I usually start with three, which I read is the first number most children learn to say. Then do this with two other numbers between zero (fist if using gestures) and ten, (or 12 if teaching telling time next). Then practice the three numbers individually, first in the order they were presented, and then in random order, until they seem to have mastered those. Then say all three and have students show you the three in the order you said them. When enough of the class does this successfully, add in other numbers in twos or threes, repeating the process (present, practice gestures, "show me three") until they seem to get them.

Now, what else is there to do, besides playing Bingo/Lotería (some unique variations on those later in this chapter) or Uno? Try these:

- *Never* have students just count from one to ten (or whatever number). Make them do it backward. Doing it backward shows that they can connect the sound of the word with its meaning as well as where one word begins and ends. [CCSS: SL 4; ACTFL: 1.3; DOK 1]

- Each day, give students a short form to fill out, on which they must ask five classmates their name and one of the following: their telephone number, their address, their shoe size (use international sizes, usually written on most athletic shoes), their height (use metric measurements, and have them measure themselves on a "growth chart" you have drawn on the wall or on the board), their lucky number, their father/mother/grandmother's age, and so on. They write the classmate's name and answer down, and when the form is full, they sit down. Note: specify that no one may give more than five answers, so that everyone gets asked five times, too. [CCSS: SL 1, 6; ACTFL: 1.1, 1.2, 1.3, 3.1; DOK 1]

- Play Coquelicot or Flute (French), Clic-Clic (Spanish) Have students count, but when they hit a specified number (i.e., three, seven, or nine) or a multiple of that number, they call out "Flute" (or whatever word you've chosen) instead of the number. When they get to 30 (if the number is three), they would say, "Flute zero, flute-one, Flute-two, flute-flute, flute-four" and so on. [CCSS: SL 1, 4; ACTFL: 1.1, 1.2, 1.3, 2.2; DOK 2]

  - For a variation on this, let students decide if they would like to say one, two or three numbers . . . that way the following students don't have time to rehearse the one they'll say.
  - For another variation, have the student who gets the specified number or a multiple say "Go," "Back" or "Jump." If "go," the next person in line says the next number. If "back," the previous person gives the number, and if "jump," the next person is "jumped," and the person next to him/her gives the number.
  - To encourage speed/fluency, have students beat time: slap thighs twice, clap twice, snap fingers on right hand AND say the number, snap with left hand, and repeat.

- Similar to Rock-Paper-Scissors, have students stand in groups of four or five. On a countdown, students show one or more fingers. The first to count all fingers and say the answer in the TL gets a point. If they get too good at that, increase the value of the fingers to two or more! [CCSS: SL 1, 4 and L1; ACTFL: 1.1, 1.3; DOK 1]
- Knock loudly on your desk, having students count silently. When you stop, they shout the number in the TL. Then have students take turns doing the knocking. [CCSS: SL 1; ACTFL: 1.2; DOK 1]
- Sing the numbers to the tune of *Ten Little Indians*: [CCSS: SL 1, 4; ACTFL: 1.3, 5.2; DOK 1]

Uno, dos, tres amigos
Cuatro, cinco, seis amigos
Siete, ocho, nueve amigos
Diez amigos son.
(Eins, zwei, drei Freunde . . . Un, deux, trois camarades/copains . . .)

- Play Slapjack. Put students in groups of no more than four or five, having them push their desks together to form a playing surface. Give each group a deck of cards, and turn one card over at a time while all count aloud. If they say "three" when a three turns up, all hurry to slap the deck. Last one to slap has to take all the cards in the turned-over pile. The object is to *not* get any cards. If you have authentic (TL) cards, they'll also learn how to say jack, queen, king, and ace. [CCSS: SL 1, 5; ACTFL: 1.2, 1.3, 4.1; DOK 1]
- Have a lottery, with students picking their own numbers. Call out or draw the winning numbers each day, just like on television. Give the winner some object or privilege. [CCSS: SL 1; ACTFL: 1.2; DOK 1]
- Play Connect the Dots, but with a twist. Take a basic connect the dots picture, but number the dots randomly. Then, you call out the numbers in the order they should be connected: for instance, 15, 3, 49, 22, and so on. It is better listening and, since the numbers are random, it requires a more thorough knowledge of them, than the standard way of playing connect the dots. [CCSS: SL 1, 5; ACTFL: 1.2; DOK 1]

- Saute/Saltar: have students choose a number between one and nine, and then get together with a partner, revealing his/her number at that time. Then they put those two numbers together to make a larger number (for example, if they have a three and five, they can be 35 or 53). Then, have them stand back to back, lock arms, and jump the number of times needed to (loudly) count from one to their number. [CCSS: SL 4; ACTFL: 1.3; DOK 1]
- 11 to Win: Have students pick 11 numbers within a given range (i.e., 1–50), write them down as numbers, and all stand up. As you (or a volunteer) call numbers, students must sit down if any of their numbers are named. Winner is last one standing. This goes *very* quickly. [CCSS: SL 1; ACTFL: 1.2; DOK 1]
- Worksheets for practice (speed practice, if you prefer): Most worksheets are *not* active, but these are.

  - Pair students, giving each either worksheet A or worksheet B. Each worksheet has half the items in the classroom listed: desks, pencil sharpeners, globes, televisions, doors, blackboards, boys, girls, students, etc. Each student takes turns asking the other, in the TL, how many there are in the room, writing down the partner's answer. [CCSS: SL 1; ACTFL: 1.1, 1.2, 1.3; DOK 1]
  - Timed speed reading. Give students a worksheet with numbers (there is a good one online that will work for ANY language at https://teaching-what-works.wikispaces.com/file/view/SuperSpeed_Numbers_15–25–02.pdf). With a partner, students take turns saying the numbers. If one doesn't know the number, the partner can supply it but then the person whose turn it was must repeat the number twice before they go on to the next one. Set goals: how many lines read, how much improvement in speed, etc. [CCSS: SL 1, 5; ACTFL: 1.2; DOK 1]

- "Higher! Lower!" Have a brave person stand, back to the chalkboard. Write a number up, and have him or her guess the number in the TL, with the class shouting "Higher!" or "Lower!" Write down the time, and challenge others to beat that time. [CCSS: SL 1; ACTFL: 1.1, 1.2; DOK 1]
- For larger numbers: Also using decks of cards, remove all the face cards, and have each team lay out the cards face up so that everyone can see them. Call out a number and have the team assemble cards that add up to that number. Make everyone on the team responsible for making sure that each member knows how to say each number; stronger students seem to enjoy helping the not-so-strong ones. Call on one person in each team to name the numbers. As he or she says them, write them on the board, and add them up. This is a good way to practice the bigger numbers. [CCSS: SL 1; ACTFL: 1.2, 1.3, 3.1; DOK 1]
- Casi . . . Bueno . . . Nada/Presque . . . Bon . . . Jamais: play as a whole class or with teams. This is a great Sponge or "brain break" and great practice for larger numbers. Think of a three, four, or five-digit number and write that number of blanks on the board (similar to the start of Hangman). A student will guess a number, and you will write it as it was stated. Then, tell students: Right (if correct number in correct position), Almost (if number is in the desired number for in a different position), or No (if that number isn't in there at all). Here is a sample. I have chosen 703 to start, and write ___ ___ ___. The first student guesses 305, so I write that. Then I point at the 3 and say "Almost" (so they know there is a 3, but not as the first number), then at the 0 and say "Right," then at the 5 and say "No way" as that number isn't there. They love this game and learn the words (casi, etc.) well, too. [CCSS: SL 1, 5; ACTFL: 1.1, 1.2; DOK 2]

- Play Penny Toss. Write the numbers on a large paper or poster board. Have students toss a coin (peseta, euro, etc.) onto the paper, calling out the number it lands on. To practice larger numbers, play this in teams, with each team keeping track of their score by adding together the numbers their members call out. [CCSS: SL 4, 6; ACTFL: 1.3; DOK 1]
- Hand out M&M candies or something similar like Skittles. Have the students report how many they have, and then recount in sets according to colors. They can also subtract (by eating, announcing the number they will eat) and then report the new total. [CCSS: SL 1, 4; ACTFL: 1.1, 1.3; DOK 1]
- For a more advanced class reviewing the numbers, have them draw "phone numbers." Have two of each phone number. "Dial" a number, and have the two students with that number come to the front of the room and either have a short conversation (review of other skills from earlier years) or compete to answer a question. [CCSS: SL 1, 6; ACTFL: 1.1, 1.2, 1.3; DOK 1]
- Get pictures of desirable products (paper or on slides) and have an auction. The highest bidder for the car/cell phone/video game player/diamond ring/truffles, etc. wins. Or, like on The Price is Right (TV game show) the one closest to the actual price wins. [CCSS: SL 1; ACTFL: 1.1; DOK 1]

Telling Time

I no longer teach a unit on telling time; clocks at school, on cell phones, etc. are digital, but if you do, here are some good active learning strategies.

> CCSS: SL 1, 2, 4, RL 1, 3
> ACTFL: 1.1, 1.2, 1.3, 2.2, 4.2
> DOK 1, 2

- I have a purchased set of clocks for classroom use in practicing time, but have had more success asking students to make their own clocks: give each a paper or Styrofoam plate and a paper fastener that will poke through the plate and then split, folding each half flat on the back to hold the hands on, while allowing them to turn). As homework, have them make their own clock. If you wish, have a contest to see whose is the fanciest, the most expensive-looking, etc. Then, say a time to the class. While you are adjusting your clock to that time, or getting ready to reveal an image of a clock, the students are setting their clocks. Somehow this is much more motivating when they have made their own clock.
- The above activity easily converts to a bulletin board: Give each student a different time of the day, and a paper, on which they illustrate what they usually do at that time of the day on a weekend/vacation (otherwise, you will have many pictures of school). Then, post the picture next to the clock, adjusted to the correct time. Having the clocks on display also means they are available the next day: as the students enter the classroom, they go get their clocks.

- Use a bell, or borrow a triangle from the band. Strike it a number of times. Ask what time the "clock" just struck. The student who gets the answer first gets to strike the next time. This is especially great in the grade school and middle school levels.
- Another activity that works well with young students or with an older group that is kinetically oriented is to ask the students to be human clocks. Have them stand and, with their arms, show the time.
- Develop a set of cards for playing "Go, Fish!" Half the cards should be pictures of clock faces displaying various times, and the other half of the cards should be the clock times, written out in the TL. Each student is dealt from four to six cards to begin, with the remainder in the center of the desks (pushed together to form a table) as the draw pile. Student A asks, in the TL, "B, do you have eight o'clock?" If B has this card, he hands it to A, who lays the pair out for the others to see, and A asks a question of B or any other student in the group. If B answers no, A must draw a card, and his turn is over, and B asks a question. The game is over when all the cards are matched, and the winner is the person with the most matches. [CCSS: RL 1, 3; ACTFL: 1.1, 1.2, 3.1; DOK 1]

A bit less active, but nevertheless good practice: photocopy or link to TV guide pages from countries that speak the TL. (Many newspapers are now on the Internet and you may easily get the schedule for the same day you do this activity, if you wish it to be current.) Not only will students enjoy seeing the 24-hour time system in use, they will enjoy seeing American shows listed, and guessing at the movies. After a few minutes, ask students to go and stand with others who want to see the same show at (x) o'clock. [CCSS: SL 1, 2, 4; ACTFL: 1.1, 1.2, 2.2, 4.2; DOK 2]

A related activity would be to locate the movie theater listings from a major city. Again, ask what they want to see, and where it is showing, and at what time, how much it costs, and who is in it, as well as how they will get there, who they will go with, and anything else you can think of.

Alphabet

Once you have introduced the alphabet, and sing the Alphabet Song, what else is there to do?

- Give each student a small cup half full of Alphabits cereal. With a partner, each will hold up a piece of cereal, say the letter in the TL, and when the partner OKs the pronunciation, he or she may eat it.
- Sing the alphabet not to the standard tune, but to the theme song from the game show, "Jeopardy" . . . and then sing the alphabet backward, to the same tune.
- Call out the initials of celebrities, and have the students guess who the celebrity is.
- Each day, read a few of the following acronyms. [CCSS: SL 1, 4 ; ACTFL: 1.1, 1.3, 3.1; DOK 1] Have them identify it, and see who can call out the long form (i.e., ESP—extra-sensory perception):

NFL	ESPN	CBS	AWOL
USA	MTV	VIP	NBA

ASAP	NCAA	FBI	DOB (date of birth)
ADHD	UFO	UPS	CIA
RSVP	UNICEF	LOL	your school initials

Try some language-specific ones, too. Examples:
French: OVNI Objet Volant Non-Identifié = UFO;
French & Spanish: SIDA = AIDS.

- Have a spelling bee, but a non-traditional one. Pass out big cards with the letters of the alphabet to the class. Call out a word, in English OR in the TL, and have the students spell the word by standing, shouting their letter and holding up the card for the class to see . . . Or have them run to the front of the room and quickly line up. [CCSS: SL 1, 4; ACTFL: 1.2, 1.3; DOK 1]

- A good follow-up, using the same cards, is to have each student take a piece of tape, and have them post them somewhere in the classroom: anywhere, even on a fellow student! Then, ask them, first, to point at the various letters, which are, of course, not in order. ("Dónde está/Où est/Wo ist_____?") Then, add more detailed questions, giving choices: "Where is the letter X? On the window or on the door?" or "What letter is on the window? S or Z?" As the students become more familiar with the locations in the TL (incidentally, this is a *great* way to introduce or practice classroom items at the same time), change to a yes/no format, with students giving the location if they answer no: "Is S on the door?" "No, on the window." You may be surprised, the following day, to see students turn to the spot where the letter had been the previous day, when you practice using one of the other activities in this section. [CCSS: SL 1, 4; ACTFL: 1.1, 1.2; DOK 1]

- Using the same cards again, sing either alphabet song, but students must stand up with their card held high when their letter is sung. Even high school seniors seem to like this. [CCSS: SL 1, 4; ACTFL: 1.2, 1.3; DOK 1]

- A variation I found called Schreibmaschine (Typewriter) involved assigning each student in a team or row a certain number of letters of the alphabet (can use the cards again if you wish!). When another team (or the teacher, or a student on the team drawing a slip of paper from a dish) calls out a word, the team must immediately spell it, each student contributing his/her letter when it is needed, but staccato (with no breaks) just like a typewriter: "bleiben." "B—L—E—I—B—E—N" "Richtig, nächste Gruppe!" [CCSS: SL 1, 4; ACTFL: 1.1, 1.2, 1.3; DOK 1]

- This one is well suited for the energy level and cooperativeness of grade school (FLES) or middle school students, I think: put the students in groups, move the desks and chairs out of the way, and, as you call out letters of the alphabet, have the students actually make that letter with their bodies, either standing up or lying on the floor. Reward the fastest. [CCSS: SL 1, 4; ACTFL: 1.3; DOK 1]

- Begin spelling the name of a student in the class. When he/she recognizes his/her name, the student raises his/her hand and completes spelling the rest of his/her name. [CCSS: SL 1; ACTFL: 1.2, 1.3; DOK 1]

- An old game we used to play on long car trips works well here: Have one student say a word in the TL; the next student must say a word that begins with the last letter of the preceding word (Note: in French, ban words ending in –x, and be ready with lots of suggestions for "e"; in Spanish, lots of "o" and "a" words). [CCSS: SL 1, 4; ACTFL: 1.2, 1.3; DOK 1]

- Play Hangman in small groups, using TL vocabulary. For extra culture, give them the names of famous people of TL origin or descent, well-known places, or products from the target countries. [CCSS: SL 1, 4; ACTFL: 1.2, 1.3; DOK 2]
- Play Wheel of Fortune with the same topics as those listed for Hangman.
- Make an Abécédaire (French for ABC book), an illustrated book that lists something for each letter in the alphabet: A is for Alligateur, B is for Bacon, and so on. (This will be good dictionary use practice, also.) Then have students read them, or read them to each other. If you are working on verbs at the same time, why not tell them to use verbs instead of the traditional nouns, or adjectives/nationalities/foods, depending on the unit? [CCSS: RL 1; ACTFL: 1.3, 2.1, 2.2, 3.1; DOK 1 making the book. CCSS: SL 1, 4, RL 1, 4; ACTFL: 1.2, 1.3; DOK 1 reading the book.]
- Have each student write out his name and address. Pair each student with another. Tell them they have to phone in their name and address to (country that speaks TL) in order to receive a free gift, but they only have enough money for a 90-second telephone call. Have one of them give their name, spell it, and then their address, spelling it also, to their partner. Stop them after 90 seconds, and have them compare the information their partner wrote with the correct address and spelling. Repeat with the partner dictating. [CCSS: RL 1, SL 4; ACTFL: 1,1. 1.2, 1.3; DOK 1]
- Prepare a letter, gearing the difficulty and subject matter to the level of the class. Fill the letter with names, places, etc., which will need to be spelled. Have one student as the boss, and the other as the secretary. (I usually make the student who is a weaker speller the secretary.) The boss dictates the letter, spelling any words the secretary asks to be spelled. Give the original to the secretary, and have her tell the "boss" what went wrong where, if there are errors. [CCSS: RL 1, 4 and L2; ACTFL: 1.1, 1.2, 1.3; DOK 1]

  – Variation: Partner A is "boss" for half the letter, and then switch roles for the last part.
  – Variation: Post the letter on the wall, so the "boss" has to memorize it, and run back to the "secretary" and dictate as much as they remember.

- Learn ASL from a book in the library. As you say the letter, sign it also. This is a little "extra" for students who pick up on it: visual learners will associate the sign with the letter. Hearing-impaired students will definitely love this. [CCSS: SL 2; ACTFL: 1.1; DOK 1]
- Since many letters, especially the vowels, have the same name as the sound they make, there may be more activities in the Pronunciation section that you could use for the alphabet.

Family

What do you do after everyone has read and drawn a family tree?

- The first day of this unit, my students begin a "Me Book" online—we use Voicethread— but this could be done by stapling together several pieces of paper. [CCSS: W2, L1, L 2;

ACTFL: 1.1, 1.3; DOK 2] On the front page, they leave space for a photo, and write their name and their French/Spanish/German name they have chosen. As they learn more vocabulary, they add to it their nationality, hair color and other description, likes and dislikes. Then they add their entire family (or imaginary family; my goal is to practice the vocabulary, so if they have no brothers or sisters or pet, they invent them or choose a celebrity) to the book, one page for each family member. They may put in actual photos, or cut and paste them—many kids' mothers seem to bear a strong resemblance to Taylor Swift lately—and then describe their family in the same way they have described themselves. Throughout the unit, we add to the book, and it becomes both a graded portion of their final exam and part of their student portfolio, as well as something their classmates like read during free time, and good show and tell for parent conferences.

- Give students a description of a person, asking them to draw that person (we often use whiteboards for this). [CCSS: RL 1, W 2; ACTFL: 1.1, 1.2, 1.3; DOK 2] Using their picture, they will then try to locate other members of their family. The descriptions they were given had carefully chosen characteristics (i.e., long curly dark hair, or a dimple on the chin, or ears that are long and large) that will help them locate the other family members. The drawings will also help establish who is the father, mother, brother and sister. They then make up a story about their family (last name, where they live, etc.) and then introduce themselves to the class. Variation: project a picture from a site like awkwardfamily photos.com and describe the photo for the partner to draw, then compare with the original.

Calendar

- In Spanish, French, and German, with very little difficulty, the days of the week can be sung to the theme song from *The Flintstones*. Try it!
- Make dominoes. Cut colored paper into equal-sized pieces (or use a template found online). Draw a line down the center. Each one should have a day of the week in English on one half and in the TL on the other (note: not usually the same day, but combinations like Dienstag/Friday, lundi/

> CCSS: SL1, 4, RL1, 4, W3, L1, 2
> ACTFL: 1.1, 1.2, 1.3, 4.1, 5.2
> DOK 1, 2

Sunday, and viernes/Tuesday). Divide the students in teams, giving each a set of "dominoes." Play this exactly like dominoes, with each drawing four or five pieces to begin. Students should match the word in the TL with its English equivalent, moving in a straight line or to the side, until all pieces are used up. This could also be done for the months. [CCSS: RL 1; ACTFL: 1.2, 5.1; DOK 1]
- Make a crossword, but with no clues. Fill in 1 month to begin, and have students fill in the others based on the length of the word in the TL, the letter "clues" that filling in other months have given them, and so on. I usually give this activity as homework. This can also be done with numbers. [CCSS: RL 1, 4; ACTFL: 1.2, 1.3; DOK 2]

- Pair students, giving them an envelope with the months written on little strips of paper. At your signal, they will open their envelope and see which group can put them in order fastest. As a variation on this, the envelope could contain seasons and holidays to match, or months and typical activities for each. [CCSS: RL 1; ACTFL: 1.2, 1.3; DOK 1]
- Pair students, giving them an envelope with the months (or days) cut up into individual letter "tiles" as for Scrabble. Call out, in English, a month (or day) and see who can assemble it, spelled correctly, the fastest. Let them call out the next one.
- In Four Corners, the teacher "labels," either orally or literally, the four corners of the room with the four seasons, and instructs the students to get up and move to their preferred corner. Once they are in that corner, have them discuss activities to do during that season or weather to be found during that time, clothes to wear, food to eat, and so on.
- Make Story Calendars: run off a calendar page for each one for the current month. Have the students cut each square so that it opens like a door in an Advent calendar, and then paste it to a blank sheet of paper. Under each door, have them write a sentence in the TL. Sentences could involve what they will do on that day, or they could make up a completely different story for each week, while keeping each very short and simple: on Sunday, Juan got a bike, on Monday, he rode it, on Tuesday, he crashed, on Wednesday he was in the hospital, and so on. Then have them show their calendar to others in the class, having the partner name a date, and having the student open the door to the date named, so both are still practicing the vocabulary. [CCSS: SL 1, RL 1, W3, L1, L2; ACTFL: 1.1, 1.2, 1.3; DOK 2]

Weather

- Duplicate the weather pictures that you intend to use when testing (especially important, so that students recognize them easily). Make Bingo-style cards with the weather pictures on them, a different picture in each portion. Make several different variations of these cards. Beneath these, list how to say "Put," "square," and other words they will need for this activity. Play Bingo, or Four Corners or other variations (see more in Chapter 4). Have volunteers "call" the phrases.
- Also make blank Bingo grids, and envelopes with the weather pictures in them. Pair students, giving one a filled-out Bingo grid, and the other one a blank grid and an envelope. Student A will describe his grid to Student B, in the TL, until Student B has the same illustration. This is great for practicing prepositions: "Put 'it is snowing' to the right of 'it is sunny'." [CCSS: RL 7, SL 1, 4; ACTFL: 1.1, 1.2; DOK 1]
- SPONGE activity: Use the pictures from the text or online to make a slide. Ask students to look at the screen and name the weather expressions. When you are ready, turn the screen off, remove a couple illustrations and rearrange them a bit, and then turn it back on and ask which ones are missing. [CCSS: RL 7; ACTFL 1.2; DOK 1]

- This activity requires some clothing: get donations from students, relatives, go to garage sales or resale shops, whatever. Divide these into piles, with the same items in each pile. Divide the students into as many teams as there are piles, give each student a number. Say a weather expression and a number, and the designated student from each time will run to the team's clothing pile and select items appropriate to wear for that type of weather, and put them on. The first team whose delegate is correctly dressed and who sits back down with the team gets a point. (Bonus point to name the clothing items as he/she removes them?) [CCSS: SL 1, 4; ACTFL: 1.2, 1.3, 3.1, 4.1; DOK 1]

- Have students take turns giving weather reports each day, using props. Don't tell them when their turn will come; draw names daily, so every day when they enter, they will check what the day, date, weather, and so on is. Have them begin with a greeting and their name, just like a weatherman, and then do the date and weather. If you want, also have them give one item of news, like "Today I am playing basketball" or a classmate's birthday. [CCSS: SL 1, 4, 5, 6; ACTFL: 1.3, 3.1, 4.1; DOK 2]

- Give students a whole-country weather map (TL countries, too!) Describe the weather for one city or region, and have the students write down/indicate which one you described. [CCSS: SL 1, 3; ACTFL: 1.2, 3.1, 4.1; DOK 1]

- Have students in groups illustrate a five-day weather forecast for a city (in a TL country perhaps!) hard copy, slides or online, with a different type of weather depicted for each day, and represented by a large symbol. Each day would also be labeled in the TL. Have students present their weather forecast, with the poster as a backdrop, live or via video. [CCSS: RL 1, SL 2, 4; ACTFL: 1.2, 1.3, 3.1, 3.2, 5.2; DOK 2]

Nationalities

We all know how difficult it is to teach nationalities, with students' generally poor backgrounds in geography. I wish I had a nickel for every kid who, when presented with the sentence, "Hilda is from Bonn. Hilda is_____," in which he is expected to fill in the nationality, looks at me and assures me he doesn't know of any city on this planet named Bonn.

I have no real solution for that problem, but here are some fun activities to add to your repertoire when practicing nationalities:

- Have each student select a different famous person, and then introduce themselves to the class as that person. For instance: Hello, my name is _____. I am from (city) and I am (nationality). Variation: using the name given, have the class guess the nationality. [CCSS: SL 1, 4, 6; ACTFL: 1.3, 3.1; DOK 1]

- This is a great motivator for all ages, and especially for shy students. Give each a stuffed animal. (I use my now-adult daughter's collection, but you could pick them up cheaply at garage sales, or have students bring in their own—but be sure to have a few extra for students who forget.) For their animal, they make up a name, address and nationality (plus any other information you would like them to practice.) Then, have each circulate freely in the room, introducing their "friend" to each other's "friends." Even the shyest kid will talk, because it's not about himself/herself. [CCSS: SL 1, 4, 5, 6; ACTFL: 1.2, 1.3, 2.2, 3.1, 5.1; DOK 1]

- Another variation on the above activity is to make paper bag puppets. Buy those inexpensive brown lunch bags and have students, either in class or as homework, decorate them with a face, arms, and whatever they wish. I would suggest writing a good rubric or checklist for this activity (see the chapter on assessments.) Maybe you'd even like to have a beauty contest for these, or prizes for most creative, prettiest, ugliest, and so on. Once each student has a puppet, have the class proceed as stated above: invent a name, and so on. One advantage to these puppets is that they fold flat and may easily be stored, either in the classroom, or in the student's folder or book, for use during later units. For example, during the food unit, the puppet may be brought out once again to talk about food he or she likes and hates. [CCSS: SL 1, 4, 5, 6; ACTFL: 1.2, 1.3, 2.2, 3.1, 5.1; DOK 1]

- My students really like this game, which provides for purposeful student movement as well as practicing vocabulary: I call it Exchange Students. Each student quickly draws a strip of paper from a bowl. On the strip of paper is the name of a city. Give the students a few seconds, if needed, to find out what country that city is in, and then they stand and, in the TL, try to locate people of the same nationality. Please note the word "nationality." I make sure that each student has a *different* city, so that they must use the nationalities rather than the cities. This encourages a little bit more of the geographical aspect, too, as I have overheard students saying, "I never knew (city) was in (country)!" I like to have students from the same country link arms as young people do in many countries, and have some sort of reward for the most numerous nationality (which is determined by fate, as I always have more slips of paper than I do students.) I know some teachers do this early in the year, and have the "families" work together for an extended time period for projects (i.e., a weather report, food and dress from their country). [CCSS: SL 1, 2, 4, 5, 6; ACTFL: 1.1, 1.2. 1.3, 2.1, 2.2, 3.1, 5.1; DOK 1]

- I call this game Suitcases. I put the students in teams, swear them to secrecy, and give each team a nationality and an old suitcase. They have overnight to come up with some items which are typical for that nationality, and then bring in, draw pictures or make a slide show of them. For instance, for the nationality "English" students may produce Big Ben, a tea bag, a British flag, or other stereotypical items. Then, the next day, they show the contents of their suitcase, one at a time, to the other teams, with points for the first team to identify the nationality the suitcase contains, in the TL, of course. For even more vocabulary learning, have the students name the items as they produce them from the suitcase in the TL. It's great CI, as the item is displayed as the word is pronounced, and many kids will easily acquire new vocabulary well before it is introduced in the text. [CCSS: SL 1, 2, 4, 5, 6; ACTFL: 1.1, 1.2. 1.3, 2.1, 2.2, 3.1, 5.1; DOK 1]

- A similar activity is to play You Don't Say with nationalities. Give students cards with a nationality written at the top, and a list of places, people, and items that are typical. They read these clues aloud one at a time, trying to get their partner(s) to say the nationality. [CCSS: SL 1, 4; ACTFL: 1.2, 1.3, 2.1, 2.2, 3.1, 5.1; DOK 1]

Food and Drink

Obviously, tasting and cooking ethnic foods is a popular activity, and well worth the class time (see Chapters 2 and 4 for recipes) but there are other, authentic and just as educational things to do.

- Have a Market Day. Have students sign up to bring a vegetable and a fruit or other food item that does not need refrigeration (rice, yogurt, hard-boiled eggs, etc.) Make sure there are no duplicates. Give them a date to have these in class (make it several days ahead to give them time to shop.) They also need to have the name of the food and its cost (changed to the equivalent in money from a country that speaks your TL) on a card, as well as a shopping bag or basket. On the appointed day, divide students into Shoppers and Sellers, and have them walk about and purchase food, either singly or in teams. When the activity is over, each must show the class what they have bought (in the TL, of course) and the vendors compare profits. Things like grapes and berries may be tasted by all, and everyone takes home a purchase, with instructions to teach parents or siblings how to say it in the TL. [CCSS: SL 1, 4, 5, 6; ACTFL: 1.1, 1.2, 1.3, 2.1, 3.1, 5.1 and 5.2; DOK 1]
- Give students a quiet, writing activity to practice this vocabulary (or as a game or a quiz or a journal entry.) [CCSS: W3, 4, L1, 2, 3; ACTFL: 1.1, 1.3, 3.1, 5.1; DOK 1] Give them one point for each correct answer, and minus one for inappropriate ones. Try some of the following writing prompts:

> You run a sandwich shop. List the choices of sandwich fillings for your customers.
> Write out a shopping list for making a really fancy fruit salad.
> You are a chef. List what you might use for making an omelet.
> You are choosing a dessert at a restaurant. What choices do you have?
> I'm thirsty, and it's summer. What advice could you offer me?
> Doctors say a balanced diet has five servings of fruits and vegetables each day. List 3 days' worth, with no repeats.

I have had, however, more success with more unusual writing prompts:

> Tell things you would never want to see/use in a sandwich.
> List all the people in your family, and a food and beverage each one hates.
> Make out the strangest possible menu for a meal (i.e., roast beef in raspberry jam)
> Write drinks that athletes should probably never drink.
> List all the foods that a vegetarian would despise.
> Make up the most colorful meal possible.

For journal writing, more open questions encourage higher-level thinking:

> I saw Godzilla/Thor/Super Mario, and he was eating . . .
> Holiday meals are always memorable, because . . .
> I visited a (French/Spanish/German/Italian) restaurant, and saw . . .

- This activity requires either plastic (play) food, or cards with large pictures of food on them. I cut some nice photos from food magazines over the years and laminated them on colored paper, and these work well. Have everyone sit in a circle. Explain the rules to the class: you are going to hand out several items of food to every second or third student, evenly spaced around the circle. The student with the picture will try to give it to the student next to him, but that student will refuse to take it, saying, "What is it?" or "What is that?" The first student must tell the second what that food is, in the TL. They must repeat this conversational exchange three times, before the second student is allowed to take it. He or she then tries to give the food item to the next person. To make it even more difficult, send some items to the left, and some to the right. [CCSS: SL 1, 3, 4, 5, 6; ACTFL: 1.1, 1.2, 1.3; DOK 1]

Clothing (Ropa/Vetements/Kleiderspiel)

- Buy a bag of clothespins, and write the name of an article of clothing on each. There are several activities to use these. One would be for students to move about, pinning the clothespin on someone who is wearing that article of clothing. Another would be to provide a clothesline with the pins already on it, and to have students look through a bag of old clothes, hanging each item up with the pin with that article's name on it. (Toddler clothes are smaller and perhaps easier to use for this.) If a lot of old clothes aren't in your budget or storage capability, have the students look through old magazines, cutting out pictures of those articles of clothing and pinning those to the clothesline. [CCSS: RL 1; ACTFL: 1.1, 1.3, 3.1, 4.2; DOK 1]
- Why not use the clothes they just cut out of magazines in the above activity to make mobiles? Glue the pictures to cards or pieces of paper, writing the word for the clothing on the back side. Suspend these from an X-shaped hanger device with string, thread or yarn, and hang them from the ceiling. Don't forget to take them down before the test, though. [CCSS: W 2, L 2; ACTFL: 1.1, 1.3, 2.2, 3.1; DOK 1]
- Have your students look at classmates and jot down what they are wearing, then take turns describing each other's clothing. First one to guess who is being described, wins. [CCSS: W2, L2, then S4; ACTFL: 1.1, 1.2, 1.3, 3.1; DOK 1]
- Using what the students are wearing that day, have them stand, and tell them to exchange any clothing possible, including accessories. They must keep track of who has their stuff. After a few minutes (use your judgment on how on-task they are), have them stop, and report, orally or in written form, where their items are: "Mark has my left shoe, Anne has my right shoe, Bob has my watch, Mike has my shirt." The oral version of reporting has a

slightly interesting aspect, as the person they gave it to may have given it to another person: "Mark has my shoe," to which Mark would reply, "No, I don't have your shoe; I gave it to Paul," which is not only a wonderful conversational simulation but which also requires the use of a direct object pronoun. [CCSS: SL 1, 4, 6; ACTFL: 1.1, 1.2, 1.3; DOK 1]

- Have two or three volunteers stand in front of the class for 30 seconds or so, then go out in the hall, into the closet, or somewhere nearby, and change three things about what he/she is wearing: take off jewelry, pull sleeves up or down, exchange shirts, and so on. When they come back into class, have the class tell you what is different. [CCSS: SL 1, 4; ACTFL: 1.1, 1.2; DOK 1]

- Play Name It or Wear It. First, you need to go to garage sales, resale shops, Grandma's attic, or other places to find a variety of clothing in outrageous sizes (from tiny to huge) and colors, preferably in styles long obsolete. To play, hold up an item, and name a student. If the student cannot name the item in the TL, he or she must wear it. After you are finished, have a fashion show. Maybe even take Polaroids, or use the Snapshot and make a PowerPoint presentation for review. Some kids miss on purpose, just so they can model. [CCSS: SL 1, 4; ACTFL: 1.1, 1.2, 1.3; DOK 1]

- A variation on Name It or Wear It would be to get three volunteers to pull items from the bag. Holding the item up, they would ask a classmate (or teammate) to name both the item and its color. If the student can do this, the item goes into a discard pile, but if they can't, the volunteer has to put the item on, somehow. Then after all the clothes have been taken from the bag, as a review of items missed, the volunteer will undress, and the group will describe them once again. If playing this with teams, make sure each team's bag has similar items. [CCSS: SL 1, 4; ACTFL: 1.1, 1.2, 1.3; DOK 1]

- If you have learned body parts, add that to the game. Tell them to put the glove on their head, or the shoe on their hand. After a few minutes, let students give the commands. For a treat, let them give *you* the commands. [CCSS: SL 1, 4; ACTFL: 1.1, 1.2, 1.3; DOK 1]

- Send the kids to the Internet to buy an outfit. Every language has online catalogs with full-color pictures, where the kids can "shop." Just Google to find department stores with online sales sites. Have them send you a screen shot of their final selections. Some of mine have actually found and bought clothing online after this. [CCSS: RL 1, W7; ACTFL: 1.1, 2.2, 4.1, 5.1, 5.2; DOK 1]

- Have students stage a fashion show. That's a logical activity, but I have a suggestion: have your students help you write the rubric for this activity. Let them decide how many times each should talk, if everyone has to model, and so on, and you will get a lot more cooperation. Also, give them the option of doing the show live, on PowerPoint, or on videotape; shyer students will thank you. Each show, however, must have a theme: winter, sports clothes, hippie garb, retro fashions, or whatever. Letting students have a say in deciding what is done has wonderful results; they have a firm recollection of what is required, and do better shows, and you get to give more As on the results. [CCSS: W 2, L 2, then S 4, 6; ACTFL: 1.1, 1.2, 1.3; DOK 2]

- Have a magazine Scavenger Hunt for clothes. Give students a list in the TL of things like a red shirt, a green dress, blue socks, purple shoes, or whatever, and turn them loose with a bunch of old magazines to hunt for them. [CCSS: RL 1; ACTFL: 1.1, 1.3, 3.1, 4.2; DOK 1]

- Post several similar pictures cut from magazines. Tell the students that one of these people has just committed a crime. Describe the criminal for them, using as many negative statements as positive ones, i.e., He is wearing a hat. The hat is not black. He is not wearing a raincoat. He is wearing a brown jacket, etc. Have them help you "catch" the criminal. [CCSS: RL 1, SL 1, 3; ACTFL: 1.1, 1.2, 3.1, 4.1; DOK 2]

- Have a more advanced class make a page of fashion "do's" and "don'ts," illustrated from magazines. This practices the command form of verbs, also (or the subjunctive, depending on how you structure it). [CCSS: W 1 or 2, 4, 6 and L 1, 2; ACTFL: 1.1, 1.3, 3.1, 4.2; DOK 2]

Colors

TPR is usually the best way to go to introduce colors. Take sheets of construction paper in various colors, and introduce the colors two or three at a time. Circulate through the class, asking students within reach to "Touch the orange paper" or "Point at the blue paper." This is a very low anxiety activity. Then, get another set of papers in the same colors and shapes, but smaller, and introduce the words "big" and "little," as well as adjective placement. Practice again for 10 minutes or so, wandering about the room, and, for your visual learners, putting a vocabulary list you have prepared beforehand onto the screen, or on the board. Then try one of these activities:

- Flyswatter: tape the papers to the board (or, attach them with magnets)—give them some practice time with a partner while you set this up—and send two student volunteers to the front of the room, arming each with a flyswatter. Say, "Touch the big green paper" and the first student to swat the correct paper wins. (See Chapter 2 for more on how to play Flyswatter.) [CCSS: SL 1, 3; ACTFL: 1.1, 1.2; DOK 1]
- Play Elimination. Have the entire class stand. Call out a color, or, to seem less biased, have bowl full of strips of paper with the colors written on them and draw a paper from this bowl. Students wearing this color may remain standing, and others must be seated. If some sort of reward or privilege is connected to this activity, I find the students who are "out" stay involved in their desire to monitor the honesty of the students who are still playing. Continue until most of the students are seated, reward the remaining students, and start over, or go on to another activity. They will beg to play this again. Be sure you replace the strips already used; fate determines the winners (or, those whose tastes run to wildly colored clothing.) [CCSS: SL 1, 3; ACTFL: 1.1, 1.2; DOK 1]
- A wilder variation of Elimination, and which has no winners or losers, is to call out a color, and anyone wearing that color has to switch seats. To make it more interesting, remove one seat so one student will be left standing. Let him or her pick the next color. To practice clothing, name a color and an item, i.e., "White T-shirt." [CCSS: SL 1, 3; ACTFL: 1.1, 1.2; DOK 1]
- Play I Spy: say, in the TL, "I see something that is (color)" and have students guess what it is: "El globo?" . . . No . . . "El mapa?" . . . No . . . and so on. [CCSS: SL 1, 3, 4; ACTFL: 1.1, 1.2; DOK 1]

- Bring in fruits of different colors, and teach the fruit's name and color as you cut them up. Give kids pieces, as they tell you what fruit and color they would like to eat. [CCSS: SL 1, 4; ACTFL: 1.1, 1.2, 1.3, 5.2; DOK 1]
- Buy a bag of multicolored balloons, enough for each student to have one. At your signal, have them blow up and tie off their balloon, telling what color it is. Then, they throw it into the air, and bat it from student to student, calling out the color before they touch it. This gets pretty noisy (expect a balloon or two to pop), but kids of all ages enjoy it. [CCSS: SL 1, 3, 4; ACTFL: 1.1, 1.2; DOK 1]

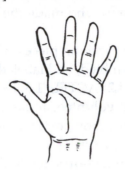

Body Parts

Besides Simon dice/Simon dit/Simon sagt:

- Take turns singing, Head and Shoulders, Knees and Toes (to the tune of There's a Tavern in the Town): Head and Shoulders, Knees and Toes, Knees and Toes (touch these parts as you sing)—repeat the first line again—Eyes and Ears, and Mouth and Nose, Head and Shoulders, Knees and Toes. In French, the third line is rearranged so it rhymes: Les yeux, le nez, la bouche et les oreilles . . . Sing this over and over, and faster each time. See who can sing it the fastest. [CCSS: SL 4; ACTFL: 1.1, 1.2, 2.1; DOK 1]
- Lead an exercise class. This will teach body parts as well as verbs, prepositions of location (up and down) and a review of the numbers. After this, it is fun to assign groups of students to make their own exercise videos, and then show one each day whenever the class needs a break from sitting (or at the beginning of the hour, especially first thing on a Monday when they are fairly lethargic). I even encourage them to use finger-lifts, eyebrow raises, and other silly things as a small part of the routine, as those practice the more obscure body parts. [CCSS: SL 1, 4; ACTFL: 1.1, 1.2; DOK 1]
- Have student volunteers go to the board. Give each a piece of chalk, blindfold them, and then have them draw a person. Have the other students in the class tell them what body part to draw. (They may also use adjectives: a big hand, a small nose.) The class is usually enthralled while watching these masterpieces develop. [CCSS: SL 3, 4; ACTFL: 1.2, 1.3; DOK 1]
- Place a common object (plastic spoon, cup, stuffed animal, etc.) on a chair or desk between two students. Call out body parts randomly, and have students touch that part, until you call the object's name ("Spoon!"/"Cup!") and they have to try to grab it first. The loser is out, and the winner finds a new partner, until you have a class champion. [CCSS: SL 3, 4; ACTFL: 1.2, 1.3; DOK 1]
- Divide students into groups, giving each group a large piece of white bulletin board or butcher paper and markers. One of each group will lie down, and either you or a person

in the group who the student trusts to do this will outline his or her body. Then, they color themselves, and label body parts. Specify how many parts must be labeled. [CCSS: W2, L2; ACTFL: 1.3; DOK 1]

- Using Post-It notes, have students write one body part on each piece, and then stick them onto the appropriate parts of a volunteer from their group. If he or she prefers, the volunteer may stick them onto himself/herself. Give a certain number of participation points for this. Then, the volunteers go to another group, which removes and reads the papers aloud, checking the spelling and grammar of the other group. Points are given for finding errors, and points deducted from the group who made the errors. [CCSS: W2, SL 4, L2; ACTFL: 1.1, 1.2, 1.3; DOK 1]
- Make a collage "Frankenstein" of various pieces of people taken from different photos (from a TL source if possible), assembled, and labeled in the TL. This makes a high-interest bulletin board. [CCSS: W2, 8 and L2; ACTFL: 1.3; DOK 1]
- Play Mannequin—Have a student volunteer to be the mannequin, and another who will pose him as you instruct: bend the elbow, extend the finger, place one hand on the knee, etc. [CCSS: SL 3, 4; ACTFL: 1.2, 1.3; DOK 1]
- Have a mock disaster drill: assign roles—rescuer, Red Cross worker, doctor, injured person (identify the injury, don't let them choose). Pick a somewhat exaggerated event: avalanche, asteroid hit, volcanic eruption—something not likely to occur where you live. You can even do fake blood (rags painted red to tie on various places). Give vocab like "Can you move your leg?" or other things said to test injuries, as well as things for the injured to yell: "I'm stuck under this boulder" or "My head hurts," etc.) Keep it as melodramatic as possible and this could be a great video! [CCSS: SL 1, 3, 4, 6; ACTFL 1.1, 1.3; DOK 3]

Prepositions

- Hide-the-Pencil: Have a student volunteer give you a pencil or a pen. Send him or her from the room, and hide the object somewhere in the room. Have the student come back in and ask, "Where is the pencil/pen?" (Wo ist . . . Où est . . . ¿Dónde está . . .) The students answer using the prepositions: "behind Sam, far from the teacher, to the left of the clock" and so on. The clues may not repeat any prepositions; if one has been used, students must think of a clue using a different preposition. After five clues, if the student has not found his object, show him where it was, and let him or her select the next student volunteer. You can play, too. [CCSS: SL 1, 3, 4; ACTFL: 1.1, 1.2, 1.3; DOK 1]
- If you are lucky enough to have a lot of old Mr. Potato Head pieces around, or can acquire them from friends and family, great! Otherwise, here is a substitute: using felt, cut out a head shape, ears, eyes, nose, mouth, and other face parts. Felt pieces usually cling together, especially if they are assembled on a desk top or other flat surface. Using either set (the real ones, or the felt), have students assemble a person while you describe. Or, have one student describe to a partner while the partner assembles it. Or, display a face with parts in unusual places, and have the students tell you where they should go. [If you describe: CCSS: SL 3, 4; ACTFL: 1.2, 1.3] [If they describe: CCSS: SL 1, 3, 4; ACTFL: 1.1, 1.2, 1.3; DOK 1]
- Give students a drawing of an empty classroom. Below it is a series of sentences telling what objects to draw, and where to draw them: "Put the book on the desk. Draw a map to

the right of the window. Put a desk in front of the window." Use as many prepositions as possible. Have students compare drawings to see if they correctly followed directions. [CCSS: R1, 2, 3, 4; ACTFL: 1.3; DOK 1]

- Try origami. Get a book on origami and tell the students how to make something. My two most popular shapes so far have been a bird that flaps its wings if you pull the tail, and a box that is flat when finished, but which you inflate by blowing into it. (We call it a "balloon.") [CCSS: SL 3, 4; ACTFL: 1.2, 1.3; DOK 1]

- Get a map of Madrid/Paris/Berlin/Tokyo (any major city in the TL) and have students plot a route from a place you have predetermined to a major monument. If you have a laminated map, have them trade instructions and draw their route (following the instructions as written). Or, use a student volunteer and a map projected on a screen. Have the volunteer(s) try to follow directions given by classmates. [CCSS: W2, L2; ACTFL: 1.1, 1.2, 1.3, 2.2, 5.1; DOK 1]

- Tell students they must help a new exchange student at school. Giving each group a different class schedule, have them write directions from before school when the student gets off the bus, to all his/her classes, and back to the bus at the end of the day. This also practices time expressions. [CCSS: W2, L2; ACTFL: 1.1, 1.2, 1.3, 2.2, 5.1; DOK 1]

- Record directions within the building and have students listening to it follow a route through the school to a "treasure" (cookies?) you have hidden somewhere. I suggest not sending groups out all at once. [CCSS: SL 1, 3, 4; ACTFL: 1.2, 1.3; DOK 1]

Object Pronouns

Here are a couple of ideas that are low-prep:

- Lost-and-Found: Have people exchange things they personally are wearing or brought to class with another person, and then have that person exchange with a third classmate. Go to each student and ask if they have lost something and they will answer: "Mark has my calculator," to which Mark would reply, "No, I don't have your calculator; I gave it toPaul," which requires the use of a direct object pronoun (and gender practice for the noun).

> CCSS: SL1, 3, 4
> ACTFL: 1.1, 1.2, 1.3
> DOK 1

- No Sir/Ma'am!: This game is fast-paced and practices the pronouns, over and over: After numbering the chairs in your room, have students sit while you announce, "The King of (TL country) has lost his (object) and number (say a seat number) took it!" The person in that seat number must stand and say, "No, Sir/Ma'am, I don't have it—number (says a different number) has it!" and the newly accused person stands up, denies it, and accuses another, until someone doesn't react fast enough (or stands up when it wasn't their number called, calls his/her own number or one that doesn't exist i.e., 21 when there are only 20 students). Then students with lower numbers all shift up one seat, and that person goes to the end (largest-numbered seat). Change objects lost to practice a variety of pronouns. To win, students must try to trip up others with numbers lower than theirs so they may move up. Fast-paced and practices the pronouns, over and over.

Asking Questions

CCSS: SL1, 3, 4
ACTFL: 1.1, 1.2, 1.3
DOK 2

- Help students better understand the structure of a question with a learning game sort of like Jeopardy. Using any sort of game board (tic-tac-toe, horse race, escargot, etc.) divide the room into teams. You will need a large number of fairly complex sentences, such as: Maria goes to the mall on Saturday to buy a pretty red dress. If desired, dictate the sentence to the students. Then with each team in turn, give them a part of the original sentence and have them tell you (or write) what question that part would answer. (i.e., "to the mall," with the answer "Where does Maria go?") If they answer correctly, they win the square, move their token, or whatever, depending on the display method chosen.

- Celebrity speed dating. Assign every class member the name of a secret celebrity, and a list of the names of classmates. They may need a little research time to find out more about their celebrity, or have more names than students so they could exchange for a new, known name. Using a 2-minute paired session of questions and answers between both, each student should answer as accurately as possible whatever his celebrity would answer, while at the same time trying to guess who their partner is. At the end of 2 minutes, each moves to sit with a new partner, until all have had a chance to speak together. At the end of the event, reveal the secret identities and see which student guessed the most correctly.

Activities that Work for Any Subject

I am assuming that we all know how to do board races, crossword puzzles, Go Fish games and word searches, as well as online sites like Kahoot, Quizizz, and Quizlet. Here are some more creative and active low-or-no-tech ways to practice vocabulary and concepts covered in class.

Variations on Loto/Lotto/Bingo
- **Strip Bingo** (The name immediately arouses interest!) Give each student a strip cut lengthwise from a piece of blank paper. Fold the strip in half three times (giving eight squares). Each student chooses eight vocabulary words, writing the English translation in the boxes. The teacher (or a selected student) reads the entire vocabulary list aloud, while each student concentrates on hearing the ones for only the first and last ones on his/her strip. When one of those two is heard, that box is torn off (so another word takes its place). Note: have students keep the boxes removed so you can check for accuracy. When the reader reaches the end of the list, the reading begins again at the top. The winner is the student with no words left. To make the game last longer, do not say a word that you think most students will have on their list as often as other words. [CCSS: SL 3, 4; ACTFL: 1.2, 1.3; DOK 1]

  – Variation: instead of folding the strip into boxes, students may write down a given number of words (i.e., 15), making sure to tell them to spread out the words so they take up the entire strip. Then play as before, tearing off the end words until the strip is gone.

- – Variation: Students may also cross words out instead of tearing them (but it is harder to verify who is telling the truth about having all the words used when doing that).
- – Variation: Use the words *in context* (sentences, or a short paragraph) and have students listen for them.

- **Body Bingo**: Students pick a given number of vocabulary words, writing them down (or drawing a picture) so they can remember their "picks." Have all stand up. Draw vocab words and, as they are read aloud, if one of their words comes up, they must sit down. The winner is the last one standing. This is a quick (5 minutes or less) activity. [CCSS: W1, 4, L2, SL 3, 4; ACTFL: 1.2, 1.3; DOK 1]

- **Tic-Tac-Toe** (Noughts and Crosses): Draw a nine-square grid and number each square from one to nine. Divide the class into two teams. Have the starting team choose a square, and ask a question. If they give the correct answer, they win the square. If not, the other team may try to "steal" the square. Then Team two chooses a numbered square for their turn. [CCSS: SL 3, 4; ACTFL: 1.2, 1.3; DOK 1]

- **Mobiles**: Cut pictures out of any category: clothing, colors, food, family members, professions, animals, transportation, or whatever unit you wish. Paste them on cards, writing the word for the picture in the TL on the back of the card. Make an X-shaped hanger from dowels, pieces of coat hanger, plastic drinking straws or anything else rather stiff, and hang the items using thread, string, or yarn. Hang them from the ceiling, where they will catch the eye, and reinforce the vocabulary. Don't forget to take them down before the test, though. [CCSS: W1, 4, L2; ACTFL 1.1, 1.3; DOK 1]

- **Circle Sheet**: Write the vocabulary all over a paper, in both languages or just the TL, making sure there is an uneven number so there are no ties when playing. Pair students, giving each a different colored pen, pencil, marker or crayon. (I prefer crayons as they don't mark on skin or clothing or pierce skin; this game can get pretty wild if you have fierce competitors!) Someone can: call out the vocabulary OR say it in English, or give a hint (i.e., You put it on a toothbrush) and they race to see who can find and circle it first. [CCSS: SL 1, 3, 4, 6; ACTFL 1.1, 1.2, 1.3; DOK 1]

- **Hot Potato**: Set a timer, without telling the students how much time it was set for. Choose an item, and hand it to a student. In order to pass it to someone else, the student must correctly answer a question. The student caught holding the item when the timer rings is the loser. To keep students on task, have everyone take notes, or review their notes as the questions are asked. I suggest you place a time limit for answering questions, so that students don't spend a long time looking through their notes for the answer. [CCSS: W1, 4, L2, SL 3, 4; ACTFL: 1.2, 1.3; DOK 1]

- **Black Box**, or Poison Box: A variation on Hot Potato, with no timer. Give a student a box, telling him or her only that inside it is a slip of paper. Written on that paper is a task. If the student correctly answers a question, he or she may pass it to someone else. Once all your questions are used up, the person holding the box will open it, and perform the task. Examples of tasks: go up to the blackboard and write your name, holding the chalk in your mouth, with your hands behind your back. Walk to the door and back like a duck, singing *Frère Jacques*. Sing or lip-synch a song in the TL for the class (or, dance to a song). [CCSS: SL 3, 4, L1; ACTFL: 1.2, 1.3; DOK 1]

- **Round the World**: Prepare a series of questions or a list of vocabulary. (You might even ask the students to submit these the day before the activity is scheduled, or at the beginning of the hour, as homework they turn in to you.) Give everyone a review sheet. Have one student either in the front or back of the room stand next to the person seated closest to him or her. Tell them you are going to ask a question, and whichever person says the answer first, gets to move on to challenge the next person in the row, and so on around the room. Anyone who makes it all the way around the room wins. [CCSS: SL 1, 3, 4, 6. L1; ACTFL 1.1, 1.2, 1.3; DOK 1]
- **Twister**: Use the purchased party game mat, which works for colors, but can be converted, with words written on paper and taped to the circles, as practice for almost any vocabulary, as well as body parts, left and right. [CCSS: R1, SL 1, 3, 4; ACTFL: 1.1, 1.2, 1.3; DOK 1]
- **¡Caramba!Flute!/Verflixt!/Darn!**: First, either type a list of the vocabulary you wish to practice, leaving enough space between the words so they may be cut out, or print them on cards. (I use a Business Cards template that spaces them for me.) Include one card with the word "Darn" in the TL for every four or five vocabulary words. Cut these apart, and place them in an envelope. You will need one set for every two teams of students. If you want, you can write the definition of the word on the back, or have the students do this.

  To play, a student from Team A draws a word from the envelope, and Team B has 5 seconds to give a (upper-level) definition or (lower-level) translation of the word (if the cards are double-sided, go with the side up as it is pulled from the envelope. If the side up is in English, they must give the TL word. If the TL side is up, then they give the English.) If Team B correctly translates / defines the word, they keep it, and then decide to either pass, or continue. If they continue, Team A draws another word, and they continue to answer. Once a team decides to pass, the envelope changes hands, and the round is ended.

  If Team B answers incorrectly, Team A has a chance to steal the word. If they successfully translate the word, they not only keep that word, they may take another from Team B's pile, and the envelope changes hands, with Team B reading the next word.

  If one team draws the word "Darn" from the envelope, the other team loses all it has accumulated during that round (it is important to keep cards from different rounds separate from each other), puts them back in the envelope, and the envelope changes hands. The "Darn" card makes the game unpredictable enough to keep one team from monopolizing the entire game.

  A variation of this game that works for all levels is, instead of providing a definition of the word, to ask the students to use the word in a sentence. Using vocabulary in context is, after all, one of the main goals of most state or national standards. [CCSS: SL1, 3, 4, 6, RL1 and L1; ACTFL 1.1, 1.2, 1.3; DOK 1 or 2]
- **Bang!/Pan!/Paf!**: Have students stand back to back, "guns"(pens, if using paper) ready. Give them a phrase to translate. They whirl around and race to see who can do it correctly, first. [CCSS: SL 1, 3, 4, 6, L1; ACTFL 1.1, 1.2, 1.3; DOK 1]
- **Casino**: Have students take out a piece of scratch paper, making three columns labeled "Bet," "Answer" and "Total." Then, have them number from one to ten (or whatever number) down the side of the page. At the top, have them write "100 euros" (pesos, Marks, yen, etc.) Before you read or show question #1, have them place a bet—any amount, but if they go broke, they lose their participation points for the activity, or just say they can't

bet it all until the final question (This way, they don't bet too wildly). After they have all written an amount, the first question is read, and they write down their answer in the Answer space. Then, the teacher reveals the correct answer. If students answered correctly, they add the amount they bet to the original 100. If they answered incorrectly, they subtracted that amount. This seems to get even the unenthusiastic students excited about reviewing vocabulary. [CCSS: SL1, 3, 4, 6, L2; ACTFL 1.1, 1.2, 1.3; DOK 1]

- **Fortune Tellers** (sometimes called Cootie Catchers)
  Note: If at all possible, give the following directions in the TL:

  1 Start with a perfect square of paper. Fold it in half, side to side, forming a rectangle. Unfold.
  2 Fold it in half the other way. Unfold.
  3 Fold it in half diagonally, forming a triangle. Unfold.
  4 Fold in half diagonally the other way. Unfold. The paper will be very creased.
  5 Fold each corner point into the center. Crease well.
  6 Turn the paper over, so the folded parts are not visible. Again, fold each corner point into the center, and crease well.
  7 Flip the paper back over. Slide the thumb and forefinger of each hand into the four open square flaps, bringing your fingertips inward to meet each other . . . and voilà!

  Now that you have the paper made, you must decorate them. As a child, we used these to tell fortunes: We would say a number, and then open and shut the device, alternating opening it keeping the top and bottom flaps together, and shutting it, then opening it again, keeping the left and right sides together, counting as we did so. On the inner flaps were numbers or nouns or adjectives, and when a choice was made among those visible, the flap was lifted to reveal a "fortune." Use your imagination: write an adjective on the inner flap, with a profession below it: You will be a fast race car driver or a famous scientist. High school students get really creative with these. If you don't wish to use the future tense, have them "describe" objects: You have a green car or a mean dog. [CCSS: SL1, 3, 4, 6 and L1; ACTFL 1.1, 1.2, 1.3; DOK 2]

- **Pancho Camancho/Jean Valjean/Walter der Alter**: This game works for any vocabulary for which you have a picture card. Give each student a picture card, and have everyone stand or sit in a circle so everyone can see everyone else's card. Let's pretend the category is food. You start, by saying, "Pancho Camancho come (food that Student A is holding a picture of)." Student A would quickly reply that, no, Pancho Camancho is not eating (food A), he is eating (food that Student B is holding a picture of). Student B would continue by saying, no, Pancho Camancho is not eating Food B, but he is eating (another food whose picture is held by another student). That students would deny/accuse, etc. Of course, my French classes say, "Jean Valjean mange . . ." And German classes use Walter der Alter. This game works well for other things besides food. Action verbs are easy to teach using this: "Jean Valjean is skiing." "No, he's not skiing, he's swimming." "No . . ." And this is really helpful when you have to teach direct object pronouns. [CCSS: SL1, 3, 4, 6 and L1; ACTFL 1.1, 1.2, 1.3; DOK 2]

- **Jeopardy**: Just like the game show. I use a PowerPoint template, and we play using an inexpensive buzzer-lockout set (to avoid arguments as to who was first). Instead of questions, there is an answer and the student thinks of a question. For example, if the screen shows bathing suit, the student might say: What do you wear when swimming?

More difficult statements are worth more points. If they get it wrong, they lose that amount from their total, and another team gets a chance to answer. The team with the most points at the end wins. [CCSS: SL1, 3, 4, 6 and L1; ACTFL 1.1, 1.2, 1.3; DOK 2]

- **$25,000 Pyramid**: Give students a category, and they must describe to their partner things that belong to that category in order to get the partner to name the category, or give the students a list of items, having them read them aloud one by one as the partner guesses the category. A version of this, called Taboo, gives the student a list with the category and five words about it, none of which the student is allowed to use when describing the category. For example, the category is "dinner" and the student is unable to use the words meal, plate, lunch, evening, or time as clues to the category. This really encourages circumlocution. [CCSS: SL1, 3, 4, 6 and L1; ACTFL 1.1, 1.2, 1.3; DOK 2]

- **Flyswatter**: Write vocabulary words on a piece of butcher paper, or on a PowerPoint slide projected on the wall. Send two kids to the paper/screen/wall, giving each a flyswatter, plus a stern lecture on what will happen if they use the flyswatters on each other or the floor. Call out a word in English, and they compete to see who can locate and swat the word in the TL first. This also works great for irregular past participles (you call out the infinitive form), comparative words in Spanish, numbers, colors—anything that you could make flash cards for. To have more of the class participate, have more papers (and more flyswatters). The students don't even care about keeping points, they are having so much fun swatting (and learning). [CCSS: SL1, 3, 4, 6; ACTFL 1.1, 1.2, 1.3; DOK 1]

- **Human Swatter**: We use a sponge baseball bat, very soft. Students sit in a circle with pictures they have drawn of vocabulary words. One student sits in the middle, with the bat. To begin, a designated student in the circle would look at the pictures, and say another student's vocabulary word. The student in the center would try to strike the picture (or desk of the student with the picture) with the bat, before the student with the picture named says another person's vocabulary word. If he is able to do this, the student with that vocabulary word takes the bat, and the seat in the center. It is against the rules to swat humans, but it sometimes happens by accident; that's why the soft bat is important. [CCSS: SL1, 3, 4, 6 and L1; ACTFL 1.1, 1.2, 1.3; DOK 1]

- **Darts**: Get a magnetic dart board at the dollar store or online, or if your classroom board is magnetic, you can just buy magnetic darts, and draw or project the dart board, and organize students in teams. Have a list of questions on the unit; teams that answer correctly can throw a dart and get the number of points depending on where the dart lands. If you draw your own dart board, you can place categories on the sections and have teams throw a dart to get a question in that category, and a point for a correct answer to the question. [CCSS: SL 1, 3, 4, 6 and L1; ACTFL 1.1, 1.2, 1.3; DOK 1]

- **Angel and Devil**: If the vocabulary lends itself to opposites (fat/thin, tall/short, black/white) have two students volunteer to dress up: a halo or horns, with glitter pipe cleaner or a pitchfork (shop the after-Halloween sales), and wander the room, taking turns selecting a classmate to speak. If tapped by the angel, the word must be something good (intelligent); the one tapped by the devil must say the opposite. A variation would be to have a male/female student use the glitter "wands" and students would, if tapped by the male, say the masculine form (uncle) and if tapped by the girl, say the feminine (aunt); this would work for irregular adjectives, too. [CCSS: SL 1, 3, 4, 6, L1; ACTFL 1.1, 1.2, 1.3; DOK 1]

- **Battleship** (Acorazado/Bataille Navale/Schiffenversenken): Like the game, you start with a grid of squares. Students should have two grids: one for their own ships, and one for locating their partner's ships. Ten by ten would work well for numbers review, 15 by 15, or 20 by 20 work better for other subjects. Students draw in ships that cover two, three, four, or five spaces, horizontally or vertically (not diagonally). They should have four or five ships, if you are doing the 20 by 20 size. If you are doing topics other than just numbers, fill in the grids with vocabulary in categories, or don't fill in the grids: instead, write numbers across the top and letters down the side (students would ask for space A-2, for example), or nouns at the top and adjectives down the side (students would have to make the adjective agree correctly to score a "hit"), or write verbs across the top, and subjects down the side (students would have to conjugate the verb correctly to score a "hit"). Student A would begin by requesting a square in the grid, and Student B would answer "Hit!" or "Miss!" Then it would be Student B's turn. If a student incorrectly answered a grid square, and that square involved a ship, that ship would then be unsinkable. In order to sink a ship, all two, three, four, or five questions would have to be answered correctly. The first student in each pair to sink all his or her partner's ships would win, or the student sinking the most of his or her partner's ships would win. [CCSS: SL 1, 3, 4, 6, L1 and L2; ACTFL 1.1, 1.2, 1.3; DOK 2]

- **Jenga**: At the dollar store I bought a small wooden set of Jenga-style blocks, and numbered each block. Students play a regular Jenga game, but before they may remove one of the blocks, they must answer a question. Put questions on one numbered sheet and answers on another, and pass the papers in a circle so everyone has a turn. With the blocks numbered, you can use the Jenga blocks for multiple units. [CCSS: SL 1, 3, 4, 6, L2; ACTFL 1.1, 1.2, 1.3; DOK 1]

- **Word Blocks**: (I use Duplo blocks as they are larger, but Legos work, too). To help students form sentences, print labels and stick them to the blocks, coordinating block color to part of speech. Then have students put them together. You can specify the color pattern to follow, see who can make the longest sentence, etc. You can write on the blocks with a Sharpie marker, but labels are easier as you can stick new ones on to reuse the blocks. [CCSS: SL 1, 3, 4, 6; ACTFL 1.1, 1.2, 1.3; DOK 1]

- **Scavenger Hunt**: Compete to see who can gather information the fastest. Make sure the list includes not only information to be found in the text, but things they may see posted in the classroom, look up in a dictionary, ask you or a specified class mate (i.e., birthday, father's name, shoe size). Can be done outdoors, on a nice day, or inside a TL magazine (find a picture of a red-haired girl, a boy in a blue sweater, etc.) if there's bad weather. [CCSS: SL 1, 3, 4, 6; ACTFL 1.1, 1.2, 1.3; DOK 1]

- **Dice Game**: Divide the students into pairs and give each pair some dice. The dice must have words taped over the numbers, or (this is easier) there is a list of numbered words on the board or screen. For example, if the student throws two dice, getting a three and a two, they must make a sentence using word #2 and word #3, and dictate it to their partner, who writes it down. They take turns doing this until they have written 10 to 12 sentences, which they hand in as an assessment for the teacher to look at and grade. Note: putting the dice in small paper cups, and having students throw them into shoe box lids saves a lot of chasing after dropped/wayward dice. [CCSS: SL 1, 3, 4, 6, L2; ACTFL 1.1, 1.2, 1.3; DOK 1]

- **Concentration**: Play this just like the old TV game. Approximately 20 to 30 numbered cards arranged in a square are chosen in pairs by designated students. If what is written on the back of the cards is the same, a match has been made, and the cards are removed, revealing part of a phrase written behind the playing surface (or a blank if that is a space between words in the phrase). If what is written on the back is different, the cards are turned face down, and a different student takes a turn. The student or team who correctly guesses the phrase written behind the cards first is the winner. As a vocabulary review, the numbered cards would, of course, have vocabulary words written on the back. Note: this may be done using technology; there are quite a few free Concentration templates available online. [CCSS: SL 1, 3, 4, 6 and L1; ACTFL 1.1, 1.2, 1.3; DOK 1]

- **You Bet Your Life**: This is played like the Groucho Marx show. Pick a "secret word" from the chapter vocabulary, and write it on a card. Then have students do a speaking activity, using the vocabulary list at the end of the chapter. The first to use the "secret word" wins. [CCSS: SL 1, 3, 4, 6 and L1; ACTFL 1.1, 1.2, 1.3; DOK 1]

- **Basketball**: Divide the class into teams, and have each use scrap paper to make a ball. Put the trash bin or recycling bin in the center and ask a question. Teams answering it correctly get one point, and an extra point if they can throw the paper ball into the "basket." [CCSS: SL 1, 3, 4, 6, L1; ACTFL 1.1, 1.2, 1.3; DOK 1]

- **Snowball Fight**: Give each student a small square paper, and a partner. Give each group of partners a vocabulary word: one will write the word on the paper, and the other its definition, and then both wad them up into two "snowballs," and each will go to an opposite side of a line (tape, yarn, etc.) and when the teacher says "Go," begin to throw the snowballs. The winning team will have the least number of snowballs on their side when the teacher says "Stop!" Then, every student will take one ball, unfold it and find a new partner, matching vocab word with definition, for the next activity. [CCSS: SL 1, 3, 4, 6, L2; ACTFL 1.1, 1.2, 1.3; DOK 1]

- **Picture Grid**: Give students a paper with ten squares. As homework, they must pick ten vocabulary words and, for each, draw a picture. On the back of each picture, they must write the word. The next day, they cut these pictures apart, and arrange them on the desk. Their partner will then attempt to guess what vocabulary word the picture represents. If they are able to correctly guess and spell the word correctly, they keep it. When one person's pictures are done, they trade roles. The one with the most pictures at the end wins. [CCSS: SL 1, 3, 4, 6, L1; ACTFL 1.1, 1.2, 1.3, 2.2; DOK 1]

  Afterward, reuse the pictures—have each student draw two, and create a sentence using them, and continue until they have written five sentences for you to look at as an assessment. [CCSS: add L2 to the above; ACTFL stays same]

Finally, let me say that some of these games take a lot of time to prepare the first time you do them. Either grin and bear it, telling yourself you'll have these for many years to come, or do the following: assign the students to make games, as a graded project. They are just as creative as you are, and will undoubtedly come up with games you and I would never have thought of, and which will be valued additions to your repertoire. Many of them will undoubtedly involve students kinetically, which at least half of the above do not do. Let your students come to your rescue. The more they do themselves, the more they learn (remember Glasser's and Marzano's findings). You can always recycle their favorite games for other chapters by updating the questions.

Using Whiteboards

Whiteboards can be purchased anywhere they carry school supplies, but many teachers take a piece of poster board or cardstock and slip it into a page protector for a very inexpensive, much thinner and portable version. Another way to get a set is to go to a building supply store or lumberyard and purchase a sheet of shower board: pressed fiberboard with a white, slippery coating on one side, usually used for bathroom walls. Have them cut the sheet for you into 20 to 24 (or more) pieces. If you tell them it is for your classroom, they may give you a break on the fee for cutting. The edges are not sharp at all.

Some people store theirs on the rack under students' desks. Others punch holes in them and run a string through at least one hole, for hanging on the wall, or through two, for hanging around students' necks. I keep mine on an old overhead projector cart, along with the markers and erasers, which is another topic. Some teachers purchase dry erase markers (or require the students to do so). In my room, we just use the darker-colored crayons. To wipe off the marks, many people use a bag of the unmatched socks they have collected over the years. Those work well, but lacking enough of those, I just cut up old flannel sheets and shirts. Either way, it is quite easy to launder the whole bag occasionally. Crayon just melts right off the fabric and disappears. It takes a bit more effort to erase, but my students have plenty of energy that needs to be used up. I also paint numbers on the back of my whiteboards, for games we play, which are described in the next few paragraphs.

What are whiteboards for? Anything that can be done on paper may be done on a whiteboard, and somehow it feels more "fun" to do it. Here are some ways I use mine:

> CCSS: SL1, 3, 4, 5, 6, L1, L2
> ACTFL: 1.1, 1.2, 1.3
> DOK 1, 2

- Play Draw What I Say, with body parts, clothing, and other vocabulary.
- Have students draw their favorite meal and then hand the boards from person to person, having them "read" the board aloud.
- Have students draw a family member, listing some personality characteristics. Pass these around, having students compare this person to their own family. I usually make them write these comparisons on a separate sheet of paper, numbering each according to the number on the back of the whiteboard they are looking at.
- Ask students to draw something that represents them on the board. Have them share this with a partner. Collect the boards and post them on the chalk rail, writing a number above each. Have students try to guess whose drawing each one is. (This is good at the beginning of the year, to get to know each other.)
- My students love to play Family Feud with whiteboards. I give them a category such as "Dairy Products" and 17 seconds to write (or any number that is not a multiple of five). Then, I call a number, and the student whose whiteboard has that number on it shares his or her answer. Anyone whose written response matches that answer gets a point (or a point for their team).
- Ask students to draw three items in a category: hobbies, clothing, weather, sports, food, etc. Then tell each student to take a card; each has two question words on it. Half the students stand up, and move about the room, asking questions of the seated students, using those question words. The seated students must respond. After a few minutes, have them hand their card to a seated student, and return to their seats; repeat the activity.
- Add-ons: Have students all draw the same body part and label it, or (more variety) write the same part of a sentence (i.e., a noun), or part of a meal, or one item in a room, then pass the board to the next student, who names/reads the first item and then adds another item.

Continue until several students have contributed, and then pass the boards around until each student gets his or her original board back. You can even write poems this way.

- One student will quickly sketch a table with food on it/a family member/a room in a house/a picnic with several different sports. Then, the student describes his drawing to his partner. When they are done, they compare drawings.
- Verb drills: Call out a subject pronoun, verb, and tense. See who can get the correct answer fastest—have them hold up their boards. After a certain amount of time, hold up your board, so they can check their answer.
- Start with one whiteboard per row of students, but everyone has a crayon or marker. Call out a verb and a tense. The first person writes the first person form (je/yo/ich), and passes it to the next person, who writes the second person form (tu/du), and passes it, continuing until all six forms are written. The first row that gets the board back up front for the teacher to check, and who has all the forms written correctly, wins.
- After assigning a translation, done individually, put students into groups, assigning each a sentence or two, and giving each group a marker board for each sentence they are assigned. They must share their translations, and agree on what to write on the whiteboard. When it is done, they put it on the chalk rail for the class to compare with their own translations.

Flashcard Activities Galore

Teacher-Driven

- **Pick-Up**: Teacher tells a story or reads individual sentences and the students pick up the corresponding vocabulary word.
- **Categories**: Teacher gives a category and students point to or pick up all the words or phrases that match that category.
- **Mindreading**: Teacher holds a set of flashcards, and students have to guess which on is on top of the pile.
- **Award Winner**: Teacher writes random numbers (including negative numbers) on the board and covers each with a flashcard. Students (alone or for a team score) take turns naming the items on the cards, and if correct, remove the card and those are the points they get.

> CCSS: SL1, 3, 4, 6, L1
> ACTFL: 1.1, 1.2, 1.3
> DOK 1, 2

- **Flyswatter** (Tapette/Matamosca): Place flashcards on the board or wall, and give students a flyswatter. When the teacher names (or gives a hint or riddle) about a term on a card, the first one to slap the card with the flyswatter gets a point.
- **Round the World**: Choose a student to start; she/he stands behind or beside another student. Teacher holds up a flashcard. The first one to say the word or phrase stands behind the next student, moving in a circle. If the sitter is the first one to speak correctly, the standing student sits in the winner's seat. This continues until one student makes it completely around the room.
- **Ticket In** (or Ticket Out): Teacher stands by the door, holding up flashcards for each student. To enter, or to leave, the student must correctly name the flashcard.
- **Intelligence**: All students stand. Teacher shows a flashcard and names it. Students repeat the word or phrase . . . except sometimes the teacher says the wrong word/phrase. In that case, students should remain silent. Any student who speaks is "out" and must sit down.

Individual

- **Pick Three**: Students randomly pick three cards and write a sentence using all three of those words or phrases.
- **Speak Three**: Students randomly pick three cards and tell a story using all three words or phrases or phrases.

Partner Games

> CCSS: SL1, 3, 4, 6, L1, L2
> ACTFL: 1.1, 1.2, 1.3
> DOK 2

> CCSS: SL1, 3, 4, 6, L1,
>   RL1, 4
> ACTFL: 1.1, 1.2, 1.3, 4.1,
>   possible 4.2
> DOK 1, 2

- **Tic-Tac-Toe** (FR Morpion-cartes/SP Tres en raya contar-jetas/GER Drei gewinnt): Each partner puts nine flashcards in Tic-Tac-Toe formation (a 3 x 3 grid). Students do Rock-Paper-Scissors to decide who goes first. First person chooses a card and has to say the TL word for it to win that space. If correct he/she puts an X, if not the other player tell what the answer is, and puts a new card down on that space. The first to win three in a row wins.

- **Beat the Clock** (Non-TL side up): One partner is the timer. The other partner has 1 minute to go through their stack of cards giving the TL word earning one point for each correct word. The timer must check the words or phrases. Switch. The timer becomes the player, and the player becomes the timer.

- **Partner Race Complete** (Non-TL side up): One partner is the timer. The other partner has to go through their stack of cards giving the TL word for each. If he/she misses the card goes to the bottom of the pile and has to start again. The person with the shortest time wins. The timer must check the words or phrases. Switch. The timer becomes the player, and the player becomes the timer.

- **War**: Partners hold their own cards in their hands with the TL side up. At the same time, partners flip over their cards so that the non-TL side is facing upon the desk. Students race to call out the other person's vocab word in TL first. Winner gets a point. If the same vocab word appears for both partners, another word is thrown down and students race again to see who can say that word in TL first. Winner gets two points.

- **Partner Bingo**: Partners put a certain number of vocab words or phrases down on their desks with the non-TL facing up. Teacher calls out the words or phrases like bingo. If a student has that word he turns it over to the TL side. Winner is the partner who has all his/her words or phrases called first. Note: throw in "verb," "noun," etc., or certain sounds within the words or phrases: "starts with ___, has a ___, ends in ___," etc.

- **Slap/Point**: Students lay out the same set of vocab words or phrases with the non-TL showing. The teacher says a word in TL. The first person to slap or point to the word gets a point. Descriptions can be used instead.

- **¡Ay Chihuahua! Oh La Vache!**: Each player chooses ten flashcards. Teacher runs off pictures of a Chihuahua/Cow so that each student has two. Make sure the pictures are not dark so they cannot be seen through the card or paper. Players tape each of the two pictures to two of his/her flashcards on the TL side and place the cards on a desk non-TL side up. The partner chooses a card to say in TL. The player then turns the card over to check the answer. If they get it right it is worth ten points. If they get it wrong, it is minus five points. If the card has a Chihuahua/Cow on it, the partner loses all his/her points.

- **Rock and Roll Vocabulary**: Each partner chooses 12 cards and places them in four rows of three. Number the cards from 1–12. Roll a die to see who goes first. The first player rolls either one or two dice. That person has to say the TL for the card that equals the number that shows on the die (dice). If correct, he/she gets to remove that card and put it in a win pile. If not, the other player gives the correct answer, and puts a new card with the same number down. The first person to win all 12 cards wins.

- **Flashing Flashcards**: Each person chooses ten flashcards to show their partner in English. They stand back to back. The teacher will count to three in TL. On three both partners turn and face each other. Whoever says the partner's word in first wins that card and puts it in a win pile. The player with the most points wins.
- **Mark It**: Students lay out the same set of vocab words or phrases with the English showing. The teacher says a word in TL. The first person to put a chip on the word gets a point. Descriptions can be used instead. Markers may be actual chips or plastic discs, pieces of cardboard, dried lima beans, etc.
- **King of the Hill** (non-TL side up): Each person will build a pyramid with flashcards as follows: Each partner will take turns back and forth saying his/her partner's cards following the numbered pattern below. If she/he gets one right, she/he gets to remove that card and add put it in their win pile. If she/he gets one wrong, the partner will put down a new card for the next turn. No one can go on until they win the previous card. Whoever answers number 15 first wins.

Figure 3.1 King of the Hill

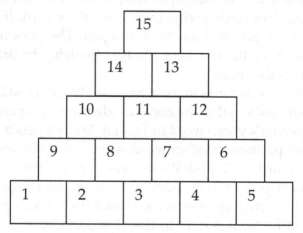

- **Dots**: Start with a sheet of dots, at least 15 x 15. Student and partner take turns showing a flashcard in non-TL to each other. If she/he says it correctly in TL, she/he gets to draw a line to connect two dots. The person with the most boxes when the time is done wins. May be done as a class on the board.
- **Word of the Week**: Do Rock-Paper-Scissors to see who is going to go first. The first person shows the second person a vocabulary word in Non-TL. If the other person says it correctly in TL, the person showing the card gets the letter. If he/she answers it incorrectly, he/she gets a letter. Play goes on until someone spells the word. The first person to spell the whole word loses. Take turns.
- **Hangman**: Each player draws the hanging gallows on paper, screen, or whiteboard. Do Rock-Paper-Scissors to see who goes first. The other player shows a card in Non-TL. If the first person says it correctly in English, nothing happens. If wrong the other player gets to add a body part. Each person is trying to hang their partner's man before he/she can hang

his/hers. Less ghoulish variations: draw a turtle instead of a hanged man, or a flower and erase a petal or leaf at a time.

- **Hopscotch**: Students lay out cards on the floor, and then take turns to call out the order in which their partner must jump onto each card.
- Dice: Students do Rock-Paper-Scissors to decide who goes first. Partner A rolls the die. Partner B shows as many cards as there are dots showing on the die to partner A, one at a time. A gets one point for each card said correctly in TL. His/her turn ends when he/she misses. Then they switch roles, adding up points as they continue. [CCSS: RL 1, 4 and L1; ACTFL 1.1, 1.2, 1.3; DOK 1]
- **Pictionary**: Group of three. Students do Rock-Paper-Scissors to decide who goes first, second, and third. First person looks at his/her top card. He/she draws a picture while the other two are trying to say the word in TL first. The person who does gets a point. Second person draws then the third person draws. Players not drawing are guessing. The person with the most points is the winner. [CCSS: RL1, L4; ACTFL: 1.3, 4.1 possible 4.2; DOK 1]
- **Sentence Six**: Each partner starts with six flashcards, face up on the desk. They stack the rest of the cards face down between them. On each turn, they draw a card and decide whether or not to exchange it or discard it. Each is trying to make a sentence that would use all six flashcards (with additional words or phrases supplied to supplement as needed). When one has a sentence, they call the teacher over to judge/award points. [CCSS: RL 1, 3, 4, 6; ACTFL 1.1, 1.2, 1.3; DOK 2]

Larger Group Flashcard Activities

- **Pass the Bomb**: Give groups of four to six each a set of flashcards and a "bomb" (an eraser or small object). When you call "Start," the student holding the "bomb" picks a card and names it. If she/he gets it right, the "bomb" is passed to the next student, who picks a card and names it. Students must get the word or phrase correct to pass the object. When the teacher calls "Stop" (after a minute or less whoever is holding the "bomb" gets a point. The object is to not get any points. When the teacher decides the game is over, students with the lowest score win.

CCSS: SL 1, 3, 4, 6
ACTFL 1.1, 1.2, 1.3
DOK 12

- **Scavenger Hunt**: Place flashcards all around the room: on walls, hidden, stuck under desks or chairs, etc. Give each student a list of TL words and have them find the ones on the list.
- **Scavenger Hunt II**: To introduce new vocabulary, hide/place flashcards with a picture and the TL word—give the same list in English to all, and have them find the translation.
- **Board Games**: Teacher provides a board (I use a Jeu de l'oie or an escargot; easy to find online), a set of markers (one for each player), and a die. Players roll the die to see who goes first. First person takes a card, says the word correctly in the TL and moves the number of dots that were on the die. If the player misses, he/she stays on the same space.
- **Big Memory**: Give each group a bag of flashcards. The first student takes a card from the bag and names it in the TL, passing the bag if correct; if wrong, she/he pulls another card until s/he gets one correct. The second student pulls a card, naming the first person's card and then the new card, and so on, until all the cards are gone. There can be duplicates in the bag for larger groups.

- **Claque-Claque** (or Pega-Pega): Teams of three have two sets of flashcards on a desk, picture side up. Teacher calls out a word or clue, and all three try to slap the card (but only two can). Successful students keep the card to count as a point. Note: students only can use one hand, and must not hover over the desk. Any student arguing will not get a card. Don't call the last one or two cards as it gets too crazy/wild. For a final "sudden death" round, use only one deck.
- **Hot or Cold**: While one student is in the hall, the other students choose a card to hide in the room, and then invite him/her back in. The class has to chant the word or phrase, focusing on pronunciation. Students chant louder when the student gets closer to the flashcard, and quieter if s/he gets farther away, until the card is located.
- **Memory**: Students lay out a number of cards on a desk, and then all but one close their eyes. The one left removes a card, and then instructs them to open their eyes. The student who correctly identifies the missing one keeps that card, replacing it with another and is the one who removes a card in the next round. [CCSS: RL 1, 2, 3; ACTFL 1.1, 1.2, 1.3; DOK 1]
- **Human Sentences**: Students hold up flashcards and stand in order to make a logical "human sentences." [CCSS: RL 1, 2 and L1, 2, 3; ACTFL 1.1, 1.3; DOK 2]
- **Heads Down, Thumbs Up**: Six students stand at the front of the class, each with a different flashcard. The rest of the students put their heads down and their thumbs up. The six flashcard students go around the class and each touches the thumb of one student, returning to the front. The students whose thumb was touched guess who touched them, by saying the flashcard that student is holding. [CCSS: RL 1, 2, 3; ACTFL 1.1, 1.2, 1.3; DOK 1]

Pronunciation Skills

Too often we leave students to figure out the pronunciation rules of a language for themselves. I like to incorporate a short unit at the first-year level, starting on day one, when students choose names. On that day, I teach that the letter "a" sounds like "ah" and "i" sounds like "ee." (The "i" rule would not be true for German, of course; perhaps German teachers would teach that a "w" sounds like a "v" and a "v" sounds like an "f.") We then read through the lists of names, pronouncing them, and notice that there are no exceptions to this rule. On day two, as the students enter, their first activity is to read the list of words on the board. These are words we use in English but which are from the TL (in my case, French) and which maintain the pronunciation rule taught the day before:

       garage   visa   Adidas   chalet   fiancé

Spanish teachers might use:

      patio   adios   taco   piñata   amigo

We would then try practicing some other words that have "a"s and "i"s in them, but which are not used in English.

Every day I introduce two or three more sounds, and we practice pronouncing unfamiliar words with those sounds in them, until the students know the pronunciation rules. I tell the students that they must be able to pronounce unfamiliar words if they want to ask about them: for example, ordering in a restaurant, asking for directions when lost, asking for a ticket to the movies at a multiplex.

Then, the next few days, I set up short classroom simulations where they need to do just that. Of course I, as the French person, don't understand them until they can correctly pronounce the word they need. [CCSS: SL 1, 3, 4, 6; ACTFL 1.1, 1.2, 1.3; DOK 1]

To forestall complaints that the foreign language is "funny" or "stupid," I like to share the essays by Richard Lederer (easy to find on the Internet) called "English is a Crazy Language I" and "English is a Crazy Language II," as well as my own experiences teaching English in France, as a foreign language.

- Give your students a copy of the Pledge of Allegiance in the TL (see Figure 3.2), but take out all the vowels. Say the Pledge for them, having them fill in the vowels. It is fun to see their faces light up as they begin to recognize what it is. When they are done, have them say it with you. Begin class with it at least once a week. Have them memorize it for extra credit. Follow this up with any poems, or other short sayings. Some private schools have students learn the Lord's Prayer. All can be found on the Internet. [CCSS: SL 4, L1; ACTFL 1.1, 1.2, 1.3, 2.2, 3.1 or 2, 4.1, 5.1; DOK 1]

Figure 3.2 The Pledge of Allegiance

En Español:
"Yo prometo la lealtad a la bandera de los Estados Unidos de América, y a la Republica que representa, una Nación bajo Dios, indivisible, con libertad y justicia para todos."

Auf Deutsch:
"Ich gelobe Treue auf die Fahne der Vereinigten Staaten von Amerika, auf die Republik, die eine Nation unter Gott ist, vereinigt durch Freiheit und Gerechtigkeit für alle."

En français:
"Je prête serment au drapeau des États-Unis d´Amérique et à la République qu'il représente, une nation sous Dieu, indivisible, avec de la liberté et de la justice pour tous."

In Latin:
"Fidem meam obligo vexillo Civitatium Americae Foederatarum et Rei Publicae, pro qua stat, uni nationi, Deo ducente, non dividendae, cum libertate justitiaque omnibus."

- Teach pronunciations through songs. Find a song and play it for them. Then, teach the words little by little. The ideal song is one that starts slow, and then gets fast. Students will be so proud of themselves when they learn to sing it. Then, and only then, show them the words in written form. They will immediately notice that some words are not spelled like they thought they would be, and will internalize some valuable pronunciation rules. See Chapter 2 under Musical intelligence, also.

Dictionary Skills

When I was in middle school, we would all get a dictionary, and the teacher would call out a word, and we would compete to see who could find it fastest, holding the book up in the air, open to be checked. With online dictionaries, teachers need to use different ways to practice.

- I go over standard abbreviations from the dictionary, for example, vt: transitive verb—I tell them just to know that v stands for verb. We also practice the abbreviations n., m. and masc., f. and fem., adj., pl., pret., and any others we will soon need. Then we look up some words like "fly" (an action, an insect, or part of a pair of jeans, among its uses) or "fork," which can be something you use to pitch hay or eat with (nouns), or an action people do, or roads do (verbs). We look up words like "gun," whose listed translations will range from a cannon to a handgun, and learn how to double-check all words before we use them by not just looking in the English-to-French portion, but checking the one we decide to use in the French-to-English portion. [CCSS: RL 1, 3, 4, 6 and L1; ACTFL 1.1, 1.2, 1.3; DOK 1]

    The activity in Figure 3.3 teaches students to look for synonyms. This worksheet is usually followed by a writing assignment such as to tell me what they "got" for Christmas, or to list items they will "get" for their family. [CCSS: RL 1, 3, 4, 6 L2; ACTFL 1.1, 1.2, 1.3; DOK 2]

Figure 3.3 Dictionary Work

Handout 4: Dictionary Work

Translate each of the following sentences by looking up NOT the word in quotation marks, but another word that you could substitute in place of it (a synonym) and which would have the same meaning.

1. I want to "get" a job.
2. I need to "get" up earlier.
3. I study to "get" ahead in school.
4. My classmates "get" together after school.
5. Tomorrow I "get" a new car.
6. My brother said he would "get" me for that prank.
7. My sister has the ability to "get" on my nerves.
8. You need to "get" out your homework now.
9. I "get" to go to a party tonight.
10. We "get" into trouble sometimes.
11. I'm going to "order" a pizza.
12. I put my books in alphabetical "order."
13. The teacher gave an "order" to line up.
14. He "found" a wallet on the sidewalk.

The next step is to learn how to take a verb and add –ing, and –ed to it.

- For written work, circle in pencil all incorrect word choices students have made using the dictionary, and mark with a "D." Give them a second chance to get the right word before counting it wrong. Students forced to do this will be more careful in their future dictionary use, as it causes them extra work. [CCSS: L1, 2, 3, 6; ACTFL: 1.2, 1.3; DOK 1]
- Have students make unusual nametags. [CCSS: RL 1, 3, 4, 6 L2; ACTFL 1.1, 1.2, 1.3; DOK 2] First, they write their name downward. Then, they use the dictionary section of the text (or a dictionary) to find an adjective that uses each letter, and add that. For example: Marc would write

Magnifique

Aimable

ARtistique

Charmant

Your students will learn a lot of new vocabulary that day.

- Have your students start a "Dictionary" portion of their notebook, where they write words they had to look up, the sentence the words were found in, and an original sentence using the word. Writing them a second time, in context, and taking a little class time to review them (we often do this after a test, while slower students are still finishing) seems to be helpful. Require a certain number of words each grading period. This will also help you see words that many of them need to learn or review, providing useful feedback for future classes.

Making Technology Use Less Passive

Active use of technology does *not* involve digitized worksheets, apps, and software that just practice basic skills, or using technology to read or watch content produced by others. Those might just as well be on paper, and also show little impact on student learning.

I have several ways to incorporate more activity into use of technology. One is to have my students rotate between stations: in some, they get direct instruction focused on content, in others do an online simulation, or connect with an outside expert, or craft a digital presentation to show what they had learned.

Another is based on the Substitution, Augmentation, Modification, and Redefinition (SAMR) method and which I have linked to my use of IPA (see Chapter 1) by using authentic digital/online resources. The idea is to not do Substitution tasks like those listed in the first paragraph of this section, but to do tasks that are not possible without technology. This takes time and thought.

Some examples of Augmentation: responding to an audio recording not made by the teacher, using spellcheck or word count or a thesaurus or online dictionary when writing, designing a brochure, invitation or other print task using a template.

Examples of Modification: listening to or viewing other's work and responding to it, creating a multimedia story using a site such as Flipbook, or creating a travel guide using Google Earth that incorporates student recordings or videos.

Redefinition might be done in one of the following examples: converting a speech to a song or rap (we have used Songify or Autorap), using Twitter (or writing a tweet on paper), writing a continuation of a collaborative story, using a concept mapping tool to trace the main events or ideas in something read or viewed, supporting an idea with interviews/opinions of others found online, or creating an interactive timeline (or bibliography) complete with digital stories and links.

4

Celebrations

Celebrating holidays, birthdays, and other events according to the culture of the language you teach is one of the most enjoyable activities in the foreign language classroom, and often one the students remember best, and comment on most. This chapter will give you some ideas and resources for organizing your own celebrations. I will list these in the order they occur during the school year.

Activities that Work Any Time

Twitter Search
One of my absolute favorite authentic-resource activities for any holiday is to do a Twitter search with a hashtag and the name of the holiday. You will find pictures, descriptions, and more, many in the TL. These can be copied and pasted and used for reading and up-to-date info on how people in the TL countries celebrate the holidays. There are always lots of postings.

CCSS: RL 1, 7
ACTFL: 1.1, 2.1, 2.2
DOK 1

Bingo
Give the students an empty Bingo grid, having them fill in vocabulary typical for that holiday or paste pictures of typical holiday items in the grid for Picture Bingo, and play Bingo.

CCSS: SL1 and L2
ACTFL: 1.1, 1.2, 2.1 and 2.2
DOK 1

Vocabulary Wordoku, Word Search, or Crossword
Use vocabulary from the holiday. I have posted free wordokus (sudokus using words rather than numbers) in Spanish, French, and German for every major holiday and back to school on teacherspayteachers.com. Search using my name. Warning:

CCSS: RL1, L2
ACTFL: 1.2, 2.1, 2.2
DOK 1

some clues are in English, because that forces students to think of what the words actually mean (and it makes the puzzle a bit harder). There are some great free sites to easily make a word search or crossword online.

<table>
<tr><td>

CCSS: W1, L2
ACTFL: 1.1, 1.3, 2.1, 2.2
DOK 1 if list, 2 if creative

</td><td>

Poetry

Have students write poems about the look or emotions of the holiday, or simply have them write a "listing poem" with the first letter of each line spelling out the name of the holiday, such as "Weihnachten."

</td></tr>
<tr><td>

CCSS: RL1
ACTFL: 1.1, 1.2, 2.1, 2.2
DOK 1

</td><td>

Dominoes

Domino-making apps are easy to find online; dominoes should be a mix of pictures and vocabulary in the TL. Print on card-stock, laminate, and play.

</td></tr>
<tr><td>

CCSS: RL4, W3, L2
ACTFL: 1.2
DOK 1

</td><td>

Mad-Libs

These are short stories (a ghost story, a description of how a holiday is celebrated, the history of a holiday tradition, and similar topics) in the TL with key words omitted, and with blanks inserted. Each blank has a description such as: "plural noun," "verb in the future tense," "a boy's name," and so on.

</td></tr>
</table>

Have the students choose words for each blank, and then provide the story. The results can be hilarious! It also practices awareness of parts of speech, verb endings, and so on. See New Year's for an example of this.

<table>
<tr><td>

CCSS: SL1, L2
ACTFL: 1.1, 1.2, 2.1, 2.2
DOK 1, 2

</td><td>

Venn Diagrams

Have students do Venn diagrams (two interlocking shapes, usually circles, but for Halloween it could be pumpkins, for Valentine's, hearts, etc.) Using these, they compare and contrast the American way of celebrating with the foreign way; customs

</td></tr>
</table>

both have in common go in the center area where the shapes overlap. This could be done in English or in the TL.

Video Skits

Have students record a skit of something that could take place on the holiday: a tradition, how to make a food, a song to sing, decorations, and so on. If shy, instead of a skit they could make a Powtoon or Animoto, but that's much less active. See Christmas for another skit idea.

Internet Sources

Sites for most major holidays with a variety of activities are a good starting place:

French: www.teteamodeler.com/dossier/fete.asp or http://fr.hellokids.com and Marie Ponterio's French pages: http://web.cortland.edu/flteach/civ/fetes/fetes.htm.
Spanish: www.guiainfantil.com or http://es.hellokids.com.
German: http://de.hellokids.com.
Youtube.com is also full of great holiday videos (songs, stories, etc.)

There are many great TL country sites designed for children. My students have decorated Halloween pumpkins on a Canadian site, looked at masks for Mardi Gras, and watched parades for various holidays, live. Online newscasts or Tweets (search with a hashtag and the name of the holiday) in the TL on the Internet will yield many items for advanced classes to read and discuss.

If you're not sure what holidays your target countries celebrate, or want to look up some of the more obscure ones, try this website: www.lonelyplanet.com/places and then do a search for holidays in the country you want to know about.

Note: if these contain reading/writing/listening, I'll list the CCSS and ACTFL standards but many are just forms of celebrations and don't correlate with those; of course, *all will be ACTFL 2.1 and 2.2 because they are holidays!*

September

National Hispanic Month

National Hispanic Month takes place in the United States is in September. Contact a local Hispanic group and see if they have someone who could come share the culture via a talk, slides, dance, food, etc.

September 5: Dia de los Ninos Heros

This Mexican celebration is a day to read/learn about child heroes, or talk about something brave each student did. Ask your media center specialist for help finding a book about a child hero.

A great site from Spain is www.wincalendar.com/es/Dia-de-los-Ninos-Heroes.

September 16: Mexican Independence Day

This holiday is a good excuse to learn a bit about the history of that country. This website tells the story of Independence in Spanish and has lovely illustrations of Padre Hidalgo, Juan Diego, etc.: www.mexicodesconocido.com.mx/la-independencia-de-mexico-1810–1821.html.

Les vendanges (dates Vary According to the Region)

In France, many high school and college kids pick up a little extra spending money right before school begins by working the grape harvest: www.reussirmavie.net/Faire-les-vendanges-ou-et-quand_a206.html.

Sip some grape juice and surf the Internet to festivals in Quebec: http://fetedesvendanges.com/en/, or Paris: www.fetedesvendangesdemontmartre.com/ and Belgium http://france3-regions.francetvinfo.fr/grand-est/vendanges-au-tour-belges-1103783.html. Other TL countries, including Spain and Italy—any place known for its wine—will have a harvest festival.

La Fête de la Gastronomie

A fairly recent French holiday, it is celebrated from Friday to Sunday toward the end of the month of September in many countries, with fine dining and the careful preparation of delicious food, enjoyed in groups. My classes plan and prepare a menu of traditional French foods; I arrange the classroom to look like a restaurant, and we learn a bit about each dish, and then taste them. www.economie.gouv.fr/fete-gastronomie/homepage?language=en-gb.

October

October 5: World Teacher Day

Why not assign a teaching activity, or an activity that has students remember good teachers they have learned from?

Columbus Day (US): First Monday in October

Make cupcakes and decorate them with toothpick masts with paper sails attached, and the names of Columbus' ships; eat them, sell them as a fundraiser, or give them to the other teachers for some positive PR for your subject area. Here are some Internet sites with information about Columbus' life (and there are good videos on YouTube):

> www.ibiblio.org/expo/1492.exhibit/Intro.html with information in English.
> www.educapeques.com/lectura-para-ninos/momentos-de-la-historia-el-descubrimiento-de-america.html in Spanish.

> CCSS: W2, L2
> ACTFL: 1.3, 2.1, 2.2
> DOK 1

Thanksgiving in Canada (Action de Grace): Second Monday in October

Canada has celebrated Thanksgiving since 43 years before the Pilgrims landed in Massachusetts. They celebrate it much like the USA: turkey, football, and family time. Have your students make a "verb turkey"—like a hand turkey you make in kindergarten, but give each student a different verb and have them write its forms on the finger part of the turkey, the infinitive on the body, and make the turkey do something in the drawing, to show the verb's meaning.

Figure 4.1 Verb Turkey

Make a Difference Day (US): Fourth Saturday in October

This sounds like an interesting possibility for community service-based projects. See Chapter 2 under Interpersonal Intelligence for some ideas on types of projects to do. A video about this day, in Spanish, can be found at: www.youtube.com/watch?v=t8pL4JHMlj4.

Oktoberfest: End of October (Germany)

This German festival typically features copious amounts of beer and Gemütlichkeit. Although the beverage won't be possible in a school situation, the songs and traditional dances and clothing are possible.

- Use two squares of cloth and two strips of ribbon to fashion the traditional Lederhosen suspenders or the dirndl bib, and use safety pins to dress the class.
- Learn traditional songs such as "Du, du liegst mir im Herzen" or the "Schnitzelbank" song.
- Dance the Chicken Dance. The kids will love it!
- Make your own pretzels.
- Have a "coaster flip" competition (with real German beer coasters if possible). Find rules at: https://coasterflip.com/ and videos on YouTube.

On a more serious note, this is also a good time to study Munich, via a movie, text, slides, or filmstrip.

There are sure to be several Oktoberfest sites on the Internet, also, but be very careful to preview them before turning your class loose as there may be inappropriate pictures (due to the connection with drinking for this holiday).

October 31: Halloween

- Give students a list of Halloween vocabulary, which they look up and include in a "scary" rebus story (a story made up of pictures connected by words—for example, instead of writing the word pumpkin, they draw one). Then groups take turns reading these to each other.

> CCSS: SL1, 4, L1, 2
> ACTFL 1.1, 1.3, 2.1, 2.2
> DOK 2, 3

- Have students create a witch's brew recipe from icky ingredients (spiders, etc.)
- Have lower-level students draw monster faces.
- Translate one of the children's poems, like "Three Little Pumpkins": "Three little pumpkins, sitting on a gate. The first one said, 'Oh, my, it's getting late' . . ." Check the local library or see an elementary school teacher for some ideas. If they have actions that go with them, it's even better. For Spanish, why not teach the students some sayings involving "Calabazas" (pumpkins), like: Calabaza, calabaza, cada uno a su casa or Que te pasa, calabaza?/Nada nada, limonada?
- Even my high school students also like doing the "Eensy Weensy Spider" in French—in Spanish, La Araña Pequeñita—not really Halloween, but spiders are scary! [CCSS RL1, W2, 3, L2; ACTFL 1.1, 1.3, 2.1 and 2.2; DOK 3]
- Have upper-level students write or read scary stories.
- For French teachers, Canada's http://jeu.info/halloween.htm website has Halloween games for French children (good for elementary level and up). Halloween is spreading to France. Reports of costume parties and town-organized dances are becoming more and more common, with pumpkins for sale in supermarkets and a few decorations for sale. A good article in English about this may be found on the Internet at: www.frenchtoday.com/blog/halloween-in-france-toussaint and a resource sheet maintained by a group of French teachers is at: https://docs.google.com/document/d/1zYlxA15d10Ni0L-SW9sJuGsNT0OAhUiF6iLmsx_l16Q/edit.

November

> CCSS: RL1, 7, W7, SL1, 4,
> L1, L2
> ACTFL: 1.3, 1.3, 2.1, 2.2
> DOK 2

November 1: All Saints Day (La Toussaint/Die Allerheiligen)

This is usually a day for family to visit graves to weed and decorate them. They also get together and share fond memories of the departed. A variation for the classroom could be to give each student the name of a famous dead person, research and then "reminisce" about that person, what they did, etc. (see Dia de los Muertos below for similar activities). An interesting variation is for every student, after research, to write one fairly easy question about that person, and have them prepare a tombstone with the person's name, birth and death dates, and the question. Turn off all the lights, play some somber music by a French/German composer, and have the students do a "Roam around the Room," answering the questions about each person as best they can, on a worksheet provided. Reward the student who gets the most answers correct. This is even more fun when done with the lights off, using flashlights (or the one on their cell phone).

November 2: Dia de los muertos (Mexico)

The Day of the Dead is one of the quintessential Mexican holidays, and many teachers enjoy celebrating this. Emphasize that in most countries, it is just a day to go to the cemetery and *limpiar las tumbas*. The Mexican celebration is not a universal Hispanic celebration.

- For this holiday, there are several traditional foods: sugar skulls and skeletons, made of a sugar paste put into molds and decorated (you could use chocolate or Rice Krispies in the same molds—not as authentic, but easier); and also "pan de muertos," or Dead Bread.
- Decorations usually include papier-maché skulls and skeletons, marigolds (the traditional flower), and a traditional altar (ofrenda). The ofrenda must contain the following:
  - picture of the famous person;
  - arch done in marigolds or tissue paper flowers on a chicken wire frame (the scent of marigolds is supposed to help the souls of the dead find their way back to the living);
  - sugar skulls (use recipe above, or substitute shaped Rice Krispy treats). These often have the names of friends written on them, and are traded like we do Valentines;
  - Pan de los Muertos (a sweet, anise-flavored bread—for a recipe, lesson plans and other activities, go to this Internet site: https://spanishplans.org/2011/10/26/dia-de-los-muertos/);
  - glass of water (for the dead to drink);
  - candles (to light the way back to the land of the living);
  - tablecloth;
  - table with shelves (a card table with boxes on it will work, when covered with the tablecloth);
  - fresh fruit such as apples or oranges;
  - nuts;
  - items associated with the deceased or that the deceased would have liked.
- Create your own cemetery. Have students select a famous dead Mexican or Spanish person, and create a self-standing "lapida" and mini-ofrenda to place around it. The tombstone can be made from a shoe box, with biographical information written or painted on the bottom,

Figure 4.2 Recipe for Sugar Skulls

Ingredients for Dough:
1 tablespoon powdered egg white (available at health food stores and supermarkets)
1/4 cup water
1 1/2 teaspoons vanilla extract
8 cups powdered sugar
2 cups cornstarch

Ingredients for Royal Icing:
1/2 teaspoon powdered egg white
3 tablespoons water
11/2 cups powdered sugar
3 drops red food coloring
2 drops cinnamon extract
3 drops blue food coloring
2 drops peppermint extract

Preparation:

To prepare the dough, mix powdered egg white and water together until foamy. Add vanilla extract and powdered sugar. With a spoon, and then by hand, mix until a firm dough forms. Dust a jelly roll pan with 1 cup cornstarch. Knead sugar dough in cornstarch for a few minutes until it becomes smooth and pliable. Roll the dough into a log shape. Wrap it in plastic and refrigerate it until chilled.

I also pack some small plastic knives for cutting it in class. Cut into pieces about the size of a small fist. Use more cornstarch to prevent sticking, if needed.

You can make a flat cookie-like version that looks like a skull, or mold around tennis ball sized Styrofoam balls, available at any crafts store. Scoop out eye and nose areas with a blunt knife or a toothpick. Skulls traditionally have lots of big teeth, so draw them on with a toothpick. These are generally dry in one day, but allow two to be sure.

To prepare the royal icing, beat powdered egg white and water together until foamy. Add powdered sugar and beat until smooth.

Divide mixture into two small bowls. Add red food coloring and cinnamon extract to one and blue food coloring and peppermint extract to the other. Mix to blend the colors in each bowl. Fill two pastry bags with icing mixtures. Decorate skulls with icing. Allow objects to dry. Weather conditions affect drying times. Objects may take anywhere from several hours to 48 hours to fully dry.

Makes about eight sugar skulls.

and a stone or something placed to help it stand upright. Have "DIP" (descanse en paz) on the top of each. Electric or battery-powered candles add a nice touch. Have a snack among the "graves," or have lunch there, like they do in Mexico, while students explain the items in the mini-ofrenda or talk about their famous dead person. [CCSS RL1, 7, W7, SL1, 4, L1 and L2; ACTFL 1.3, 1.3, 2.1 and 2.2; DOK 2]

- Make the ofrenda you would like to be made for yourself; invent a future for yourself, and place items on the ofrenda that would be fitting for that person. [CCSS SL1, 4, L1 and L2; ACTFL 1.3, 1.3, 2.1 and 2.2; DOK 2]

- Crafts to do could include making papier-maché flowered skulls, tin art, tissue paper flowers (marigolds), a clay censer (for incense). "Papel picado," or paper cutting, is also a traditional craft:

    – Using two to three sheets of tissue paper (some use the same color, but they may use up to three different colors), line up the edges so they are fairly even and then staple together two bottom corners which will eventually be cut off.

    – Do this separately for each piece of tissue paper used: Fold over the top edge about 1/2 to 3/4 of an inch. Place a long piece of yarn inside the fold. The yarn should stick out of both ends by at least 3–4 inches. Tape or staple the fold to the "backside" of the project (three pieces of tissue = three folds + three pieces of yarn).

    – Using straight pins or tape, fasten the tissue paper (back side down) to a piece of cardboard.

    – Have students draw the design they want on another sheet of paper for practice and cut it out. This way the student will know if there are any problems with "holes" or whatever before using the tissue. Change the design as needed. Then copy it onto the tissue paper.

    – Using an X-acto knife, or scissors, cut out the design. Remove from cardboard.

    – Tie pieces of yarn together and string up around the room.

    – An alternate way to cut out designs is to fold the tissue accordion-style three to six times (three to four is best) and cut out the design. There are videos on YouTube to help with this.

- Face painting is also a popular thing to do; skeleton faces are the most popular.
- Writing activities should include writing Calaveras (poems) that take a light-hearted view of death. Write "Calaveras en Verso" about a celebrity or teacher at school. Illustrate them and then display them in the classroom. At the end of the unit, wear black (as though going to a funeral), or have a costume party, with the kids as famous historical Mexicans. [CCSS: W2, 3, L2; ACTFL 1.3, 2.1 and 2.2; DOK 3]
- A great film short: www.pbs.org/video/film-school-shorts-program-dia-de-los-muertos-film-school-shorts/.
- An explanation in English: www.pbs.org/video/byyou-diversity-dia-de-los-muertos-celebration/.
- There are a number of great children's books (many bilingual) on this holiday that can be found online (amazon.com and other sites).

November 11: Remembrance Day/Armistice Day

Remembrance Day commemorates the armistice signed between the Allies for the cessation of hostilities on the Western Front during World War I, at 11:00 am—the "eleventh hour of the eleventh day of the eleventh month." Armistice Day is one of the most important military celebrations in France, since it was a major French victory and the French paid a heavy price in blood to achieve it. In the US and Canada, we use poppies in remembrance, inspired by the bilingual (French/English) poem by the Canadian Major John MacRae ("In Flanders fields where poppies grow . . .") which is well worth reading in both languages.

In France the blue cornflower (Bleuet de France) is used symbolically rather than the poppy, in honor of the change from red to blue uniforms for the French troops during that war, so my classes make them, out of blue felt with a little yellow, white or some black beads in the center, and wear them, telling the holiday's story to others.

Figure 4.3 Bleuets

November 24: La Sainte Catherine

November 24 is, in France and Canada, the celebration of Sainte Catherine, the patron saint of unmarried ladies. On this day, single females over the age of 24 make huge, silly green and yellow hats, and wear them to advertise that they are "available." Some websites to check for more information on this unusual holiday are (in French): www.linternaute.com/actualite/societe/1179562-sainte-catherine-2017-a-quelle-date-fete-t-on-cette-tradition/ or in English: https://vanessafrance.wordpress.com/2013/11/25/saint-catherines-day-customs/.

The traditional food is taffy, or "tire," recipe at: www.food.com/recipe/tire-de-la-ste-catherine-429302

December

December 6: St. Nicolas' day (Germany, France)

- Have students put one of their shoes outside the room and ask one of the staff to put some candy in each shoe. While they are doing this, introduce Christmas carols as an activity, or decorate the classroom.
- A French tradition my students like is to pour a thin layer of lentils or wheat in a dish, and water them. In a few days, they sprout. Traditionally, these young green plants are part of the holiday table, symbolizing the coming of life in the middle of the cold winter. My students get to water and watch them grow, and we even have a contest to see which class's planting gets the tallest.
- My students are also fascinated with St. Nicolas' alter ego/companion, Krampus in Germany, https://news.nationalgeographic.com/news/2013/12/131217-krampus-christmas-santa-

devil/), who gives bad children sticks to beat them with. The French one, Pere Fouettard, is not as demonic but still a bit scary: www.youtube.com/watch?v=rQP7PsFq_LA St. Nicolas et Pere Fouettard dans les maternelles 2011 (you can also hear the kids sing a traditional song to St. Nicolas).

<table>
<tr><td>CCSS: RL1, 7, W7, SL1, 4, L1, L2
ACTFL: 1.3, 1.3, 2.1, 2.2
DOK 3</td></tr>
</table>

December 25: Christmas

In the various languages: www.geocities.com/Paris/LeftBank/3852/christmas.html.

Why not have students write a skit based on the 12 Days of Christmas song? You could be very traditional, or do school-based items (12 thumbtacks, 11 rubber bands, 10 hall passes, 9 detentions, and so on). This could be done live, or as a video, a PowerPoint, a story board, or some other visual presentation. These can really be fun.

Noel (Francophone countries)

The traditional dessert is a cake called a Bûche de Noel. There are many good recipes for this online, including some calling it a Yule log. Some interesting sites for more on this holiday:

www.culture.gouv.fr/culture/noel/angl/noel.htm Noël in France and Canada.

https://frenchmoments.eu/christmas-in-provence-noel-en-provence/ Noël en Provence (photos included).

https://noel.tourisme-alsace.com/en Alsace calls itself the Capital of Christmas.

And there are some great videos on YouTube and TF1 as well as Marie Ponterio's site.

<table>
<tr><td>CCSS: SL1, L1
ACTFL: 1.1, 1.2, 1.3, 2.1
DOK 2</td></tr>
</table>

Navidad

- Make luminaria. The luminaria is the last in a chain of fires that light the way during posadas. I have read that originally tree branches were laid out, stacked like a little fence, into a triangle. In the center was a fire. These were placed along the path that Mary and Joseph would follow (the Posadas).
- Re-enact the Posadas. Group the students into "houses" and have them take turns visiting each other's homes, practicing greetings, exchanging holiday wishes, etc.
- Make piñatas (I suggest assigning this as homework for extra credit, or to do as a club activity outside the classroom) and have the Posadas group carry them. Then break them!

On the Internet for Navidad:

A Navidad lesson with other good links: www.ctspanish.com/christmas/christmas.htm.

Mexican Christmas Unit: http://teachers.net/lessons/posts/246.html.

Traditional foods galore: www.ibtimes.com/what-nochebuena-all-about-hispanic-christmas-eve-tradition-1763858.

The unusual Night of the Radishes (Rabanos) celebration in Oaxaca: www.donquijote.org/travel/guides/oaxaca/night-radishes.asp.

Christmas song lyrics: www.guiainfantil.com/servicios/musica/villan/indice.htm.

And don't forget YouTube as a wonderful resource.

Weihnachten (German)

- Have each student read a German story or fairy tale and rewrite it into a 1990s version, using a minimum of 15 German words and at least two illustrations in the story.
- Alternate reading, and singing carols like "O Tannenbaum" and "Stille Nacht" or "Glöckchen Kling" (Jingle Bells).
- Make lebkuchen (cookies) or gingerbread to enjoy.
- Make German paper stars: www.craftideas.info/html/german_star_instructions.html.

> CCSS: RL1, 7, W7, SL1, 4, L1, L2
> ACTFL: 1.3, 1.3, 2.1, 2.2
> DOK 2

Other Languages

- Japanese Christmas songs (links to video clips): http://muza-chan.net/japan/index.php/blog/japanese-christmas-songs.
- How Christmas is celebrated in Japan, South Korea, Thailand and Viet Nam: www.sbs.com.au/popasia/blog/2014/12/16/how-do-different-asian-countries-celebrate-christmas.
- Christmas in Africa: www.one.org/us/2012/12/17/how-africa-celebrates-christmas-2/.

January

January 1: New Year's Day

- Have students draw a symbol to represent their lives in this New Year. Some examples: an arrow for a change of direction, or a plus sign, a heart, etc. Some draw carrots (go on a diet, or eat better), or other interesting things. Give them about 5 minutes for this, and have them discuss and/or explain the symbols and why these were chosen. [CCSS: SL1, L1; ACTFL 1.1, 1.2, 1.3; DOK 3]
- Write resolutions. For my lower-level classes, we have fun doing this as a Mad Lib-type activity: I ask them for an adjective in their own gender, a number, an object, a family member, a place, something you own, etc. and then we plug those into "resolutions" such as these (written in the TL of course.)

  1 I am going to try to be more _____ (adjective).
  2 I want to lose _____ kilos.
  3 I am going to buy _____ (object) for my _____ (family member).
  4 I am going to visit _____ (place).
  5 I am going to paint my_____.

  For the class that knows the future tense, I replace "am going" with that tense. [CCSS: RL4, W3, L2; ACTFL 1.2; DOK 1]
- January is "enero" in Spanish. Have kids match definitions with words that end in "ero" . . . such as numero, mesero, sombrero, llavero, caballero, etc.

January 6: Three Kings Day (La fete des rois)

Figure 4.4 is a recipe for the northern-style "galette," or Kings Cake, of France, which is baked with a small "fève" (I use a bean wrapped in tin foil) in it. The person whose piece contains the fève is king or queen for the day, gets to wear a plastic crown, and students must ask him or her for permission to do things like go to the restroom, etc. I usually give the king or queen choices about what we do on that day, also (but choices between X or Y, not just a "what do you want to do").

Figure 4.4 Kings Cake

Ingredients:
2 1/4 cup flour
1 pinch salt
2/3 stick butter or oleo
1 1/2 teaspoon baking powder
1 cup sugar
2 eggs
1 tablespoon almond (or vanilla) extract

Preparation:
Mix all together until the consistency of thick paste or cookie dough. Form into a circular shape, about two fingers thick. Cut top in a diamond pattern and brush with egg, after inserting the fève.

Bake 350 degrees for 20 minutes, or until golden. Cool and serve.

Serves 20 (small) pieces.

In Mexico, on the night of January 5, children leave a sober, self-critical note assessing whether or not they have been good during the year, and listing the gifts they would like in case they were good enough. Here's a free lesson plan for this holiday: https://commonground international.com/spanish-teachers/tres-reyes-magos/.

And an Internet site with sample letters to the Reyes Magos: www.euroresidentes.com/ navidad/reyes-magos/carta-reyes-magos.htm.

Traditional foods on January 6 are rosca, a round cake encrusted with dried fruit (there is a small plastic figure of the infant Jesus inside, and whoever gets it must give a party on February 2, Candelaria), tamales made of cornmeal, and atole, a thick hot chocolate drink made with cornstarch.

This would be a wonderful reason for them to do a self-assessment of how they are doing in your class. [CCSS W2, L2; ACTFL 1.3; DOK 3]

January 21 (France)

Why not stage a re-enactment of Louis XVI's execution? One year, as an interdisciplinary project with the metal and wood shop classes, we researched, designed, and built a small guillotine. Now, on this day, I bring cheese sticks to school, along with decorating supplies (coconut, those small colored sprinkles used on cakes, etc.) Each student has a statement to read such as would have been said at the execution, and then decapitates (and eats) the cheese stick.

February

February 2: Candlemas (La Chandeleur in French/Candelaria in Spanish)

- On this day, crepes are the traditional food. Here is an explanation in English of both the significance of the ingredients and of the preparation of crepes: http://articles.chicago tribune.com/1992–02–27/entertainment/9201180888_1_shrove-pancake-race-crepe-pan.
- There is a poem said on this day (a tradition similar to Groundhog Day in the USA): "A la Chandeleur/L'hiver passe ou prend vigueur." People look out the window, and if the weather is good, spring is on its way; if it is bad, there are six more weeks of winter ahead.

Ya-Ya Matsuri (Japan): Held in Early February

Have students take turns yelling "Ya! Ya!" and looking fearsome, as is the custom. Make some fearsome masks, after studying typical Japanese Noh masks. www.historyofmasks.net/famous-masks/noh-mask/.

February 14: St. Valentine's Day (All Countries)

- Get a bag of those candy hearts with sayings on them ("Conversation Hearts"). Have each student take one, and translate what it says. (I usually tell students to translate the meaning, rather than just word-for-word. For example, "Honey Bun" should not be translated by the word for honey plus the word for bun.) Have them write the translation on a paper heart, and post those on the board, and make valentines. I let students take them home for their mother, and send the remainder of our valentines to a home for the elderly in Canada, where they are really appreciated. [CCSS W4, 7 and L2; ACTFL 1.3, 2.2 and 4.1; DOK 2]
- Another fun activity is the Venn diagram one, with a twist. I have students draw a name from each of two boxes: one has names of famous men, and the other, names of famous women. Using the TL, and a Venn diagram, students then list the characteristics of both, putting the ones they have in common in the center. On the back of the page, I have them write a short statement of whether this "couple" will be a good match, and why. [CCSS W1, 2, 4, 7 and L2; ACTFL 1.3, 2.2; DOK 2]
- Make Love Locks, like the fad spreading all over the world. I take cardstock in the form of a lock, have students go online to choose a poem or saying about love in the TL, and then we decorate the hall.

Figure 4.5 Love Locks

- For upper-level students, give pink hearts to each student, and have them write to "Tante/Tia (choose a name in the TL)" who gives advice to the lovelorn. Give prizes for the most creative problems. Then give each heart to a student in a different class to answer, with prizes for the most interesting answers. Staple both together for a high-interest bulletin board. Students will love reading these. [CCSS W1, 2, 4, 7 and L2; ACTFL 1.3, 2.2, 3.2; DOK 3]
- Give students a sheet of paper with the names of all the students in the class, triple-spaced. Have them write the nicest thing about that person—either a compliment, or a description of that person's best qualities. Cut these apart, recopying them to correct the grammar if needed, and give each person "their" envelope on February 14. [CCSS W 2, 4 and L2; ACTFL 1.1, 1.2, 1.3, 2.1; DOK 2]
- As students enter, they get a card with a name on it. They must walk around to find their "match": Beauty looks for the Beast, Donald Duck for Daisy, Bert for Ernie, Winnie the Pooh for Tigger, and so on. When they find their mate, both report to the teacher for the name of a real historical couple in the TL to research and report on (Abelard and Heloise, Don Quijote and Dulcinea, Diego Rivera and Frieda Kahlo, Pierre and Marie Curie, Paris and Helen of Troy, etc.) [CCSS SL 1, then W7; ACTFL 1.1, then 1.2 and 1.3, 2.1, 5.1; DOK 2]
- Have students describe themselves, likes and dislikes, favorite activities to do on a date, etc. Also have them choose an alias. Then have the class (or another class) read these, and match them up as potential dates. Post these matched sets, and watch the students eagerly read them. [CCSS W 2, 4 and L2; ACTFL 1.1, 1.2, 1.3, 2.1; DOK 2]
- I organize into pairs and have my advanced French students go to this website: poesie.webnet.fr and select a love poem. On February 14, they present these poems to each other, and vote on the best poems. The winners receive a chocolate heart.
- Listen to romantic music, like "Eres tu," and have students compete to see who can make up the most romantic lyrics. (or for laughs—The One Semester of Spanish Love Song: www.youtube.com/watch?v=ngRq82c8Baw—there's a French version of it, too).

Fasching/Carnaval (France, Germany, Mexico, and Spain)

This is a 1-week celebration that features costumes, parades, and merrymaking. There are some really good sites on the Internet to investigate masks, watch parades LIVE, and read about the history and traditions. A good site called Le Carnaval de Nice is: http://en. nicecarnaval.com/history-and-traditions (there is a version in French too).

The last day of Carnaval is Mardi Gras: a Tuesday, 40 days before Easter (usually late February).

- Make masks from paper plates. Give each student a paper plate, let them begin in class, but assign the finished masks as homework. New Orleans makes masks from window screening, with the sharp edges covered with duct tape. These are easy to see through, and really transform the face beneath. Give prizes for the funniest, most beautiful, most creative, and other categories.
- Have food: fried foods are traditional Mardi Gras foods. My classes make crepes, eat a few, and sell the rest at lunch time (we use the money earned to fix a big several-course French meal for a new September holiday). Eggs (hard boiled, and served like deviled eggs, or baked into a special bread) are also traditional.

- We watch a movie about Mardi Gras, and I give each student a doubloon or a string of Mardi Gras beads purchased from a mail order catalog.
- Have a parade through the school: use old shoe boxes as "floats" and have students decorate them. Have floats illustrate aspects of the target culture, or choose a theme. Wear masks for the parade.

March/April

March 2: Dr. Seuss' Birthday (US)

I either have my students spend some time reading little children's books in French that I have collected over the years, or take them down to one of the elementary schools to read to the children there.

March 21: The First Day of Spring

Celebrate by taking the class outdoors for a scavenger hunt. Each group should have a list, a paper bag, a dictionary, and a watch. Give them about half an hour to find as many items as possible from a very specific list of things like "three smooth stones," "a green leaf," and so on. Count out the items in French as you check them, and have a prize for the winners.

National Foreign Language Week (Usually the First Week in April)

- Label the room in the TL, and as much of everything else in the school as possible. We put a sign on every room, telling the teacher and the subject(s) taught, in French. Make posters about famous people from your language, and post them around the school. Write complimentary sayings on Post-It notes in your TL and put one on every locker.
- Talk to the cafeteria employees in advance, and arrange a menu of foreign food for one day that week (tacos, quiche, sauerkraut and sausages, egg rolls).
- Have high school students prepare a play, skits, video, or craft to present at the middle school or grade school (or on the televised announcements at their own school).
- Put a treat in each teacher's mailbox with a note, or have students prepare some ethnic food to leave in the teacher lunchroom.
- Try to schedule a movie, musical performance, or speaker for interested students some time during that week.

Easter (International)—Dates Vary

- On the Internet try this site: www.thelocal.fr/20170413/6-ways-the-french-celebrate-easter for French and www.dw.com/en/german-easter-traditions/a-1520904 for German activities and games using Easter vocabulary.
- Buy plastic eggs and have a treasure hunt through the school, with clues hidden in the eggs.
- Fill plastic eggs with vocabulary the students have been studying. After an egg hunt, have them write a story using all those words in the story. [CCSS: W2, 3, 4; ACTFL 1.1, 1.3; DOK 4]
- Fill plastic eggs with pictures representing vocabulary, and have students write rebus stories, trade them, and read them aloud to each other. When they come to a picture, they say the word it represents (good vocabulary review). [CCSS: W2, 3, 4; ACTFL 1.1, 1.3; DOK 4]

- Have students write what they are going to do over Easter vacation, put it back in an egg, and then draw one to read, and guess who wrote it. [CCSS: W2, 3, 4; ACTFL 1.1, 1.3; DOK 3]
- Have students write a command and put it in an egg. Have each person draw an egg, and do what it says to do. [CCSS: W2, 3, 4; ACTFL 1.1, 1.2, 1.3; DOK 2]
- Put a small object in each egg. Tell students it is not just an ordinary toothpick/paper-clip/ribbon (etc.) but that it has special powers. Have them tell what it is, what it does, and how they will use it (present progressive or future tense). Alternate idea to use past tense: tell students each object was used in a crime. Have them describe the crime orally, or write out the police report or newspaper article about the crime. [CCSS: W2, 3, 4; ACTFL 1.1, 1.3; DOK 4]
- Print an egg-shape on paper, and give each student one. Have them get in groups, assign them a last name, and let them decide who each egg will be, and decorate it appropriately (Papa might have a mustache and golf club, etc.) Below the picture should be a short biography: name, age, likes and dislikes, etc. Display each family on the board, each in their own paper "basket." [CCSS: W2, 3, 4; ACTFL 1.1, 1.3; DOK 2]
- Put a small object in each egg. Have students try to sell these objects to the class, convincing them that they really need that object. Have the class evaluate who does the best job. [CCSS: SL 1, 4, 6 and L1; ACTFL 1.1, 1.2, 1.3; DOK 3]

April 20: Earth Day (International)
- Plant something outdoors in the name of your foreign language club.
- Do an Internet or Twitter search for information on Earth Day in your TL.
- Read articles about pollution, or environmental concerns in countries that speak the TL. Write letters to the leaders of these countries about these concerns. [CCSS: RL1, 3, 7, W2, 3, 4; ACTFL: 1.1, 1.2, 1.3, 3.1, 4.1, 5.1; DOK 4]
- Make posters that say, "Save the Earth" and similar slogans in the TL, and decorate the school. [CCSS: W2, 4; ACTFL 1.1, 1.3 DOK 4]

CCSS: SL1, L2
ACTFL: 1.1, 1.2, 2.1, 2.2
DOK 1, 2

April 27–May 6: Golden Week (Japan)
This is actually three holidays rolled into one. First, the Japanese celebrate Green Day (try some of the Earth Day activities from above). Then comes Constitution Day. For this, study/read parts of the Constitution. Do a Venn diagram to compare it to ours. Look at the history of Japan, and the events that lead to the writing of its constitution.

The third holiday is Children's Day. If possible, invite grandparents to class. Have the children bring them tea, and have small gifts ready for the grandparents to give the children. Sing songs.

May

May 1: May Day/International Labor Day/Le premier mai (France)
- On this day, workers all over the world enjoy a day off, and parade through the streets. This would be a good day for a mini-lesson on careers.

- Make Cootie Catchers (see Chapter 3) and put careers on the innermost portion, adjectives on the first. When students pick a number, they will be told their "future": "You will be a tall architect" or "You are a thin boss."
- In France, it is traditional to offer a bouquet of *muguets* to those you love. Have students make a card for someone, with a drawing of lilies-of-the-valley on it.
- A maypole dance is also a tradition on this day, to welcome the spring.

May 10: Mothers' Day (Mexico)/Third Sunday in May for Other Countries

Make a card or a small gift for Mom. An ojo de dio, a paper flower, some Scherenschnitte, or something similar are easy to do.

Graduation/End of Year

- A final project could be a student yearbook: each student gets a page to put poetry, stories, or whatever about himself/herself. Seniors are required to write a "will." Also have a page for foreign language club activities and pictures, as well as teams and activities the students are in. Photocopy and staple these, and hand them out on the last day (or, publish online). Have them sign each other's books (in the TL, of course). [CCSS: RL2, 4, W2, 3 4, L2; ACTFL 1.1, 1.2, 1.3; DOK 3]
- Have student write about themselves (in future tense): 10 years from now, I will be . . . Or, stage a "class reunion" and have them pretend to be themselves, and talk about what they have been doing since high school. [CCSS: written W3, L2; spoken SL 1, 3, 4 and L1; ACTFL 1.2, 1.3, 5.2; DOK 3]
- Put up baby pictures, and have students guess who it is. The owner of the picture can provide three to five clues. [CCSS: RL1, W2, L2; ACTFL 1.1, 1.2, 1.3; DOK 2]
- Make a video or PowerPoint presentation, with the highlights of the year, and a short interview with each student (wishes for the class, or whatever they'd like immortalized). [CCSS: RL2, 4, W2, 3 4, L2 if oral interview SL 1, 3, 4 and L1; ACTFL 1.1, 1.2, 1.3; DOK 3]

Miscellaneous Celebrations

Quinceañeras

Here is a website with information on this fifteenth-birthday feast, usually celebrated in Mexico with a large party and other traditions: https://people.howstuffworks.com/culture-traditions/cultural-traditions/quinceanera.htm.

Saints' Days

Use a Catholic calendar, and have students choose a Saint's Day during the time they will be in your class. On that day, give them a card, have students compliment them, let them lead a game or choose an activity for the class, or make some small fuss over the student, just as they would do in countries where the TL is spoken. (Be careful, though, not to seem to promote religion.)

5

Getting Over the Rough Spots

Grammar is like poison: in small doses it can be beneficial,
but in large doses it can kill.

(paraphrased from a medical text read long ago)

We all have topics that we must teach, but with which students struggle. There's no coincidence that the majority of these situations involve grammar. In this chapter, I will offer some active learning ways that I and several colleagues have tried that have worked for us, and which could add some variety to the way you cover the same topics.

Verb Conjugation Activities, in General

- Inside-Outside Circle: Place students in two circles, one facing outward, and one facing inward, basically pairing students. Give the inner circle cards with subject pronouns on them, and give outer circle students cards with verbs written on them. Students look at each other's cards and say the correct form of the verb in the tense you are working on. You may wish to designate which students should say the verb, or have them work together to do this. Then, either have the students rotate to a new partner, or have them pass the cards to the left (or the right) to have a new situation to deal with. [CCSS: SL1, 4; ACTFL 1.1, DOK 1]
- Play Beanbag: Take a soft beanbag or similar object (my colleague Cynthia Jones uses a beach ball.) The person who begins says first person singular form of a verb in a given tense, and tosses the bag/ball gently to another student, who gives the next form (second person singular). When all forms of that verb have been correctly stated, you may start over, and speed up the throwing, or change to a different verb. Since students don't know who will get picked next, they are all on task, thinking of the next form. [CCSS: SL1, 4; ACTFL 1.1; DOK 1]

- Use two dice, preferably different colors, and a stack of three-by-five cards with verbs written on them. A student draws a verb, and throws the dice. One die will decide which subject pronoun they use (post a list somewhere where all can see: a 1 means I/je/yo/ich, and so on) and the other is the tense (1 for present, 2 for command, 3 for preterite/passé). If the student writes the verb correctly, he or she or the team gets a point. [CCSS: W2, 4; ACTFL 1.1; DOK 1]

- Put students in rows of five of six. Give the first student a paper. Say a verb. The first student writes the je/yo/ich form, passes it to the next who writes the tu/du form, and so on. It's a race. Rotate students each round, so they get to practice different forms. [CCSS: W2, 4; ACTFL 1.1; DOK 1]

- Play Reverse Hangman: Name it anything you want: I usually pick an animal, but sometimes we draw a car or a house, depending on what chapter vocabulary we are working on, as I tell them what parts to draw. Send one person from each team to the front of the room. The first to correctly write a form (or correctly conjugate the verb completely in a specific tense) can draw a part of the animal or object. The first team with a complete one wins. [CCSS: W2, 4; ACTFL 1.1; DOK 1]

- Crossword puzzles are great, because if the verb is spelled incorrectly, it won't fit (immediate feedback). Make the clues sentences, and translate the sentences so the verbs are used in context. I often use these as a race, with a small prize for the first few who finish. [CCSS: W2, 4; ACTFL 1.1; DOK 1]

- Have students write daily in a journal, on a topic of your choice. If you are working on the preterit/passé, have them tell something they did, or didn't do. If working on the imperfect, ask them about former habits, likes or dislikes. If studying the future, talk about vacation plans, and for subjunctive, provide the beginning of a sentence like "It's important that . . ." and have them also tell a reason why. [CCSS: W2, 4; ACTFL 1.1; DOK 2]

- Best authentic resource of all: *music* to practice/reinforce a verb tense. It is fairly easy to find songs using grammar. Here is a great site for French, with songs for grammar and many other categories: http://platea.pntic.mec.es/cvera/hotpot/chansons/. The AATF has also recently begun a compendium of songs (with worksheets) submitted by members at: https://frenchteachingresources.wikispaces.com/Chansons+et+musique.

  For Spanish, try: http://marcoele.com/actividades/canciones/ or Musicuentos: http://musicuentos.com/tag/songs/.

  To use music to teach verbs, provide students with one of the following:

  - the lyrics to the song, and ask students to highlight all the examples of verbs written in that tense; [CCSS: RL 1, 3, 4, 6, L2; ACTFL 1.1, 1.2, 1.3; DOK 1]
  - the lyrics of the song, with the verbs removed. In the blanks, have them write the verb in the desired tense; [CCSS: RL 1, 3, 4, 6, L2; ACTFL 1.1, 1.2, 1.3; DOK 1]
  - the lyrics to the song, cut into strips: listening to the song, have them arrange the strips in the correct order; [CCSS: SL 1, 4, 5, 6; ACTFL 1.1, 1.3; DOK 1]
  - the lyrics to the song, with verbs removed, and listed in a box above or to the side. Have them guess which ones go where, and then play the song to check. [CCSS: SL and RL 1, 3, 4, 6, L1; ACTFL 1.1, 1.2, 1.3; DOK 1]

- This one is from Faye Conway of Henrico County Schools in Richmond, VA. Choose teams of five to six students. [CCSS: W2, 4; ACTFL 1.1; DOK 1]Write five to six verbs on the board in columns. Have an entire team go to the board and stand under a verb. You call out a subject such as "tu" and everyone should write the *tu* form of the verb that they are standing under. Then everyone moves to the right with the student on the end moving to the position of the first verb on the board. You continue calling out subjects until you have covered however many persons that you wish. When the team sits down you calculate how many correct verb conjugations you have, giving them a point for each one. The next team goes to the board and you proceed in the same fashion as explained above until all teams have had a chance at conjugating the verbs. Whichever team has the highest score wins. Note: you must enforce the rule that the students may not change another student's answer. You should also limit the amount of time given to write to 10–15 seconds. This would also work as an online game, but would be *much* less active.

- There are quite a few fun activities in Chapter 3 that work great for verbs: check out Whiteboards, Battleship, and Casino, for example. [CCSS: W2, 4; ACTFL 1.1; DOK 1]
- Develop an online platform for practice activities for students. I use Symbaloo (and mine are public and searchable) but there are others (Google Classroom, Thinglink, or a personal blog or web site).
- Involve students in two key ways:

  - Humor. Have them read or write funny stories. Examples could be to tell the story of a day that went very, very badly for past tense or for reflexive verbs. Give them silly situations to react to with subjunctive advice,
  - Put their names into every worksheet (or even on the test) and they'll eagerly read and comment on what it says about them.

Future Tense

- Use Concept Attainment for this (or any other verb tense that is fairly easy to form/identify): Challenge the kids by telling them you'd like to see how smart they are. Write or show them examples of regular verbs in this tense. You may use just examples in the tense, or you may compare/contrast it with a tense with similar endings (I use present when teaching the future) while saying "This one IS the new tense/that one is not" at first, and then make it a guessing game: which one is the new tense? Do this until their body language tells you they have a theory about how this tense is formed. Then give them some irregular verbs to look at. Then give them four or five sample verbs, and have them tell you if each is or is not correctly written for the new tense. Then ask them, with a partner, to formulate a rule on how to form this tense. Test the theory with a few more examples, and then debrief: have them explain the thought process they went through to come up with the theory. This step is *very* important, as it will more firmly implant the form in their mind. Finally, ask them to generate a few examples, and check these for accuracy. This can halve the time it takes to cover a new verb tense. I recommend it highly. [CCSS: RL 1, 3, 4, L2; ACTFL 1.1, 1.2; DOK 2]
- For two irregular stems, try to make up mnemonics. A good one I remember from my studies of Spanish was a way to remember decir and hacer: "Dirty Harry"—(dir) and (har). And, of course, Dirty Harry was Clint Eastwood, so you remove the CE (his initials) from

the infinitive to get the future stem. Hopefully students still know who he is (or, there's another teachable moment!)

- For French, I dress as a gypsy, set up a small booth covered with starred fabric, and tell my students' "future" (read their palm), announcing that my name is "Madame R" . . . They all remember that name, and that helps them remember that all future stems end in an "r." They also, of course, hear and write down their future (in the future tense, of course). [CCSS: SL and RL 1, 3, 4, L2; ACTFL 1.1, 1.2, 1.3, 5.2; DOK 2]

- In Chapter 3, see the description of Cootie Catchers, which are used for predicting the future. Your students will be speaking in the future tense quite willingly, when using these. [CCSS: W2, 4; ACTFL 1.1, 1.3; DOK 2]

Reflexive Verbs

- Try the following Learning Stations activity:

  - Station 1: Have students cut out (from old magazines) a picture of a reflexive activity, pasting it to their paper, and labeling it correctly. [CCSS: W2, 4; ACTFL 1.1; DOK 1]

  - Station 2: Have students listen to a recording containing ten reflexive verbs in sentences. On their answer sheet, students must rewrite the verb they heard on the recording with the new subject indicated (either by you on the recording, or printed on the answer sheet with a blank next to it). [CCSS: SL 1, 3, 4, L2; ACTFL 1.2, 1.3; DOK 2]

  - Station 3: Given a list of verbs and a subject, students have to write a short story using all the verbs. [CCSS: W2, 3, 4; ACTFL 1.1; DOK 3]

  - Station 4: Students pair up, with each pair taking a set of flashcards. They take turns timing each other as they pair each verb up with the card with its translation on it (or, take turns quizzing each other using flashcards with English on one side, and the TL on the other). They write the score and initial it on the answer sheet. [CCSS: W2, 4; ACTFL 1.1; DOK 1]

  - Station 5: Using a set of cards, play "Go Fish," either collecting a verb in all its forms (five or six, depending on whether you use "vosotros" in Spanish), or matching a verb and a sentence, or a reflexive verb and an object (for instance, to brush teeth, and toothpaste). [CCSS: RL 1, 3; ACTFL 1.1, 1.2; DOK 1]

- Assign students to take pictures of themselves and/or a friend that illustrates "their" reflexive verb. Make this into a slide presentation, or post the pictures online, or print them and post them, now numbered, around the room, and have students do a Roam Around the Room, writing down what activity they see in each picture, in the TL. This seems to work much better than using the pictures from the text, since they are all involved! With pictures, you can practice various subjects (he/she/I/you etc.) and easily rearrange the pictures to be in logical chronological order, or one that could be funny (i.e., fix hair and then wash it, eat breakfast and go to bed, etc.). [CCSS SL 1, 3, 4, 6, L2; ACTFL 1.1, 1.3; DOK 2]

Subjunctive

- One of my favorite subjunctive illustrations is to ask what the past tense of "I am" is. After eliciting "I was," we all sing the Oscar Mayer song: "Oh, I wish I were an Oscar Mayer wiener . . ." etc. That also firmly fixes the use of the subjunctive with wishes and desires.

- A good mnemonic for this tense is WEIRDO:

  W—wishing, wanting
  E—emotion
  I—inquiry/impersonal
  R—request
  D—doubt/uncertainty
  O—order

  or the one devised by Theodore E. Rose, University of Wisconsin/Madison for Spanish:

  W—wishing, wanting
  E—emotion
  D—doubt
  D—denial
  I—in certain phrases—impersonal expressions
  N—necessity and need
  G—grief or guilt

  After introducing either one, go through the phrases that use subjunctive and list them next to the letter they belong with. Then practice writing sentences using them.
  Music is good, too: (tune of *When I Wish upon a Star*, from Pinocchio):

  When I wish upon a star,
  The subjunctive isn't far.
  Wishing, wanting,
  Doubting feeling
  Use subjunctive mood

- Once students have learned the subjunctive, have them practice it using Inside-Outside Circle. Have them stand in two circles, with the inner circle facing outward, and the outer circle facing inward, pairing the students. Give the inner circle each a "story" to read, usually a Dear Abby-type one such as, "I asked two people to the dance, and they both accepted. What should I do?" The outer circle each have a card with a phrase that requires the subjunctive, such as "It's necessary that . . ." which they must use when giving advice. You can either have the circles rotate after each exchange, providing new partners, or simply have them pass the cards to the next person (or the person to their left in the opposite circle). [CCSS: SL1,4; ACTFL 1.1; DOK 1] Figure 5.1 lists some of the situations I give for this activity.

Figure 5.1 "Dear Abby" Situations for Advice in the Subjunctive

A   I have invited two people to go to the dance, and they both accepted. What should I do?

B   I like to sing, and I want to become a superstar. What can I do?

C   I owe a lot of money to gangsters, and I'm afraid. Help me!

D   I have a crush on a guy/girl, but I'm shy. What should I do?

E   My two best friends want to get married. What advice would you give them?

F   I want to get a better grade in (name of class). What could I try?

G   I had an accident in my dad's car. What should I do?

H   I'd love to get a tattoo. What design should I get, and where should it go?

I   I am a cannibal, and I'd like to eat (someone at school)'s leg. How can I do this?

J   I want to learn how to (pick an activity: dance?) better.

K   I want to go to a concert, but I don't have any money right now.

L   I want to go to France. Do you have any advice for me?

M   Extraterrestrials want to kidnap me. What should I do?

Advice Cards:

1   It is important that . . .

2   It is doubtful that you . . .

3   I am happy/sad that . . .

4   I want you to . . .

5   It is possible that . . .

6   I'm surprised that . . .

7   I insist that . . .

8   I'd like you to . . .

9   It is necessary that you . . .

10   I prefer that you . . .

• Tell a funny story, or an interesting one: I tell my students real stories about silly things I have done (I am definitely not a very good athlete) or interesting things I have read about in the paper. If you don't want to do this, then translate one of the stories from the *Star* or another tabloid; those are usually high interest (for entertainment value). As you tell the story, have the students signal what tense the verb they hear is in: for example, clap for imperfect, hit the desk for preterit. They usually notice that the imperfect is clustered mostly at the beginning of the story. [CCSS: SL1,4; ACTFL 1.1; DOK 1]

• Show a movie: When we watch the film *Manon des Sources*, there are a LOT of subjunctives in it. I kept a running list as they watched, and occasionally stopped the movie to review where each had occurred . . . a good review of plot and verb tense!

- Have the students write a story, with a prize given for the one that correctly uses the most subjunctive verbs. Give the winning story to the class to read. [CCSS: W2, 3, 4; ACTFL 1.1, 1.3; DOK 3, 4]
- Give students a simple story that frequently uses the subjunctive tense: Have them replace several underlined verbs with more "colorful" verbs. This is a dictionary-using, vocabulary-building activity I like to do with my upper-level classes. [CCSS: W2, 4, 5; ACTFL 1.1; DOK 2]
- Have students plan a trip to a place that speaks the TL, suggesting what to take, where to go, what to do, eat, see, and so on. [DOK 3; others depend if written, oral]
- Play a version of Go Fish: give students pictures of objects. One student says, "I think you have the cat"(present tense), to which student two either says, "Yes" and hands over the card, or replies, "I doubt that I have the cat"(if they don't have it) using the subjunctive. This practices verbs of doubt, as well as object pronouns. [CCSS: SL1,4; ACTFL 1.1; DOK 1]
- Have students write ten sentences in the present tense: I play tennis, I eat pizza, etc. Then, on the screen/board, place ten phrases that require the subjunctive: It's important that, I don't believe that, I wish that, I'm happy that . . . and have students rewrite the sentences in the subjunctive, beginning number one with phrase number one, and so on. [CCSS: W2, 4, 5; ACTFL 1.1; DOK 2]

Preterit/Passé Composé/Präteritum

- Use the Concept Attainment method described in the Future section previously, and post examples of the new tense, asking students to see if they can figure out how it is formed. Check understanding by asking them to write a few examples. They'll have it in minutes.
- Music is wonderful. There are many great ones for Spanish on YouTube; just search and show them. In French, for regular verbs, we sing the following:
    (Tune is If You're Happy and You Know It, Clap Your Hands):

    For the ER verbs, e accent aigu
    For the IR verbs, just the letter i
    For the RE you add u
    And that's all you gotta do,
    Passé (hold the "Ah" for two beats)
    Composé
    C'est parfait!

    For passé composé with être, I have a lot of luck using the song two colleagues in Fort Wayne, Indiana, gave me several years ago: (to the tune of *Yankee Doodle*):

    allé, parti, sorti, venu, descendu, retourné,
    arrivé, resté, monté, tombé, entré, né et mort
    (chanted like a rah! rah! cheer): devenu! revenu! rentré! passé!

    To make things more active (and enhance long-term storage in the brain) I have added gestures with each verb, which help students remember what the verb means as well. I let the students decide on the gestures, so they have some ownership of the activity; this has made a lot of difference in the speed they learn this concept.

Imperfect versus Preterit/Passé Composé

• My favorite lesson, either to introduce or review, is one in which I provide a brief story, with its sentences scrambled (Step One: List) found in Figure 5.2, and ask students to categorize them by sentence TOPIC (Step Two: Group). After this is done (and yes, I often have teams that have categories called "miscellaneous"), we look at each sentence in a particular category, for example, "Moving around" and discover that, within that category, they are all in the same verb tense. We might also color-code each section. Then I ask them to group the categories by verb tense (Step Two B: Regroup, if necessary), and rename the resulting categories (Step Three: Label): a wonderful way for them to discover that, in French, the *passé composé* tense is used for action, and the *imparfait* for descriptive passages (Step Four: Generalize). After we voice this generalization (I say, "Look at these two groups and make a general statement about each"), we evaluate our statement by trying it on a new story, *Le Petit Chaperon Rouge* (*Little Red Riding Hood*), predicting what tense each verb would be in if it were told in the past tense, and checking our answers afterward. Using Concept Development and letting them find out for themselves how these tenses work has cut the time I need to teach this unit practically in half, with much fewer practice activities needed; since they found it out for themselves instead of my just telling them. Even though a lot of time was spent in the discovering, their ownership of the concept was much more permanent and better understood by them.

Figure 5.2 Handout for Concept Development/Used in French 2 Introductory or French 3 Review

(English added only for this book, for teachers of other languages)

1. Une fille est sortie de la maison.	A girl left the house.
2. Elle était jolie.	She was pretty.
3. Ils ont vu un film.	They saw a movie.
4. La voiture est partie très vite.	The car left quickly.
5. Il était midi.	It was noon.
6. Le garçon l'a invitée au cinéma.	The boy invited her to the movies.
7. Après, ils ont mangé une pizza.	Afterward, they ate a pizza.
8. Il faisait chaud.	The weather was warm.
9. Une voiture est arrivée.	A car arrived.
10. Elle a parlé avec le garçon.	She spoke with the boy.
11. Il portait un jean et un tee-shirt.	He was wearing jeans and a T-shirt.
12. Elle est entrée dans la voiture.	She got into the car.
13. Elle regardait le ciel.	She was looking at the sky.
14. Le chauffeur était un garçon.	The driver was a boy.
15. La voiture était rouge.	The car was red.

- On a similar note, you could have the student write their own short stories, using elements the class decides on (i.e., a banana, a sports car, and a blue raincoat) to reinforce the rules on using these two verb tenses. [CCSS: W2, 3, 4; ACTFL 1.1; DOK 3]
- Arrange an "incident."

  This can be done in a variety of ways. If you have an upper-level student that you can borrow for a few minutes, arrange for them to enter your classroom and do something outrageous. Scream at the student, throw something (or another action very out-of-character for you), escort them to the door, turn and, smiling, tell the students that they are reporters who must now write down what they have seen.

  Another variation is to get a colleague, staff member, or other adult (or two) to enter the room dressed as strangely as possible and acting strangely. Leaving this up to colleagues, I have had two people chase each other through the room, shooting cap pistols, a person in medieval armor writing "Bonjour" in pink on an old poster on the wall, a princess who handed me a rose and gave me a kiss on the cheek, and other oddities. Once again, the students use the imperfect for descriptive sentences, and preterit/passé composé for actions. (Note: if possible, video this as sometimes students are so stunned/amused that they fail to take note of the actions and can't describe them in enough detail or correct sequence.)

  A third variation I have tried is to enlist class members. Give each a slip of paper with an action, and tell them to do this action continuously until you tell them to stop. Have one eat or drink something, another dance or sing, or other actions. Then, tell them to stop. The class will then need to realize that the class members' "ongoing" actions are in the imperfect, while your command to stop and sit down were in the preterit/passé composé.

  There is nothing like real-life experience to bring home how to use these two tenses.
- For another real-life experience, weather permitting, take a short field trip to somewhere in town (usually a café). [CCSS: SL 1, 3, 4, 6, W2, 3, 4 and L2; ACTFL 1.1, 1.2, 1.3, 5.1, 5.2; DOK 2 or 3] When we get back to school, I ask the following questions: What time was the trip? What were you wearing? What was the weather like? Who did you sit with? What emotions did you feel? The students write down their answers, using complete sentences, in the TL. Then I ask: What did you order? Who did you talk to? What did (a student in the class's name) do? What time did we return? Who got back to the room last? Then we discuss how the first five used the imperfect as they were description, and the last five were actions that required the passé composé/preterit.
- Have students draw and tell a rebus story. Give them a list of the elements you want: day, time, weather, location, and ongoing activity, what happened, and what happened after that (two actions). For each element, they draw a picture big enough for the class to see. Holding these pictures, they stand up and tell the class their story, each person in the group telling about the picture they are holding. If they looked up any new vocabulary in the dictionary, have them teach it before they begin, so the others can better understand. Discuss the verb tenses used and the reasons for using it, as needed. [CCSS: SL1,4; ACTFL 1.1, 1.3; DOK 2]
- Another strategy we have tried is to imagine the story as a video with the sound off. If the verb would be a visible movement on the screen, it would be in the preterit/passé composé, but descriptive details, while being visible, would not involve movement. We often use a fairy tale, *Goldilocks and the Three Bears*, for this activity.

- Use music: here's a song my French 3 class helped me write to remember the imperfect uses: (To the tune of *Jingle Bells*, with a few extra syllables, and you need to sing the word "plus" when there's a plus sign):

  IMPARFAIT, "used to be,"
  "was/were + verb + ing"
  Regular action in the past
  Or interrupted by another thing, oh!
  Date and time, looks and clothes,
  Weather and emotion,
  Circumstances of the main event
  Description, but never motion!

Object Pronouns

My favorite tool for teaching these is a PowerPoint presentation I made, in which the brightly colored nouns in sentences "fly" away off screen, and are replaced with the object pronouns of the same color, accompanied by a loud, silly noise of some sort. Students quickly learn the idea of replacement, and note the placement of the pronoun in the sentence. This appeals to visual, spatial, and auditory learners. But watching a slide show isn't very active.

- Make the majority of the students into living sentences. Give each a large (laminated?) piece of cardstock or poster board on which a portion of a sentence is written. They must unscramble these to form logical sentences. Once these are formed, take the handful of students you reserved and given them pronoun signs, and have them find which student(s) they replace, tapping them on the shoulder, like cutting in during a dance, and they will go sit down. The sentence would then rearrange itself to accommodate the new pronoun. [CCSS: W2, 3, 4, SL1, 4; ACTFL: 1.1, 1.2, 1.3; DOK 1, 2]
- This idea comes from Jocelyn Raught at Cactus Shadows HS, Cave Creek, Arizona. It is for teaching Spanish, but would definitely adapt easily to French and possibly other languages CCSS: SL1, 4; ACTFL 1.1, 1,2, 1.3; DOK 1]: Since students tend to attain language in chunks, this rhythmic approach can help the students learn the difference between the direct and the indirect. The direct object is chanted in a two-syllable sequence to match "di-rect," while the indirect pronouns are presented in a three-syllable sequence to match "in-di-rect." What the teacher says will be in capitals, and dots represent pauses:

1 Tell the kids to listen well and repeat.
   ME—me . . . ME—me . . . TE—te . . . TE—te . . . ME TE—me te . . . ME TE—me te . . .

Call on different individuals to repeat and then return to group:
   ME TE—me te . . . LO—lo . . . ME TE—me te . . . LO—lo . . . LA—la . . . ME TE—me te . . . LO LA—lo la . . .

Put these two-syllable parts together, and repeat many times. Alternate individuals with group. Add:
   NOS—nos . . . NOS—nos . . . OS—os . . . OS—os . . . NOS OS—nos os . . . ME TE—me te . . . LO LA—lo la . . . NOS OS—nos os . . . Then say all together ME TE . . . LO LA . . . NOS OS . . .

Add:

   LOS—los . . . LOS—los . . . LAS—las . . . LAS—las . . . LOS LAS—los las . . .

Build up to:

   ME TE . . . LO LA . . . NOS OS . . . LOS LAS . . .

2 While presenting the pronouns, add hand clapping, finger snapping, swaying, etc. Make it sing-songy. It's almost a tongue twister.

3 Oral Modeling: Again, do not explain anything. Tell them to listen carefully.

   Model sentences replacing the direct object. Stress the direct object and pronoun so they may understand number, gender, and placement without explanation.

   Example: PABLO TIENE EL LIBRO . . . PABLO LO TIENE

   After about five, the quicker students start to click, more after ten, etc. Then, as you say the sentence, allow the class as a whole to replace the direct object with a pronoun. When they seem ready, call on them individually.

4 Sentence List Practice: Students see it and do it on their own. Have them underline the direct object in each of the first five, and check as a group. Then have them write the sentence replacement, and check.

5 Lo Tengo game: This is the biggest hit of all. Use sets of cards with classroom vocabulary or pictures. Put the students in groups and have them lay the cards out on the floor so everyone in the group can see them. When the teacher names one, the student that grabs it, holds it up and says, "Lo (la, las) tengo" correctly gets to keep the card. If the student uses the wrong pronoun or grabs the wrong card, another can correct him or her, and take the card.

• For French teachers: to remember the order of pronouns in a sentence, try the following song sung to the tune of "La Cucaracha" [CCSS: SL1,4; ACTFL 1.1; DOK 1]:

   me, te, se, nous, vous
   le, la, les
   lui, leur, y, en
   (repeat those three lines again)
   Les pronoms!

Try putting pronouns to some familiar tune such as Baa, Baa Black Sheep, or Jingle Bells.

• Get 20 or so objects, with equal numbers that are masculine or feminine singular, or masculine or feminine plural (i.e., for feminine plural, rosas/revistas/plumas/pelotas/llaves). Ask students individually if they want one of the objects: "Do you want the flower?" They must answer, "Yes, I want it" or "No, I don't want it," using the correct pronoun. If they don't use the correct pronoun, they don't get the object. Be sure to have some highly desirable objects such as stuffed animals, chocolate bars, or whatever you think the class would like.

• Using the same objects, have students work in pairs, asking each other if they like these objects, if they want them, or using commands such as "Give it to me."

• Have students bring in a show and tell object. They will want to see each other's. Have them trade objects: "What is that?" "It's a baseball card." "Give it to me/May I have it?" (using the correct pronoun).

- Playing the card game Go Fish requires object pronouns: Do you have "la robe"? No, I don't have it (pronoun used). Go fish. This uses pronouns in the command form.
- Also using numbers: Set up chairs in a circle, and number them; then have students sit. Start the game by announcing: The King/Queen/President has lost his/her (name article of clothing) and number (x) has it! The student in that seat number will stand up, say she/he does *not* have it (using the correct pronoun) and accuse another student, using the seat number. The process will repeat until someone doesn't react quickly enough, or stands up when their number was not called, or calls on a seat that doesn't exist, or calls his/her own number. Then everyone with a higher seat number stands up and moves one number lower, while the person who is "out" moves to the highest-numbered chair. Once everyone has moved, the teacher will begin a new round with another item named. The goal is to eliminate everyone with numbers lower than yours, so that you will be in seat one. Hint: make sure this moves quickly so students must listen carefully.
- Use gifts to show the difference between direct and indirect objects: the present is the DO, and the recipient is the IO. Put cookies, candy, and "zonks" (a rubber band, a thumbtack, or some other less desirable object) in a small bag, and write a pronoun on each. Have them give each other gifts (I give it to you) for 2 minutes, and then let them open them, and try to trade with each other for another minute or so.
- Don't forget the RID rule for pronoun order: RID stands for the order in which multiple pronouns appear in a Spanish sentence: Reflexive + Indirect + Direct + verb.

Partner Activities

When using active learning in the classroom, a lot of time can be wasted trying to find a partner, and often the same students end up working together over and over (and students usually choose others of the same ability level). To avoid all this, try one of the following pairing activities:

CCSS: SL1, 4
ACTFL: 1.1
DOK 1

Partner Clocks: Suggested for Lower-Level Classes
Use several small clocks, or one large one (There are many versions available online, free: just search for "clock partners"). Give students about 5 minutes to find partners (I call them "rendezvous" in French)—if using small clocks, find partners for 12, 3, 6, and 9 o'clock. Students would write their partner's name next to that time on their clock. If using one big clock, find a partner for each hour. Then, all you have to do is call out a time, and they know who to go to. Have them leave these in the room in their folder, or tape them in their book, offer bonus points for not losing them, or have occasional candy rewards for everyone who has his or her clock on a given day.

Partner Maps: Good Review for Upper-Level Classes
Copy a map, either of a country that speaks your TL, or of a city. Students again choose partners, writing their partner's name next to a city (if a country map) or a monument or site if it's a city map. Then, all you have to do is say, "Madrid" or "Ringstrasse" and they know who their partner is. As a sponge (and review) have them go over all they can remember about that place as they move to sit with their partner.

Passports

A particularly good activity I have implemented in my classroom for many years now is to issue every student a passport on the first day of class. For beginning students, fill in name, address, and telephone number the first day, and add to the passport (age, hair color, nationality, etc.) as that material is covered in class. For second-year students, this is a good review. Make sure their passport includes several items not covered in first year, such as their class schedule, hobbies or favorite food, so those can be added. Upper-level students will fill it in quickly as a review. You may use a form you have created, or allow students to create their own.

On the second day of class, I pose as a customs inspector, and students must enter "France" (my classroom) and get an entry stamp. After that, I tell them we are in France and must speak French, and do as the French do. This clearly demonstrates my expectation that they will speak in the TL, as well as setting a classroom atmosphere of "another world."

Once the passport is filled out, it is still useful as a conversational tool in the classroom. Have students ask each other about the basics on the passport, and also additional topics, such as, "Where have you traveled? With whom? Where would you like to travel, and why?" Our passports are also used for simulations of real-life experiences such as checking into a hotel, getting a visa, picking up mail, paying for merchandise, cashing a check, seeking employment, and so on.

My passports also have five spaces on them, and serve as the student's hall pass (with permission from my principal.) After asking me (in the TL) if they may leave, and stating the purpose, they must stamp the passport as if they were leaving the country. A student without a passport may not leave, and each passport is worth five bonus points at the end of the semester if unstamped. Students therefore carefully evaluate how often they need to leave the classroom. I also make tardy students stamp their passport to enter.

Reggie Thomson also uses a passport with his elementary classes in Japanese, ages 8 to 12. He has given me permission to list here his Internet site where an eight-page document, and full details can be found: http://reggie.net/teaching/passport.htm. It is not only a passport, but the students record daily participation points on them, and keep records of grades received, etc.

Handling Mainstreamed/Special Ed Students

With more and more states requiring a foreign language for all students, regardless of ability level, we are going to have to deal with more levels of learning abilities in our classroom. Remember, most of all:

- Repetition and memorization are very beneficial to all students, but are especially good for students who have difficulty learning.
- Use more gestures and hand signals (especially if the students are hearing-impaired)—see Chapter 1 and the research on how using gestures maximizes retention and retrieval of information.

Here are some other basic things that are good for all students, but very necessary for ADHD or other learning-impaired students:

1   Try to create a nonthreatening environment, where praise is given openly, and criticism is done privately.

2   Give a lot of oral grades, but make them low-anxiety ones by making them pass/fail, especially when practicing newly learned material. Also give "completion grades" for homework, as long as it is in the TL. This will foster a sense of accomplishment and encourage participation.

3   Try to have as few distractions as possible. Cover windows in doors. Change posters or other grammatical examples from the previous unit before beginning a new topic.

4   Encourage and reward good behavior. Make sure class rules on what behavior is expected are clear, and enforced.

5   Break tasks down into small pieces, with deadlines for each piece. Students at *any* ability level benefit from a more structured assignment. Don't give one big grade at the end, but rather make a series of partial grades (see Figure 5.3)

Figure 5.3 Culture Report Checklist

Culture Report: Written

Date due   Points

_____   1 Bring in three ideas for a project.   6

_____   2 Select one of the three ideas. Make sure no one else is
                  doing this idea. Write one paragraph about the idea.   10

_____   3 Find two Internet sources about the topic.   4

_____   4 Find two other sources of information.   5

_____   5 Take notes on this topic. Hand these notes in.   10

_____   6 Make a graphic organizer on this topic.   10

_____   7 Organize notes according to graphic organizer.   10

_____   8 Find or make a graphic for the report.   10

_____   9 Write two pages of the paper.   10

_____   10 Write the rest of the paper.   10

_____   11 Have a classmate proofread/check the paper.   5

_____   12 Write final draft of paper.   10

                                                                                 TOTAL: 100 pts.

Note: Each step is required to be completed before a final grade may be given. If Step 12 is not done, students will receive a No Grade or Incomplete for this assignment.

6   Use a variety of activities to appeal to the different senses and learning styles.

7   Pair students to do cooperative activities when first practicing a new concept.

8   Stand near students, making eye contact often, and be available for questions. Don't stand by the wall or sit at your desk.

Here are some more specific strategies for these special students:

- Give them an extra text to take home, if not using an online platform such as Google Classroom.
- Talk to the special ed teacher to make sure you completely understand what the student's special needs (and talents) are.
- Talk to the student. Ask him/her how they study, and what he/she thinks works best to help him or her study. Watch the student work on a task to get a good idea or his or her learning style.
- If possible, vary the color of paper assignments are on. This will serve as a sort of graphic organizer for the student, and will help him/her organize notes as well.
- Give all directions both orally and in writing.
- Pair the student with another who takes really good notes, and give them time to interact.
- Help the student make flashcards. They need lots of extra drill and practice, and these really help. Again, if possible, make them different colors, i.e., blue for masculine, pink for feminine, gray for neuter, and so on.
- Give the student a practice test the day before a test; make sure he or she knows exactly what will be on the test.
- Give tests in several small parts on different days, or modify the test so the student makes choices rather than just fill-in-the-blank (two choices seems to work best.) Make the test open book, or allow the student to use a review sheet or list of endings, pronouns, etc. If giving matching tests, group the matching part into sections of no more than five questions each, with lines in between. Make sure the student has extra (unlimited, if possible) time to take the test. It may be necessary to send the student to a quiet spot to take the test, free of distractions, or even to have someone read the test to him or her.

Leading researchers in this field are Richard Sparks and Leonore Ganschow, so look for articles by them. For more information and links to other valuable sites, check out this website, The Foreign Language Teacher's Guide to Learning Disorders: https://germanstories.vcu.edu/ld/ld.html.

6

Instruction and Alternative Assessments in Literature

*Picking up word meanings by reading
is 10 times faster than intensive
vocabulary instruction.*

Stephen Krashen

Teaching literature is a creative endeavor at any time, and accordingly it is probably easiest to try to implement an alternative assessment program in this area first. Later, when you have mastered the various types of assessment activities, extend these to grammar, communicative activities, and other classroom performances. Remember that the standard method of teaching literature—reading followed by worksheets or discussion—is best suited to the linguistic learners in your classroom. In order to reach *all* your students, you will have to adapt this subject matter for visual/spatial, logical/mathematical, kinesthetic, auditory, and other learning styles. After all, since all students are a mixture of several learning styles, variety will benefit everyone in your classroom. In Chapter 2, in the Linguistic section, I have already written about a four-step strategy for reading. In this chapter, I will elaborate on this, with an emphasis on checking to see that learning has occurred (assessment.) Since all involve reading, all the CCSS reading standards RL1, 3, 4, and 6 would apply to each, and any writing using technology would use W6, and ACTFL 1.1, 1.2, and 1.3 apply as well, I will only list the DOK for each.

Do a Pre-Reading Assessment

If the reading is going to be difficult, such as an entire play or a book, I do more than just ask the student to do the activities described in Chapter 2. I give the student something similar to Figure 6.1, to fill out before, during, and after the reading. It assists the student, and gives me some feedback on adaptations I could make for the next group to do the same assignment.

I have the students turn it in to me before beginning, and after completion of the reading, and give completion points for each section. I will also discuss it briefly, suggesting resources they may not have thought of (especially Internet sites.)

 Figure 6.1 Planning and Evaluation Form

Name _____

Before beginning:

Name and brief description of this assignment:

What I already know about this:

Questions I have about this:

Resources to use during this assignment:

Activities that will make me successful:

Hand this sheet in to the teacher when the above portion is done.

During reading:

USE THE BACK OF THIS SHEET to write down words you find you have to look up frequently.

Reflections upon completion of this unit:

I learned I could:

I learned I need to:

I learned these facts and concepts:

I am now curious about:

I enjoyed most:

I enjoyed least:

Stop Frequently to Process Material

In Chapter 1, the recent brain research also shows us that we must stop and use information often in order to transfer it to long-term memory. This must be done periodically during the reading process itself. In Chapter 2, in the Linguistic section, I have already written about a four-step strategy for reading, and a list of small-group discussion and written activities to do as follow-ups or breaks during reading. In this chapter, I will elaborate on the reading and post-reading portions. Here are some more activities you could use:

1 Draw a picture of the _____ scene, and explain it. [DOK 2]
2 Describe an experience you have had that was like the experience of this character. [DOK 3]
3 Discuss how this character is like or unlike someone you know. [DOK 2]
4 Start a timeline for one character, and chart the events in the book/story as they occur. [DOK1]
5 Make a graph of the character's emotions, with high representing happiness, and low, sadness. [DOK 2]
6 Explain what this character would like for Christmas, and why. [DOK 4]
7 Write five questions you would like to ask this character. [DOK 2]
8 If this character were alive now, how would he/she act? [DOK 3]
9 Pick your favorite sentence you have read so far, and make a poster of it. Be ready to explain why you chose this sentence. [DOK 2]
10 Start a list of new words you have learned as you read. [DOK1]
11 Start a list of words you have looked up more than once as you read. [DOK 1]
12 What sort of music would the main character like, and why? [DOK 3]
13 Draw what you think the main character looks like (including clothing). [DOK 2]
14 Pretend you're a character from the story, and introduce the other characters to the class. [DOK 2]
15 If you were directing a film of this story, who would you pick to play the lead characters, and why? [DOK 3]

The above is by no means a complete list, but there are elements there for artistic (9, 13, 15), musical (12), kinesthetic (1, 8), mathematical (4, 5), and other intelligences, and which cannot be done well by anyone who does not have a good understanding of the text. Several are also creative and fun enough that would encourage students to read the text in order to be able to work on the desired product or join in the discussion. The above also ask students to apply what was read to their own knowledge and experience, making it likely that long-term storage of some of it will occur. And finally, these activities often involve Synthesis and Evaluation, the two highest steps in Bloom's taxonomy (Figure 1.5 in Chapter 1.)

Assess Frequently

Just as brief activities assist in learning the material, so do short, unannounced assessments test whether learning has occurred. Of new learning, 70 to 90 percent is forgotten 9 to 18 hours after the initial learning, unless it is put into long-term storage in the brain (Sousa, 2016). Therefore, an assessment should be given within 24 hours of the reading (or any learning), and should test what you want the students to have retained. It should also be unannounced, so that you can be sure that students have stored the material in long-term storage, rather than cramming it into their working memory. Another advantage of a short, precise assessment should be that it offers immediate feedback. If students get quick, specific, corrective feedback, they are more likely to continue the task successfully (Sousa, 2016).

Here is a fun assessment activity using Inside-Outside Circle, based loosely on the game Spoons. [DOK 1] Group the desks in the room in pairs, in the form of a circle (this works well, even in big classes). For each pair of desks, provide one special item (I usually just use a highlighter marker). Prepare a list of true/false or yes/no statements involving what they have read. Students on the inside are one team, and on the outside, another. Each time you read a statement (for visual learners, I also make a slide show and project the question), students race to grab the marker each time the answer is True or Yes. The team with the most markers gets one point. If the answer is False or No, they should *not* touch the marker. The team with no one holding a marker gets one point (so both could potentially earn one point); if anyone on the team has a marker, the team loses. If both teams have a marker, the team with the most markers loses one point. If the statement is false and a student touches the marker but doesn't pick it up, the person sitting opposite them should silently stand, and the team with the student who did that loses two points.

To make it even more competitive, after every few statements, have the outside students rotate so they have a new partner to compete with. It can get noisy, but my students love this!

Students will also feel more accountable for the material if they know they can expect some sort of assessment often, and will be more likely to persevere. However, if the assessment becomes predictable, such as true-false questions or fill-in-the-blank quizzes, which test only rote memory, students will stop processing the ideas and applying them. Assessments must be creative and varied in order to create a learning climate that results in improved student performance. Here are some assessments that could be given during a reading exercise, which could be done and corrected quickly, and appeal to different learning styles as well as test a variety of more complex thinking skills:

- Compare these two characters' relationship to one in a song you've heard, or a poem you've read. [DOK 4]
- Contrast this chapter with the previous chapter, using a Venn diagram. [DOK 2]
- Pretend you're the author, and explain why you chose the title of this book. [DOK 3]
- Draw a timeline of what events have occurred so far in this story. [DOK 1]
- Draw a series of cartoons to show what has happened to the main character in this chapter. [DOK 1]
- Fill in a job application for the main character. [DOK 2]
- Compare where you live with the village in this story. [DOK 2]
- Would you like to have this character as a friend? Explain. [DOK 2]

As soon as students have done one of the above activities, there are a variety of ways to correct, reinforce success, and give immediate feedback. One way is to pick all the products up, and then discuss what elements they should have contained (the standard method.) This gives feedback, but mostly tells students what they have done wrong, and some will immediately tune out. There are several alternate ways I prefer to handle these assessments.

One is called Think/Pair/Share (TPS), discussed previously. Since the student has already done the thinking part when creating his or her product, you then pair them, and have them share products. To create a positive atmosphere, specify that they may only give compliments to each other (but, in seeing someone else's product, they may see ideas they have missed, or errors they have made.) Give students time to review and revise their product, and then collect them. You may even wish to put two pairs together for a four-way sharing session

(Think/Pair/Share/Square). Using this method, you will see fewer mistakes to correct: students are more likely to put forth more effort if their peers are going to see and/or hear their work. In addition, students will review the material several times in reading or looking at each other's products (another chance to learn), and they will be involved in each other's success (team-building). But, you say, students can cheat, and coast along on someone else's coattails? Don't let students with no product participate in the sharing sessions. The student who has produced a product, even if it wasn't a superlative product to begin with, is reading several other products and evaluating the ideas contained therein, and revising his or her product. If an initially poor product becomes better in the process, learning *is* taking place. Remember, on Glasser's scale (see Chapter 1), students teaching each other has the greatest level of retention.

A similar, more kinesthetic method, but without the verbal discussion aspect, is called Roam around the Room. Students place their products out on their desk, and silently, taking paper and pencil to jot down ideas, look at each other's work, returning to their own desk to re-examine and revise their product before handing it in. Seeing an idea another classmate has written often makes a bigger impression than hearing the teacher say it. Again, there will be fewer corrections for you to make, and any misapprehensions that survive a cooperative activity like this should be discussed the following day. Another tweak: give them highlighters and have them put a mark next to parts they like (compliments go far to encourage others!) I find that Padlet (padlet.com) is the equivalent online resource as students can post opinions, read and comment on others', but it is less active, lacking the physical motion.

Give Choices

Since students have different learning styles, if possible, give them choices when assessing them. For example, instead of the "Compare where you live with the village in this story," use:
   Do one of the following activities:

- Draw a map of the village in this story. [DOK 1]
- Write a script or a brochure for a walking tour of this village. [DOK 2]
- Make up a poem/song/rap about the village in this story. [DOK 4s]
- Discuss the items found in this village that are not found in our town. [DOK 2]
- Make a page from a phone book, listing businesses found in this town. [DOK 3]
- Compare this village to one you saw on TV or in a movie. [DOK 2]
- Do a Book Snap (choose a favorite page describing the village and post it online) [DOK 2] www.youtube.com/watch?v=V_p8S2hIVqQ.

The student can choose a product that would be easiest for him or her to do, but the information included in each would be virtually the same.

Vary Projects

Consider using a project as a final assessment, rather than the standard multiple-choice test. Figure 6.2 contains a long list of project ideas for a literature final.

Figure 6.2 Alternative Assessments

Kinesthetic products	Written	Visual	Oral
ballet/dance	advertisement	advertisement	anecdote
card game	autobiography	album	audio recording
ceramics	book report	anagram	ballad/ rap/ song
charade	booklet/brochure	animation	book report
clothing	business letter	annotated	campaign speech
collage	celebrity profile	bibliography	choral reading
demonstration	checklist	area graph	comedy act
device	comic book	artifact collection	comparison
diorama	commercial (script)	award	debate
display	comparison	banner	dialogue
dramatization	computer program	blueprint	discussion
equipment	creative writing	book jacket	documentary
etching	description	booklet	dramatization
experiment	dialogue	book mark	explanation
field trip	diary/journal	bullet chart	fairy tale/ myth
finger puppets	fact file	bulletin board	free verse
food	fairy tale/ myth	calendar	interview
furniture	field manual	cartoon	jingle
gadget	glossary	chart	job interview
game	guidebook	checklist	joke
gauge	handbook	collage	lecture
hat	headline	collection	lesson
instruments	interview script	comic book	limerick
jigsaw puzzle	job description	costume	monologue
kite	joke	crossword puzzle	narration
learning center	law	diagram	newscast
machine/invention	lesson plan	diorama	panel discussion
macrame	log	display	rhyme
marionnette	lyrics	drawing	riddle
mime	magazine article	fabric	role-play
mobile	metaphor	film	seminar
model	new story ending	flag	speech
movement game	oath	flannel board	
observation	observation sheet	flash card	
origami	outline	flip chart	
	parody	flowchart	
	pen pal letter	graphic organizer	
	petition	greeting card	
	prediction	hieroglyphic	
	puppet show	illustration	
	questionnaire	imprint	
	quiz	jigsaw puzzle	
	recipe	map	
	report	mask	
	review	mobile	
	rewritten ending	mosaic	

Kinesthetic products	Written	Visual	Oral
	riddle	mural	
	scroll	newscast	
	short story	outline	
	skit	painting	
	slogan	pattern	
	speech	photo essay	
	story problems	photograph	
	telegram	pie chart	
	travel log	playing card	
	vocab list	poster	
	yearbook	rebus story	
		scrapbook	
		scroll	
		slide show	
		stencil	
		storyboard	
		time line	
		transparency	
		travel log	
		video	
		wall hanging	
		weather map	
		word search	

Again, give students a choice of projects, such as:

- Design a book cover for your book, or a poster for the film made from this book. [DOK 4]
- Draw a comic strip version of this book. [DOK 2]
- Do an interview: you are the author. Tell what you were trying to say in this book, as well as which portion was the most fun to write. [DOK 3]
- Find an article critiquing this book, and agree or disagree with it. [DOK 3]
- You are the prosecutor at the trial of (villain in the book or story). Write or speak (live or on video) your final summation to the jury, reviewing the misdeeds, and asking for whatever punishment you feel is fair. [DOK 4]
- Write a letter to the author and tell him/her what you think of the book/story. [DOK 3]

Involve Students Directly in Creating Descriptors and Rubrics

However, choice alone is not enough to get a good project from your students. Enlist their aid in preparing a descriptor and rubric for each choice you have given them. A descriptor is what elements the final project should contain, how it should look, etc. Rubrics very much the same, but with a point value, usually from one to four, for each characteristic expected, and with a description showing the distinction between the four levels (or, if you prefer, exemplary, proficient, in-progress and unsatisfactory performances.) Rubrics should be based on national, state, and local standards, and the students helping write them should see examples of products or performances. Students, together with the teacher, should then do the following:

- Determine the essential parts of the product, using terms that are understood by all.
- Define the qualities of each part.
- Assign point value or otherwise designate the parts that are most important.

For example, for a map, bring out three maps. Ask students which one is the best, and why. As they point out the good qualities, list them on the board. When you get a complete list, i.e., use of color, print big enough to read across the room, detail in drawings, lots of buildings, overhead perspective, not messy (or whatever the students like), then announce that an "A" map must have all those listed. Have students also help decide what elements a "B" must have, and so on. This only takes a few minutes, and the dividend is tremendous: not only do more students remember what elements the map must have, but also they feel ownership for the grading scale. Parents will not question your grading of a child's product because the child will not question it, and students won't be able to validly claim they didn't know you wanted them to do such-and-such. And finally, you will have a student-written rubric that you use for

Figure 6.3 Rubrics for Postcards

An "A" postcard has:
- A detailed color illustration, not necessarily hand-drawn
- A salutation and closing, with signature*
- A destination address and addressee indicated
- At least five sentences
- Uses descriptive adjectives and colorful verbs
- In French, with no major errors in grammar and no more than one spelling error
- Indicates clearly Candide's opinion of this place
- Mentions Candide's companion and his/her actions

A "B" postcard has:
- A scene pictured which is generic, or is difficult to identify
- A closing, with signature, but no salutation
- Only four sentences
- One or two major grammar errors, and more than one spelling error
- Describes Candide's actions only
- Does not describe the place visited
- Is vague or unclear about Candide's opinion of this place

A "C" postcard has:
- Black and white picture on card
- Only three sentences
- No salutation or signature
- More than two serious errors in grammar
- No description: generic "Having fun, wish you were here" type message
- Does not give Candide's opinion of this place

A "D" postcard has:
- Incomplete illustrations
- Incomplete sentences
- Handwriting that is difficult to read
- Serious errors in grammar or spelling
- Provides very little information about the destination

An "F" postcard has:
- Words in English
- Is illegible
- Many serious errors
- Less than three sentences

---

*Note: All postcards are from Candide . . . so put your initials on the illustration!

grading. All you do is circle an element such as "Only has one street depicted" and you are justified in giving the project a C or D on that basis, as the students helped you decide.

Figure 6.3 is a rubric students helped me create for a project we did while reading *Candide*, a novel whose main character travels the world, always with a sidekick, and always having some negative experience that impels him to leave and go somewhere else. Students were given the choice of writing a new chapter, a poem, a postcard, a storyboard, or suggesting an alternative of their own devising [DOK 4]. The first time I did this assignment, of course, I had no samples to show the students, but we did look at three postcards, short stories, storyboards, and narrative poems and discuss which was best and why. In subsequent years, of course, we looked at the products from the first year. Using rubrics, the products get better every year.

Give Notebook Quizzes

To encourage students to take notes on discussions and come prepared to class, try impromptu "notebook quizzes." [DOK 1] These should be, as stated previously, brief, easy to correct, and unannounced. These take approximately 10 minutes, and may be graded by the teacher or the students. The first time, you may wish to give one as a "practice" to let students know the value you place on preparedness and organization, and use Pair/Share or Roam around the Room so they can see each other's organization methods, answers, etc.

A typical notebook quiz might ask students to quote from a handout they were given in class and were supposed to keep or from notes on projects and reports given by classmates. It might also have them translate a vocabulary word discussed in class, ask or answer a question as practiced in class, give examples of a concept (grammar or cultural) practiced in class, or simply give the answer to a specific question from a homework assignment, quiz or test that was checked or reviewed in class (a good way to check that a student corrected his/her paper as you went over the correct answers in class.) Anything a student should have in notes or on a paper he or she should have kept would be material for a brief quiz. The "brief" timed aspect of the quiz also is to encourage organizing the notebook. If a student cannot find the material easily, then it is of little value to the student, as too much time would be spent searching for it.

An easy way to camouflage a notebook quiz is to give it in the form of a crossword or word search. This also can be timed.

A notebook quiz is a wonderful way to review for a test. Give students a quiz that is very similar to what the test will be, and have them fill it out, using only their notes and not the text. This may be done on an individual basis, or use Team Test (see below).

I use notebook quizzes as part of students' participation grade. Some students' quizzes mirror their achievement on tests. Others score better on these than on tests, whether it is due to test anxiety or not memorizing enough things, but these quizzes help their overall average a little. The ones who get low scores and care enough, upon seeing their grade drop, begin to modify their behavior and organize their notes.

Team Test

In Team Test [DOK 2], after dividing the students into groups of mixed ability level, give each person a copy of the test, and have them discuss and answer each question, but only write on one copy. I usually designate the lowest-ability student as the secretary for the group as they usually need practice spelling, etc. and this will increase the student-teaching-student dynamic, but make sure they also answer some questions or they'll let the others do the thinking part; I like for them to take turns answering the questions. Everyone on the team must agree on the answer before it is written down. If this is review for a test, correct these in class, either by supplying an answer sheet, with students discussing why they got the wrong answer, and how to do better next time, or through class discussion of the answers, using Numbered Heads.

In Numbered Heads, students in each group have a number, and the teacher calls out a question and a number, and the student in each group who has that number says the answer. Next, a student picked at random from those responding must explain the group's answer. If that student cannot do so, the group loses a point, as they did not make sure everyone in the group understood the answer. This method forestalls a group simply writing down whatever the brightest student in the group says, as each member is responsible for knowing every answer. Peer coaching, according to Glasser's scale (in Chapter 1) encourages long-term memory storage of information.

Team Test is also a really good follow-up when most of the class has performed poorly on an assessment. Instead of teacher-led review, put the students in teams, and, as a team, have them take *exactly the same test* as the day before. This time, they all contribute their answers, and discuss what to write. Once they have all done this (and learned their mistakes), give back the tests. I have never had a single question about a grade when I have used this method. If you give "retake tests" (correctives), they have all just reviewed for the retake, and that could be given immediately.

This can also be Round-Robin style (with each student answering one question, then passing the test to another, who reads their answer and tells them if it is right or not, repeated until the whole test is filled out).

Give More Oral Assessments

With the increased emphasis on being able to communicate, it is important to incorporate listening and especially a speaking aspect in every unit. I like to use learning stations to practice what we are studying, and one station each time is to do a recording for me. They usually use a free app on their computer or phone my Google Voice account. At this station, students would be asked to do a brief speaking activity. Here are some examples:

- The student reads the times pictured on four clocks. [DOK 1]
- The student looks at four pictures of reflexive verb activities, accompanied by a subject pronoun, and says the correct verb for each, using the correct reflexive pronoun and ending. [DOK 2]
- The student picks up a card with four questions on it in English, i.e., asking the day, date, time, his birthday, favorite food, or whatever is in the unit. He or she answers the questions. [DOK 1]
- Looking at a picture, the student narrates a short story about it, using the past tenses. [DOK 4]

- Given a picture of a room, the student names objects seen in the picture. [DOK 1]
- The student looks at a picture of a place. He or she names the place, says he or she is going there, and what they are going to do there. [DOK 2]

Journals

Journals are useful tools for the foreign language classroom [DOK 2]. Students must think, translate, consider grammar issues, and write their thoughts for others to read. Journal entries could be to reflect on what is being read in class, or to discuss issues that pertain to what will happen in the next section of the reading, such as cultural differences or values (i.e., "Which is more important, family or friends?") Having students reread their own journal entries is also reading practice, and looking over earlier writings will show them their improvement, too.

Portfolios

My school does not require portfolios but I like to have students keep things they have written for several reasons. Literature projects make really good additions to portfolios, as the projects usually require reflection, research and creativity, and, since students usually enjoy them, they choose these to put in their portfolio.

Portfolio items are also good things to have on hand to show parents at conference time. When a student accompanies his/her parent to the conference, I always have the student share some writing, showing and commenting on each item to the parent, as I sit by. Students enjoy doing this, and parents are impressed.

However, portfolios are also excellent to use as a means of assessment, especially as part of a semester grade. Here is a partial list of items you might wish to have students put in a portfolio:

- A brief statement, perhaps in English (depending on the level), the student writes the first day stating why he or she is taking the class, and goals for this year.
- Periodic self-evaluations like Figure 6.4, and at least two of the following:
  - video or audio recordings of a speech, skit, or presentation, made especially for the portfolio;
  - a paper, quiz, or test;
  - a drawing they have done as part of an assignment;
  - their favorite creative writing assignment, all errors corrected, and recopied for the portfolio.

In addition to the student's work, a self/peer/teacher assessment could be included, such as the self-evaluation questionnaire shown in Figure 6.4 [DOK 1].

DOK 1

Figure 6.4 Self-Evaluation Questionnaire Level 1 Semester 1 [DOK 1]

Name _____

Rate yourself on a scale from 0 to 4, with 0 = can't do, 1= rarely 2= sometimes 3 = often and 4= easily

I can tell you the following in French:

my first and last names	0	1	2	3	4
my birthday	0	1	2	3	4
where I live	0	1	2	3	4
about my family	0	1	2	3	4
about things I like	0	1	2	3	4
about my city	0	1	2	3	4
about my country	0	1	2	3	4
the time, day and date	0	1	2	3	4
the weather	0	1	2	3	4
what we are wearing	0	1	2	3	4
about a typical day in my life	0	1	2	3	4

I can understand and answer questions about

sports	0	1	2	3	4
my leisure activities	0	1	2	3	4
food I would like to order	0	1	2	3	4
things I want to buy	0	1	2	3	4
how I feel	0	1	2	3	4
school studies	0	1	2	3	4

I can ask questions about

directions (where things are)	0	1	2	3	4
ask someone to repeat a word	0	1	2	3	4
ask someone to define a word	0	1	2	3	4
inviting someone	0	1	2	3	4
what someone else likes	0	1	2	3	4

I can:

write a letter about myself	0	1	2	3	4
agree or disagree with someone	0	1	2	3	4
understand a short conversation	0	1	2	3	4
read a short paragraph	0	1	2	3	4
write the correct endings on verbs	0	1	2	3	4
correctly use gender with nouns	0	1	2	3	4
correctly use adjectives	0	1	2	3	4

BEHAVIOR

I came to class on time	0	1	2	3	4
I came to class prepared	0	1	2	3	4
I was courteous to classmates	0	1	2	3	4
I asked others for help, not answers	0	1	2	3	4
I helped others participate	0	1	2	3	4

Figure 6.5 Tourism Brochure Assessment Sheet

Check that each element is present and completed.

ELEMENT	Self	Peer (Initials _____)	Teacher
Cover illustration and logo	_____	_____	_____
Map (locates site)	_____	_____	_____
Description of site	_____	_____	_____
List of amenities	_____	_____	_____
List of activities	_____	_____	_____
Complete sentences	_____	_____	_____
Verb endings correct	_____	_____	_____
No gender errors	_____	_____	_____
Pleasing layout/look	_____	_____	_____
Additional information given	_____	_____	_____

Each element is worth 10 points for a total of 100 points. Consult rubric for grading information.

Portfolios are good to review at the end of a year's studies, to see what was accomplished, and how much progress has been made.

Putting it All Together

In this chapter about assessments, remember that, while you are assessing students, you should also assess your success in using active learning strategies! I often feel overwhelmed by the variety and quantity of resources out there. This book is full of tried-and-true activities, but I would urge you to consider several things when implementing them.

1 Be choosy. Find an activity that fits your teaching style/fits your comfort level. If it doesn't, mark it as "Explore later" and find something you can easily use right now. Prioritize, and take things slowly. Choose one class and one activity, and make it yours. Try it until it works well for you . . . and then try another.

2 Consider your students' learning styles as well as your own. While we do want them to expand their skills, active learning should make things easier for them, not frustrate them. Don't forget their interests as well. I love the saying: If fishing, with what should you bait the hook: something you like, or something the fish likes?

3 Always have the end in mind: what learning outcome are you seeking? Make sure your selections are aimed at the target standards.

4 Don't "go it alone." There are lots of personal learning network (PLN) communities out there for foreign language teachers (who are often singletons in their school) and loads of material out there that is ready-to-use (and free). Teachers love to share and help each other. Join a Twitter group like #langchat and pick their brains, share your successes, etc. There are great Facebook groups for all the languages, as well as PBL and CI, and more. I would love to see you tweet or post your use of my activities in your classroom, suggest modifications and resources: get active, both in the classroom, and online!

References

Books

Campbell, Linda C., Campbell, Bruce, and Dickinson, Dee. (2004) *Teaching & Learning through Multiple Intelligences*. 3rd ed. Boston, MA: Allyn and Bacon.

Canady, Robert L. and Rettig, Michael D. (1996) *Teaching in the Block*: Strategies for Engaging Active Learners. Larchmont, NY: Eye on Education.

Ebbinghaus, Hermann. (1885) The forgetting curve. In Lester A. Lefton, *Psychology*. 5th ed. Needham Heights, MA: Paramount, 226.

Gardner, Howard. (2006) *Multiple Intelligences*: New Horizons in Theory in Practice. New York: Basic Books.

Gardner, Howard. (2011) *Frames of Mind*: The Theory of Multiple Intelligences. 3rd ed. New York: Basic Books.

Hoye, Almon G. (1991) Interaction of students and teachers with the learning environment. In *Foreign Language Education*: A Reappraisal. Lincolnwood, IL: National Textbook Company, 259–290.

Hunter, Robin. (2004) *Madeline Hunter's Mastery Teaching*: Increasing Instructional Effectiveness in Elementary and Secondary Schools. Updated ed. Thousand Oaks, CA: Corwin Press.

Kagan, Spenser. (2009) *Cooperative Learning*: Resources for Teachers. 2nd ed. San Juan Capistrano, CA: Resources for Teachers.

Lazear, David. (1999) *Eight Ways of Knowing*: Teaching for Multiple Intelligences. 3rd ed. Thousand Oaks, CA: Corwin Press.

Marzano, Robert. (2007) *The Art and Science of Teaching*: A Comprehensive Framework for Effective Instruction. Alexandria, VA: Association for Supervision & Curriculum Development.

Postovsky, Valerian A. (1981) The priority of aural comprehension in the language acquisition process. In Harris Winitz (ed.), *The Comprehension Approach to Foreign Language Instruction*. New York: Newbury House, 170–186.

Rosenshine, Barak and Stevens, Robert. (1986) Teaching functions. In M. C. Wittrock (ed.), *Handbook of Research on Teaching*. 3rd ed. New York: Macmillan, 376–391.

Rost, Michael. (1991) *Listening in Action*: Activities for Developing Listening in Language Teaching. New York: Prentice Hall.

Slavin, Robert E. (1995) *Cooperative Learning, Theory, Research and Practice*. 2nd ed. Boston, MA: Allyn and Bacon.

Sousa, David A. (2016) *How the Brain Learns*. 5th ed. Thousand Oaks, CA: Corwin Press.

Wiggins, Grant and McTighe, Jay. (2006) *Understanding by Design*. 2nd ed. Alexandria, VA: Association for Supervision and Curriculum Development.

Articles

Andrews, Tessa M., Leonard, Michael J., Colgrove, Clinton A., and Kalinowski, Steven T. (2011) "Active Learning *Not* Associated with Student Learning in a Random Sample of College Biology Courses." *CBE Life Science Education*, 10(4): 394–405.

Bal-Gezegin, Betul. (2014) "An Investigation of Audio vs. Video for Teaching Vocabulary." *Procedia Social and Behavioral Sciences*, 143: 450–457. Accessed online July 23, 2017 at www.sciencedirect.com.

Begley, Sharon. (1998) "Talking with Your Hands." *Newsweek*, November 2, 1998: p. 69.

Berne, Jane E. (1995) "How Does Varying Pre-listening Activities Affect Second Language Listening Comprehension?" *Hispania*, 78: 316–329.

Danesi, Marcel. (1990) "The Contribution of Neurolinguistics to Second and Foreign Language Theory and Practice." *System*, 3: 373–396.

Freeman, Scott, Eddy, Sarah L., McDonough, Miles, Smith, Michelle K., Okoroafor, Nnadozie, Jordt, Hannah, and Wenderoth, Mary Pat. (2014) "Active Learning Increases Student Performance in Science, Engineering, and Mathematics." *Proceedings of the National Academy of Sciences*, 111(23): 8410–8415.

Gardner, Howard and Hatch, Thomas. (1989) "Multiple Intelligences Go to School: Educational Implications of the Theory of Multiple Intelligences." *Educational Researcher*, 18(8): 4–9.

Hake, Richard. (1998) "Interactive-Engagement vs. Traditional Methods: A Six-Thousand-Student Survey of Mechanics Test Data for Introductory Physics Courses." *American Journal of Physics*, 66: 64–74.

Krashen, Stephen. (2008) "The Case against the LEARN Act." Accessed online January 7, 2018 at www.sdkrashen.com/content/articles/comments_on_the_learn_act.pdf.

Lederman, Doug. (2014) "A Boost for Active Learning." *Inside Higher Ed*. Accessed online July 12, 2017 at www.insidehighered.com/news/2014/05/13/stem-students-fare-better-when-professors-dont-just-lecture-study-finds.

Norman, Geoffrey and Schmidt, Henk. (2000) "Effectiveness of Problem-Based Learning Curricula: Theory, Practice and Paper Darts." *Medical Education*, 34: 721–728.

Perkins, David N. and Salomon, Gavriel. (1992) "Transfer of Learning." *International Encyclopedia of Education*. 2nd ed. Oxford, England: Pergamon Press. Accessed online July 23, 2017 at https://jaymctighe.com/wordpress/wp-content/uploads/2011/04/Transfer-of-Learning-Perkins-and-Salomon.pdf.

Willis, Bruce D. and Mason, Keith. (1994) "Canciones en la Clase: The Why and How of Integrating Songs in Spanish by English-Speaking and Bilingual Artists." *Hispania*, 77: 102–109.

Online Resources

American Council on the Teaching of Foreign Languages (ACTFL). *NCSSFL-ACTFL Can-Do Statements*. www.actfl.org/publications/guidelines-and-manuals/ncssfl-actfl-can-do-statements.

Ponterio, Marie. *Civilisation française*. SUNY Cortland. http://web.cortland.edu/flteach/civ/.

Ponterio, Robert. *FL-TEACH Foreign Language Teaching Forum*. SUNY Cortland. http://web.cortland.edu/flteach/index.html.

Puentedura, Ruben R. *The SAMR Model Explained*. www.youtube.com/watch?v=_QOsz4AaZ2k.